AN APPROACH TO URBAN SOCIOLOGY

b
w 31

An Approach to
URBAN SOCIOLOGY

by
PETER H. MANN

LONDON

ROUTLEDGE & KEGAN PAUL

NEW YORK: THE HUMANITIES PRESS

First published 1965
by Routledge & Kegan Paul Limited
Broadway House, 68-74 Carter Lane
London, E.C.4

Second impression 1968

Reprinted and first published
as a Routledge Paperback 1970

Reproduced and printed in Great Britain by
Redwood Press Limited
Trowbridge and London

ISBN 0 7100 3453 9 (c)
ISBN 0 7100 6896 4 (p)

CONTENTS

v

TABLES

PREFACE

THIS preface is being written late in November 1964 shortly after I have checked through the galley proofs of the book. As I have read the galleys it has become apparent that many revisions could be made to bring facts more up to date, but such a task would almost inevitably mean that as soon as one revision was made some other government announcement or publication of a report would make me want to have the proofs back again. As it is, this book has been some time in preparation and so, for better or worse, I have decided that it must now go ahead.

Nevertheless, it is important to note that things are happening fast which affect the urban setting. A new government has already placed stringent restrictions on office building in the London area. Many plans to cope with 'the motor age' are afoot. Regional planning, albeit as far as one can see yet only on an advisory basis, has come out of its lengthy period of obscurity. Reorganisation of government departments so as to work for greater degrees of coordination has been introduced. All these things will have their effects on urbanism in the months or years to come.

If the reader will accept that the manuscript of this book was completed before the change of government in October 1964 then it will be of interest to see whether some of the tentative forecasts which I have made are likely to come true.

This book covers a very broad field of sociology and, even in the specialised field of urban sociology it deals with some broad concepts. I am therefore chancing my arm with some of the ideas that I have put forward, but I hope that readers will accept that I have tried hard to be as objective as I can in a field where personal feelings often run high. I am more concerned with trying to present a sociological perspective than a guide to social policy.

My first interests in urban sociology were stimulated when, as

Preface

a newly graduated research assistant, I worked for two years for Dr. Dennis Chapman at Liverpool University. What I like to think back on as my 'apprenticeship' with him was a time when many of my ideas were formed. No one could have asked for a kindlier or more stimulating 'master'. After Liverpool I spent two years at Nottingham University as a research fellow under Professor W. J. H. Sprott who was my Ph.D. supervisor and is, of course, also the editor of the series in which this book is published. Professor Sprott has seen this book right through from the stage of the first synopsis right up to the last (I hope) grammatical error. The interest he has shown and the criticisms which he has given have been of incalculable help to me.

The ideas in the following pages are ones for which I take full responsibility, but I would like to acknowledge the stimulating ideas that I have had in discussions with Mr. R. J. Green of the Norfolk County Planning Department on town planning and with Miss B. A. Sainsbury of the Sociology Department at Sheffield University on sociological theory.

My wife has helped greatly in her attempts to improve the general standard of English in this book. If it is still not very good that is not her fault—the task was a heavy one. Mrs. Margaret Sayles of the Sociology Department at Sheffield University typed the manuscripts and worked with me on the checking of proofs. For her hard work, patience and good humour I am eternally in her debt.

As always in these cases, for any errors, omissions and so on I take full responsibility; I only hope there are not too many.

PETER H. MANN

University of Sheffield.

Chapter One

INTRODUCTION TO THE PROBLEM

I HAVE entitled this book *An Approach to Urban Sociology* because it is seriously intended to be an approach. That is to say that the way in which the problem is tackled is, I hope, not quite the same as may be found in a number of standard texts on urban sociology. Indeed, it was deliberate policy in beginning this book to try to get away from the conventional text-book formula which appears to require an introductory chapter on the history of cities, and finally a chapter on either town planning or 'social change and the city'.

The purpose of this book is to try to introduce an element of theoretical consideration into the study of urbanism in contemporary Britain. If this sounds a grandiose purpose it is certainly not meant to do. But it does seem to me that British urban sociology, itself a comparatively neglected field, tends to be greatly tied up with social policy, town planning and various aspects of social work. If urban sociology is worthy of the name sociology it should be more than any of these, even though it may well include such details within its purview.

Professor Ginsberg once wrote, 'Probably a great deal of the opposition to sociology as a branch of learning is due to the fact that for philosophers it is not philosophical enough, and for empirically-minded scientists it is not scientific enough'.[1] To this could probably be added that for historians it is not historical enough and for geographers it is insufficiently geographical. Perhaps in giving too much consideration to what others think of them, sociologists have diluted their own interests in an over-zealous attempt to be of interest to others.

This book is not written especially for any group of readers other than sociologists, but I hope it may interest others, even if only to stimulate them to disagreement. My aim in the following chapters is to consider urbanism as a field of sociology. In doing this I have attempted to bring together certain empirical findings that are relevant to problems of urban sociology. I have also used theoretical propositions in sociology and applied them to urban questions. In this process I am not trying to please philosophers, empirical scientists, town planners, social workers or even sociologists. Indeed, such are the further unsolved problems that are stimulated in the author's mind by the writing of a book that I have certainly not pleased myself.

Urbanisation is one of the major phenomena of social development over the past hundred years in British society, and today Britain is one of the most urbanised countries in the world. Yet, given these undoubted facts, there is wide agreement with Ruth Glass when she writes that, 'British anti-urbanism has a long history' and that 'The absence of any general British texts on urbanism . . . is undoubtedly in keeping with the native dislike of towns'.[2] Indeed, the popular reaction to a recent American book by a woman who actually likes living in the heart of New York was one of amusement as much as anything. Certainly, at a recent conference, I found a very eminent architect and a hardly less eminent town-planner, neither of whom would publicly acknowledge this work to be other than ,a rather amusing piece of nonsense. In Britain 'urbanism' is almost synonymous with slums, overcrowding, traffic chaos and, currently, land speculation. Just as the American citizen was supposed to have lived twenty years before he learned that 'damn British' was two words, so might it be suggested that for the British citizen he might live the same time before he learned than 'urban' and 'problem' were not the same thing.

The history of British urban sociology is essentially one of the study of social problems raised by urban development. Right from the reform movements of the nineteenth century, with their genuine concerns for the evils which attended urban growth, British sociology has rarely detached itself from problems of social policy. There can be few fields of specialisation within the general body of sociology in which impartiality, objectivity and detachment have been so little sought. Perhaps it is foolhardy to attempt impartiality in this field, but if urban sociology is to be something other than the study of problems standing in the way of social reform, then some serious attempt at detachment must be the aim. I cannot claim that I am completely free from value judgments about urbanism, and many must inevitably show through in this book. As a townsman born and bred, but who has lived very happily in a village, I can merely claim some personal experience of living in a range of environment from village, through a variety of sizes of town to larger cities. In all of them I have known happiness and sadness; in all of them I have found things to admire and things to deplore. So it is with us as a society; we have our likes and dislikes, and these are part of the data upon which the sociologist draws. But rather than take sides in any battle, I see the function of the sociologist as being that of the observer who can present the analysis for the use of any interested party.

The following chapters, therefore, are an approach to the analysis of urbanism, especially in Britain. Rather than being a campaign to 'sell' a plan for a better urban life, this book is concerned with stock-taking. It is as a piece of urban sociological stock-taking that it is offered.

Chapter Two

DESCRIPTIVE COMPARISON OF
RURAL AND URBAN

THE highly urbanised form of so much of Western civilisation
is a phenomenon of fairly recent development and it is not
surprising that the method of contrasting rural and urban
groups has been used for a better understanding of changes
that have taken place and which are still continuing today.[1]
So long as we are clear in our minds as to just *what* we are
comparing, the method can be extremely valuable. However,
there are two pitfalls which must be carefully avoided if true
justice is to be done to the method.

The first pitfall comes with working with the four factors,
rural, urban, past and present. The danger lies in comparing
rural and urban without taking care to remember (or specify)
whether the comparison is at a given time or over a period of
time. For example, one can compare the present village with
the past village (defining, of course, with what period in the
past one is concerned). One can also compare the past village
with the present city. Any comparison using these four variables
is a valid one, so long as the time aspect is made clear. But it is
not uncommon to find that a comparison of rural and urban
is made in which the reader (and perhaps the writer too) has
little idea of *when* the comparison is being made. As one
example, we find Thomas Sharp saying, 'Now the point about
the agricultural village, for my present argument, is that it is,
or at least was a comparatively simple social organism'.[2] Such
an argument, ignoring the time factor, must be suspect, since
the writer is admitting by implication that a change has taken
place in the village and we cannot be sure just where in time
he is basing his statements.

The second pitfall, closely linked with the first, is that of

4

dealing in stereotypes rather than generalisations. By this we mean to refer to two allied problems. Firstly there is the problem of knowing just what a person is meaning when he refers to a rural community: it may well cover anything from a primitive village in Africa to a village inhabited wholly by wealthy commuters not far from New York. In general this problem is covered to some degree by the implication normally made that the reference is to a village in Western society based mainly upon agriculture as a way of life. This vague definition in itself covers a wide range of differences, but for most general purposes it suffices. The second point concerns the attitudes towards rural communities that are held by many writers. Here we find a wealth of value judgments that are not always made explicit, and it becomes evident that many writers, consciously or unconsciously, are 'anti-urban' and 'pro-rural'. By this we mean that in comparing village and city there is a glorification of rural life which at times is based purely on sentiment, and at times pretty sickly sentiment at that. The thatched cottage, with roses round the door and honeysuckle in the garden is a favourite picture used in greeting cards, calendars and so on. This writer has yet to see a birthday card where a large block of flats is the central pictorial theme. In song and story, and film, the 'country life' is the one for me, and 'my home town' is always a *small* place, never sounding larger than an overgrown village. The 'local yokel' is a figure of fun, but the laughter he arouses is essentially friendly in its spirit: he may be simple, but he is good hearted. His counterpart the city wage-slave never ever raises a joke, he is far too drab and uninteresting, and even if he should show signs of life he is likely to be portrayed as a fat, self-indulgent moron or a slick spiv-like character.[3] It would be an interesting topic for research to make a detailed analysis of the various stereotypes such as are mentioned above in the rural-urban contrast. But perhaps the most dangerous aspect of it all lies in the constant emphasis upon urbanism and urban life as a *problem*. Perhaps in the U.S.A. where rural sociology is more advanced, and where rural problems have been very great in fairly recent years, the attitude is more realistic and a better balance is kept. Upton Sinclair's *The Jungle* may be balanced by John Steinbeck's *Grapes of Wrath*. But certainly the position in Great

5

Britain seems to be heavily weighted in favour of the 'truly-rural'. It will be our contention in future pages that the attitudes of 'for rural' and 'against urban' do much to obscure the true understanding of both rural and urban life, and place a wholly undue emphasis upon the *problems* of city life. This is not to say that, allowing everyone his own value judgments, there should not be preferences for rural or urban life. The present writer has lived in city and village, and finds much that is attractive in both, with, if anything, a preference for village life. Where the danger lies, surely, is in the idea that city life is very busy and complicated, whereas the village is simple and cosy. It then follows that it would be ideal for us all to live in villages, and, if we cannot do this, then we should try to make our cities as much like villages as possible. Such an argument, we contend, is positively dangerous and can lead to a complete lack of any sensible orientation towards studying the form and structure of urban society. The viewpoint is distorted, and the city stands condemned before it is even put on trial.

The glorification of the rural community is further linked with a harking back to 'those good old days' so beloved of song-writers whose memories, or knowledge of facts, appear to be highly selective. Here the two pitfalls join together to make one large hole, and we find a blind groping after a form of life that probably never existed in the past, and certainly could never exist in present life.

If we can avoid the two major errors referred to above it should be possible to make an objective and impartial comparison between rural and urban forms of community. In doing this we shall use the method of the polar contrasts, linked by a continuum. As T. L. Smith points out,

> Rural and urban do not exist of themselves in a vacuum, as it were, but the principal characteristics of each may be found shading into, blending or mixing with the essential characteristics of the other . . . Rather than consisting of mutually exclusive categories, rural and urban, the general society seems to resemble a spectrum in which the most remote backwoods sub-rural [*sic*] settlements blend imperceptibly into the rural and then gradually through all degrees of rural and suburban into the most urban and hyper-urban [*sic*] way of living. If such be the case, a scale, rather than a dichotomy, would

6

provide the most satisfactory device for classifying the population or the group according to rural or urban characteristics.[4]

(It is interesting in passing to note that in the above passage Smith gives the prefix 'sub' to the most extreme rural pattern, and the prefix 'hyper' to the most extreme urban. Perhaps this is meant to imply the development of urban from rural, but it is worth noting as just one example of the way in which attitudes to rural and urban influence the selection of terminology.)

Using the method of analysis put forward by Sorokin and Zimmerman we can see how, 'through the classification of a complex and uninterrupted series of phenomena into a few types or classes, they (scientists) overcome the complexity of the concrete reality and give its important traits in the form of a few classes or types of phenomena'.[5] Sorokin and Zimmerman consider the principal criterion of difference between rural and urban society to be *occupational*. From this basic difference a further series of differences can be developed, most of which are related in some way to the basic one. Eight characteristics in all are given as a means for comparing what are called the rural and urban 'worlds', they are (1) Occupation, (2) Environment, (3) Size of Community, (4) Density of Population, (5) Heterogeneity and Homogeneity of Population, (6) Social Differentiation and Stratification, (7) Mobility, (8) System of Interaction. In this chapter we shall give each characteristic, with the comparative illustrations made by Sorokin and Zimmermañ, and, with each, develop the contrast for our own purposes. In the following chapter we shall attempt to make rural and urban comparisons using quantitative data for this country.

RURAL-URBAN DIFFERENCES SUGGESTED BY SOROKIN AND ZIMMERMAN

(1) *Occupation*

Rural—Totality of Cultivators and their families. In the community are usually few representatives of several non-agricultural pursuits.

Urban—Totality of people engaged principally in manufacturing, mechanical pursuits, trade, commerce, professions, governing and other non-agricultural occupations.

Since agriculture is concerned primarily with the cultivation of crops and the breeding and rearing of animals, the typical rural work is out-of-doors and requires comparatively large areas of land. There is, from this, a further requirement that at least some of the labour force shall live close at hand to the land or, particularly, animals, and it becomes apparent that large communities of agricultural workers are highly unlikely. Rural work also tends to call for a high degree of adaptability; the general farm worker is a man with a variety of skills who can fulfil a number of functions. (It is always a wonder to me, after spending two summers as a student working on farms, that agricultural workers are considered to be unskilled: the man with five years' experience of farm work is surely at least as skilled as the fitter or turner in an engineering works). Conditions vary according to place, but, in general, the agricultural worker is employed in a relatively small labour unit. The 'family farm' often has as its only labour force the farmer, his wife, his sons and, possibly, his daughters. Even where outside hands are employed the numbers are still generally small and a comprehensive personal relationship between the farmer and his men is possible. The continuous and relatively unchanging needs of farming make for a tradition which often results in the land being worked by succeeding generations of families. This, in turn, leads to training for farm work beginning at an early age and work and home are closely linked. An example may be cited of a farm known to me, where the farmer, an oldish man, was helped by his three sons, one of whom was married and had twin sons. At the age of four, both the boys could handle a farm-tractor and were capable of carrying out many routine farm jobs. It is not suggested that all farms have such a tradition, and the growth (as it appears) of managed farms owned by absentee city businessmen may cut across this pattern. Nevertheless, in contrast to the industrial type of occupation, the above picture may be used.

With urban occupations a very different system operates. The home and the family group rarely have any direct connection with the occupation of the wage-earner or earners. Few industrial workers have a traditional occupation into which it might be said that they 'grew'. It is often suggested that coal-mining, dock-work and a few professions such as the church

8

and the armed forces, do have a father-to-son tradition. But even if this is so, the home is not the occupational centre, and in the case of the professions particularly, the following-on of the son in his father's profession may well necessitate his leaving home altogether. Work unit and home unit no longer have the same tie as in agriculture. In the urban setting the choice of occupation open to the young school-leaver is much wider than in the rural area, and the human-industrial structure is correspondingly more complex, depending as it does upon the integration of a huge network of interrelated occupations and processes. Such an organisation makes it extremely difficult for the ordinary worker to understand anything but a small part of the whole, and the possibility of primary relationships on an occupational basis for the *whole* urban group becomes manifestly impossible. Added to this, the breadth of initial choice often leads to rapid specialisation, so that the young man who trains for a particular skill may, in effect, be commiting himself, at an early age, to a particular occupation for life. It is often said that the craftsman has the advantage that, in a slump, he always has his craft, whereas the unskilled man has nothing in particular to offer, but the fact remains that once a skill has been gained the craftsman can rarely change his job (*not* employer) without having to take a less-skilled occupation. The electrician cannot change to plumber, nor the fitter to blacksmith, and in this restriction of occupational movement (which would appear to be increasing as restrictive practices on the part of trades unions grow) may be seen a trend towards immobility. It is worth noting that in the 'recession' in the British motor-car industry in 1956 it had to be impressed upon men being laid off that 'full employment' did not mean that a man could expect the same job with the same employer for ever and ever, and this was a hard fact which did not appear to be easily digested by some. It would therefore appear that full employment, coupled with an urban industrial structure, has varying results on particular types of workers. Some may move around regularly in search of better conditions or wages whilst the demand for their services is great. Others, particularly the less-skilled, may prefer to remain in the one place, enjoying the fruits of security coupled with good pay. But given the set-back of a fall in demand for labour, the necessary

9

mobility between *types* of job of an unskilled sort may be difficult to get. The pattern is, indeed, much more complex than is found in the rural area.

(2) *Environment*

Rural—Predominance of nature over anthropo-social environment. Direct relationship to nature.

Urban—Greater isolation from nature. Predominance of man-made environment over natural. Poorer air. Stone and iron.

Because it is based upon a *physical* difference, the contrast between rural and urban environment is perhaps the simplest one to understand. Urban problems resulting from the unplanned and relatively uncontrolled development of large cities, with their resulting overcrowding, dirt, noise, and so on, are known to every thinking person, whilst the absence in some rural settings of many of the amenities expected of a modern society is not overlooked by most people. The advantages and disadvantages of the two environments as places for living are not new problems, and perhaps Ebenezer Howard's diagram of the town and country magnets is the most well-known representation of the forces of attraction and repulsion. His solution, the 'garden city' is, of course, world famed.

If we accept that the contrast between rural and urban environment brings forward the problems of what is the 'best' physical environment, we are likely to become bogged down in a host of value judgments and conditional clauses. Obviously, occupations that are linked completely with a rural environment cannot be carried out in the town: the farmer needs open land for his work, the hunter would get a poor bag stalking along the concrete pavements. Similarly the driver of a London underground train would be hard pressed to find a similar job in the heart of Cornwall. But leaving aside the obvious limitations of environment, we come to the problem of what is, to put it bluntly, the most desirable environment, in general, for the bulk of the population of this country. We know that we are a highly urbanised country, and we know that only a minority of us have occupations that could be called rural ones. Yet we know also that the countryside has a great attraction for us; witness the streams of cars that swarm out of the town on any sunny weekend, at times so thick that the countryside becomes more congested than the town itself. We have seen how the desire for space and gardens has led to widespread developments of suburbs with a very low building density: such areas as are common on the outskirts of the town. These residential areas are not rural in any way (although they may be very near to the open country) yet they have vestiges of rurality in an attempt to make them less urban. The grass verges along the roadside so as to add greenery, the trees planted along the pavement edge, the 'cottage-style' modern houses, at times with thatched roofs, all testify to the desire for a layout and a house-design which imitates the rural environment.

We have already mentioned the suggestion that the general population of this country is anti-urban, and when we consider the problem of environment there is ample evidence to support this hypothesis. Howard's idea of the garden city was a brave attempt to gain the best from both worlds, urban and rural together. Yet can it really be said that the idea succeeded? Critics of the garden city concept regard it merely as a delaying action fought against the many factors driving our society towards a more urban mode of life. Whilst not by any means denying the need for plans to control the development of the size of cities, these critics regard Howard's plans as having given rise to the unhappy compromise of the 'garden suburb', wasteful of land and creating distances from city centres which appear to be needless. Thomas Sharp says we have created 'Neither-Town-Nor-Country'.[6] To Sharp, town is town and country is country, and never the two should be confused.

It is interesting to note how urban imitation of rural life is generally an imitation of the past. It is common in city suburbs to find houses built in the 1930's in the 'Stockbroker's Tudor' style, and interiors fitted with panelling (wood or plastic) and hung with horse brasses. In the villages themselves the new fits oddly with the old in many cases. An old village, with a higgledy-piggledy lay-out, may have added to it a new council estate that is no different from one in the centre of any large city. In the villages that have been taken over by city-dwellers and converted into dormitory villages or weekend retreats the houses may be given a new lease of life, with careful restoration and good maintenance. Yet, the 'improvements' that are made (windows enlarged, with the addition of steel frames and bottle-glass panes, concrete-block garages added to the brick houses) result in a blurring of the distinction between urban and rural. Perhaps the most notable of all coalescing of rural and urban is to be seen in our seaside resorts, in particular in places where a small village has become a popular holiday resort. Here we find the sweep of sands with its ice-cream vans, its iron piers and its border of concrete promenade, the old fishing village with its host of curio shops and street upon street of boarding houses and hotels. Such places are extremely popular since there is always something to do, even when it rains. One can sit on the sands for hours on end, if one so wishes, but when one tires of sands and sea there are many other attractions of the man-made variety.

In such ways this country is moving towards a position where rural and urban differences are becoming more and more blurred. But the movement is predominantly one of urban superimposed on rural. In this country the rural 'predominance of nature over anthropo-social environment' is a waning predominance, and the 'direct relationship to nature' is becoming more and more indirect.

If this picture seems harshly drawn, let it be remembered that we are dealing here with what we began by describing as 'perhaps the simplest' difference to understand, being based upon a physical criterion.

(3) *Size of Community*

Rural—Open farms or small communities: 'agriculturalism' and size of community are negatively correlated.

Urban—As a rule in the same country and at the same period, the size of urban community is much larger than the rural community. In other words urbanity and size of community are positively correlated.

The problem of 'size of community', as a distinguishing factor between rural and urban, is primarily a problem of deciding to what factor the word 'size' is to be applied, since 'community' can be employed to refer to an area of land as well as a group of people. We shall be led into confusion unless the distinction is made clear. Obviously it would be simplest to lay down an arbitrary boundary line on the map, and say that within this boundary lies our community, urban or rural. But we are then faced with the problem of deciding whether the physical boundary line has any real social meaning, and particularly does this problem arise when we have to deal with village, town or city boundaries where there is an 'over-spill' of population. Thus, for a village we might take the boundaries of the parish council, for a town the boundaries of the municipal or county borough. But this method, useful though it may be for the employment of statistical data collected for official purposes, may lead to incorrect readings of the true social composition of the community. We may find that the village boundary, so drawn, excludes the family at the 'Big House', or the distant farmer who is an integral part of the village life. In the city there may be excluded the large council estates built outside the city boundary because of shortage of land in the city: it may well also exclude leaders of the community who live in the country villages and commute daily to the city. The problem has been recognised too with regard to the use of census data for cities and towns which form large conurbations; for example, the areas loosely referred to as 'Liverpool' or 'Manchester' are, in fact, conglomerations of large cities and towns, with no open country or visible marks of division between them. Even on a smaller scale it is difficult to know if any real social distinction can be made in many cases of cities which have a 'halo' of urban districts around their boundaries.

Thus the arbitrary choice of limits to the physical community is a choice that is often forced upon one if certain data are required, but in the broadest social meaning these boundaries may be quite misleading.

If, then, the difficult problem of laying down the community boundaries can be satisfactorily solved, the factor of size of community may be considered. Wirth[7] noted the obvious point that 'to say that large numbers are necessary to constitute a city means, of course, large numbers in relation to a restricted area or high density of settlement'. Thus Wirth's definition of the city as a 'relatively large, dense and permanent settlement of socially heterogeneous individuals', covers three of Sorokin and Zimmerman's criteria of rural-urban differences, but as Wirth adds, there are good reasons for treating the criteria separately. However, when Wirth considers details of population size most of his discussion falls under Sorokin and Zimmerman's later heading of system of interaction. We will also leave such aspects until later, and note only in this present section that communities of 500 and 500,000 people are both composed of individual persons: yet, by the very nature of the community size the lives of the individual persons will differ. The reciprocal conditioning effects which operate between community size and, for example, industrial-occupational structure, leisure activities, housing lay-out and so on, require little elaboration for us to grasp the fundamental ideas. But it is sometimes overlooked that sheer population size alone makes some things possible and others impossible. Many of the benefits and drawbacks of urban and rural life derive basically from population size. A small village could rarely hope to support its own concert orchestra or repertory theatre: a large city must be divided up into small units (e.g. parishes, wards, school districts) with the inevitable differences in social relations from a unit where all things relate to all the people.

Thus, whilst realising that population size in itself is nothing more than heads counted, we must beware being so concerned with the consequences that we forget the basic structure.

(4) *Density of Population*

Rural—In the same country and at the same period the density is lower than in urban community. Generally density and rurality are negatively correlated.

Urban—Greater than in rural communities. Urbanity and density are positively correlated.

One of the problems arising from a discussion on density is to be sure of what we are describing in terms of density. If we accept the dictionary basis of density as a mass : volume ratio, we must consider with what units we are dealing. Density of population may be expressed as so many persons to the acre or square mile, whilst density of dwellings may deal with so many dwelling units (suitably defined) to the acre or other base. With increasing ability to build living accommodation upwards, a ratio of persons to land may be quite misleading unless some further details are given of *how* people are accommodated. One may take a number of examples which could mislead. In many a country village the houses or cottages tend to be small and often crowded together. In a village in which I lived gardens, on the whole, were small and many people had allotments in a field just outside the village. The point now arises in describing density of population and dwellings, what area do we use to compile the ratio? The political-administrative area of a village may well cover several square miles, since farm land will be included, and no land, no matter how useless, will belong to no one. It may well be, then, that a village of a few hundred people which, in living accommodation, is packed tightly round a church or cross-roads, will appear to be very thin on the ground if the denominator for a ratio calculation is the whole area within the political boundary. In urban areas things become very complicated when one tries to compare 'high-density' flats with 'low-density' houses. To try to overcome this difficulty a 'net residential density' figure may be used which is 'the average number of persons per acre of housing area; which comprises the curtilages[8] of the dwellings, access or internal roads and half the boundary main roads up to a maximum of 20 feet, where these are contiguous to residential property'.[9] Distinct from this is 'gross density' which is 'the average number of persons per acre of the whole neighbourhood'. Accepting the value of the distinction here made between net and gross, one is still left with a need for a filling-out of the description of density when an urban residential area is described. We need to know, for any given area, (a) the types of dwellings in which the people live, (b) the use made of land not occupied by the actual buildings themselves, and (c) the division of land between private and public ownership. The principal distinction made between net and gross densities is the restriction of accountable land in the calculation of net density to that which can, in general, be called 'residential'. But it would be possible to take people from semi-detached houses with reasonable gardens, and re-house them in a single block of flats with a large communal garden round it, and still maintain the same net density. Obviously the environment and mode of life will be changed enormously. For another example, one may consider 200 people living in a city slum, with very small gardens or perhaps only yards. Their net density may be the same as that of 200 people living in a huddle of small terraced cottages in a beautiful village. Yet the one group is surrounded by more slums, factories and shops, whilst the other is surrounded by fields, meadows and woods.

Thus one sees that although the factor of density can be of value in differentiating between rural and urban, one must take care that the basis for whatever statistic is used is clearly understood. There could easily be cases which would qualify for inclusion as awful examples in Darrel Huff's delightful book *How to Lie with Statistics.*

(5) *Heterogeneity and Homogeneity of the Population*

Rural—Compared with urban populations the populations of the rural communities are more homogeneous in racial and psycho-social traits (negative correlation with heterogeneity).

Urban—More heterogeneous than rural communities (in the same country and at the same time). Urbanity and heterogeneity are positively correlated.

Sorokin and Zimmerman refer to 'acquired socio-physical characteristics, such as language, beliefs, opinions, mores, patterns of behaviour and so on'.[10] In so far as racial traits are concerned, this is a matter which is more to the fore in the U.S.A. than in Great Britain, though it is noteworthy that the centres of negro, Chinese, Indian and other Asiatic settlements in this country are all in ports and/or larger cities. Very rarely does one come across a person from another race settled in a country village; even more rare is an ethnic group within the village.

Viewing the rural-urban difference from a somewhat historical point of view, Angell suggests that,

In earlier, simpler societies the local community was equally important as the family and religious institutions in supplying the individual with a sense of basic common values. And it was much more important than the larger society itself which, because communication was poor, could foster such values only in the most general and abstract way. But the local community had worked out a way of actual common living. It was a world whose culture was in part unique. Over a period of time this culture had come to embody the values that were implicit in the mode of life. People accepted these values as they grew up, just as they did the kind of food they ate or the methods of agriculture they used. Each member of the community was accorded his place in the whole through the operation of accepted principles. He felt himself a member of a moral community.[11]

Angell considers this type of community to be almost extinct today. 'The improvements in communication and transportation, the growth of large-scale capitalism and increasing social differentiation have produced a type of life antithetical to this old-fashioned community'.[12]

Although it is true that many trends have combined to break down the isolation of the village and thus to reduce its homogeneity of thought and action, nevertheless the straightforward factor of population size can produce homogeneity. In the ordinary agricultural village there is a narrow variety of occupations. Kinship groups may be based largely upon a few well-established families. Religious affiliation locally is limited to 'church and chapel'. Participant leisure activities may be limited to football and cricket, church youth club and Women's Institute. In political affairs, the parish meeting, or the annual meeting of the parish council, makes for the possibility of verbal exchanges between all interested parties; there is no need for 'spokesmen' since all can be present to speak for themselves.[13]

The development of transport and mass-media such as radio, television, popular press and so on, has resulted in a broadening of village life which is antithetical to the suggested homogeneity. With mass culture the villager becomes progressively more a man of the world and less one of the village. The eight a.m. bus to the nearest town, with its load of clerks, craftsmen and typists resounds with discussions of the previous evening's television panel game, or the latest offer of the women's magazine (readership $1\frac{1}{2}$ millions).

The rural village today, then, is a composite entity. It retains some of its older characteristics, as the stranger or 'comer-in' may all too quickly find. It is still necessary in many a village to live there for twenty years before one is accepted, and a careless word spoken about Mrs. A. to Mrs. B. may well be received with the news that 'Mrs. A.'s husband is the brother-in-law of my mother's cousin, and don't you speak about my family that way'. Yet it would be stretching things too far to say that beliefs, opinions, mores and patterns of behaviour derive from the village itself. Even the village school is being replaced by larger, more efficient schools at selected points, fed by the school bus. In so many ways the functions of the village are being taken from it, that it is sometimes difficult to talk of 'the village' as a unity at all.[14]

(6) *Social Differentiation and Stratification*

Rural—Rural differentiation and stratification less than urban.

Urban—Differentiation and stratification show positive correlation with urbanity.

It is perhaps misleading to talk of there being 'less' differentiation and stratification in the rural setting than in the urban. Quite obviously the social differentiation is not of the same type in both areas. The class system of the urban environment, based greatly upon secondary social contacts does not operate in the same way in the village. The village does not have its different types of residential areas to anything like the degree found in the city. There are not large aggregates of professional men, business men, clerks, industrial workers and so on. Whatever there is of an associational character in the village, there is likely to be only *one*, so that membership of the 'X' tennis club cannot carry more social status than membership of the 'Y' tennis club, since there is only the 'Z' tennis club for everyone. Perhaps church and chapel may be regarded as sources of differentiation, socially as well as religiously and if there should be local branches of the political parties here too there may be consideration of status. (In the village in which I lived Conservatives and respectability were regarded as practically synonymous: Socialism was only for the untouchables in the new council houses.)

In the village, however, differentiation and stratification are much more personal matters. One does not see a large Bentley or Jaguar purr past and wonder who the prosperous well-dressed man at the wheel may be. One knows that he is the new owner of the old rectory who bought the farm on the hill (which he now has run by a manager) and that he is really a director of a hire-purchase finance company at the near-by city. This gentleman's status in the village would probably be a rather peculiar one, since he would be 'in' the village, but hardly 'of' it. But for the people who do function in the village —the parson, the teacher, the doctor, the postman, the grocer, the butcher, and so on, all these people are known as people, and not merely as representatives of a particular socio-occupational class. If we accept, then, that in the small village everyone will, literally, know everyone else's business, then the *need* for differentiation on a class basis (i.e. by categories) will be much less.

Given the recognition of a hierarchy of occupations, even though there may be only one representative from a particular category, the social relations will still differ between rural and urban, since in the rural setting knowledge of other people in the village will be much greater.

A further development of the greater personal knowledge in the village setting is the handing down of status from one generation to the next. The village system has certain elements of a caste system within it. As T. L. Smith suggests, 'the caste principle is not so rigid in urban as in rural societies. . . . Movement from one class to another is easier than in rural society where intimate social contacts make a person's antecedents well known to all members of the community and cause one's position to be largely determined by the status of his immediate ancestors than is the case in the city".[15] Although the concept of a caste system is rather too strong for this case, the idea of a person being born to a certain status is more recognisable in rural than urban life. In the urban setting, with its greater anonymity and social differentiation based more on material goods than antecedents, the individual is judged and classified greatly by what he has attained for himself. Probably his father's occupation would be unknown to 99 per cent of his acquaintances. In the village, however, the web of kinship and the general knowledge of family standing marks a person for life. So the bright boy who goes to grammar school, university and on to a professional position in the large city is admired by the rest of the village, but he remains, for them, his father's son. In the city, both where he works and lives, he will be accepted much more by virtue of what he has attained and his village background will be an insignificant factor in the general sum.

With the greater division of labour in the urban setting and the wider field of occupational opportunity open to the individual it can readily be appreciated how the occupational role becomes so much more important in the ascription of social status. In the urban environment, with its great contrasts in occupations, incomes, standards of living, homes and neighbourhoods, primary contacts with all members of the community are obviously impossible. So, with the permanent need for adjustment between individuals, which is facilitated by the ascription of what we call social status, the shorthand symbols of occupation, income, education, place of abode, dress and accent become important reference points.

(7) *Mobility*

Rural—Territorial, occupational, and other forms of social mobility of the population are comparatively less intense. Normally the migration current carried more individuals from the country to the city.

Urban—More intensive. Urbanity and mobility are positively correlated. Only in the periods of social catastrophe is the migration from the city to the country greater than from the country to the city.

Sorokin and Zimmerman in their comments on mobility deal with several aspects of it; migratory movements, movement from occupation to occupation, or job to job, and social movement as characterised by rising or falling social status.

It is customary to think of rural-urban mobility in the migratory sense as being from country to town, although the opening up of the American frontier was a movement in the opposite direction. In general, however, there is a steady continuing movement from country to town, or at least from rural to urban. It must be remembered, though, that any movement can be obscured by arbitrary definitions. If a city overflows its boundaries and builds housing estates in its surrounding country area then the houses may well be located in the X Rural District, but the result is not a movement from urban to rural, rather it is an urbanisation of what was previously a rural area. In the case of professional and business people who choose to live outside the city in country villages, it is a further aspect of urbanisation of the rural. The business man, with his car, or daily train, continues with his urban occupation, whilst the family leisure may be split between town and country. It is by no means uncommon today to find villages and small towns where considerable numbers of inhabitants are really more attached to the near-by city than to the village or small town. The increased mobility brought about by car, bus and train has made distances merely relative. Positioned on the right side of the city for easy access to his work, the commuter may find the journey from village to office an easier one than from a suburban district on the other side of the city from his office. A further class of people affected in the mobility problem are those who depend upon local authorities for their housing. The tenants of 'council' houses can only have tenancies in accordance with the planning of the local authority. Thus, the applicant for a council house cannot choose for himself where he wants to live—he is limited to the estate built for him and his like. The result may be that a person living in a country town may be offered a council house on a new estate built to expand a particular village. The man may then decide to accept the house, since it offers good cheap accommodation, but to retain his present work in the town, perhaps by choice, or perhaps because the village may not have any vacancies in his particular calling. Council development of this sort can bring about a physical mobility from urban to rural, but socially the migrants become rather divided in their loyalties. I have met people, particularly the housewives, who find this enforced village life tedious and dull, and would give anything to get back to the larger town.

In general, then, it can be seen that there are a number of cases of 'false' mobility which should not be accepted without careful scrutiny. It might be said that mobility only really occurs when the individual moves his home *and* occupation from one environment to the other, thus becoming wholly dependent upon the new locality for livelihood and principal social contacts. Living in the one place, be it rural or urban, and travelling daily to the other is not true mobility, though it may result in constant movement.

The 'drift from the countryside' to the major towns and cities is likely to attract two particular types of rural person—the best and the worst. As has been mentioned, the 'bright boy' who gets a good education is unlikely to find the job he wants in the small village. To 'get on' in the world he must move out to work for the large industry or government department. The country-bred bright boys are a considerable gain for the city. At the other end of the scale are the village ne'er-do-wells and misfits. For them the village is too small because their doings are always noted, whereas the city offers the blessing (for them) of anonymity and 'mind your own business'. The city, then, gets two particular types for whom the problem of adjustment raises quite different questions.

The conventional considerations of mobility sometimes tend to ignore, or at least, underplay the importance of inter-urban and intra-urban mobility. It is a well-known problem to town planners that work-people cannot be made to move to carefully sited industries. Attempts to 'redistribute' the urban population have not met with resounding success. For some reason the worked-out, depressed and depressing colliery town remains more attractive to its sons than the carefully planned and hygienic new town. Yet, given the problems of moving work-people en masse, there remains the constant movement as individuals of people in the higher social classes. Bank employees, insurance men, managers of 'chain' stores, teachers of all kinds, and every type of local government officer, may have to move either at the instruction of the employer or to attain personal promotion. Perhaps the most publicised directive towards mobility in recent years has been the memorandum from the Home Secretary to Watch Committees making the explicit recommendation that Chief Constables should be appointed from *outside* the local force. Whilst most Chief Constables are fortunate enough to have houses provided for them, many other less well assisted people may have the worry and financial strain of selling and buying houses each time they move. Some

industrial firms, commercial companies and even local government bodies have recognised these problems but for many
unfortunates a sum of well over £100 must be put aside for
legal and removal costs. A 'moving increment' of £50 (taxed)
is little inducement in such circumstances.

Mobility within the city is a further point which should not
be ignored. In the village a move from one house to another
(perhaps from a condemned cottage to a new council house)
cannot be an enormous move by the very limitations of the size
of the community. In the city, however, a move may be over
several miles, with consequent breaking of old neighbourhood
relations and a building up of completely new ones. Intra-city
mobility may affect several types of people; the occupant of the
slum house resettled on the suburban council estate; the couple
living in rooms who move to a new block of flats; the flat-
dwellers who move to a house because they are starting a
family; the expanding family who move to a larger house in
search of more space; the declining family, whose children have
left home, who seek the small bungalow for retirement. In all,
it would be quite reasonable to expect a person who lives his
whole life in one city to live in upwards of four dwellings[16]
during his lifetime merely for accommodating himself and his
family in a dwelling of appropriate size. If mobility brought
about by a desire to live in a higher status residential area is
considered, then there may well be more moves. As Park
comments on the American scene,

> Change of occupation, personal success or failure—changes of
> economic and social status, in short—tend to be registered in
> changes of location. The physical or ecological organisation of
> the community, in the long run, responds to and reflects the
> occupational and the cultural. Social selection and segregation,
> which create the natural groups, determine at the same time
> the natural areas of the city . . . In great cities the divergences
> in manners, in standards of living, and in general outlook on
> life in different urban areas is often astonishing . . . this
> emphasises the importance of location, position and mobility
> as indices for measuring, describing and eventually explaining,
> social phenomena.[17]

In all, the picture that the modern city brings to mind is one
of a restless, ever-moving population, constantly on the go for

one reason or another. Indeed, it is one way of expressing success to describe a person as 'getting on'. Mobility at all levels and in a host of ways is a part of city life. This is best seen perhaps in the unique situation in London, where it may be said that many daily travellers make a rural-to-urban move each morning, though perhaps it would be truer to call it suburban-to-urban, or even urban-to-urban. We have in the Greater London area the peculiar phenomenon of thousands of people daily moving great distances from home to work; distances which in the provinces would probably be regarded as quite beyond contemplation.[18] Yet with the transport system geared to this principle hardly a thought is given to the daily invasion and retreat, so dulled have our senses become to it.

Mobility, then, is of the very nature of the urban environment. Ranging as it does, however, from migration from one country to another down to a bus-trip to the cinema, we have here a concept which is so great as to require further, more detailed consideration. We shall return to this question later.

(8) *System of Interaction*

Rural—Less numerous contacts per man. Narrower area of the interaction system of its members and the whole aggregate. More prominent part is occupied by primary contacts. Predominance of personal and relatively durable relations. Comparative simplicity and sincerity of relations. 'Man is interacted as a human person'.

Urban—More numerous contacts. Wider area of interaction system per man and per aggregate. Predominance of impersonal, casual and short-lived relations. Greater complexity, manifoldness, superficiality and standardised formality of relations. Man is interacted as a 'number' and an 'address'.

In this concluding category the basic argument is quite simple, indeed obvious. If you live in a small isolated community you will know fewer people than you *could* know in a large city. But the people you *do* know in the small community you are likely to know more fully, more intimately and (if the idea of stability is accepted) for a longer period of time. In the city you 'know' a vast number of people, but most of these people are likely to be known superficially or in a segmentary, single-role way. Thus, in the city, the postman is the anonymous man who delivers the letters and to whom we give a tip each Christmas. If the delivery is early in the day we may rarely see him. We are unlikely to know any details of the postman's life. His name, address, marital status, leisure interests and so on will all be a closed book to us. In the small community with one postman we are likely to know the postman as 'George Brown', father of two boys and a girl, brother of the garage mechanic, captain of the church bell-ringers, ardent follower of the hunt, etc. etc. In fact, we shall know the postman as a 'whole' person.

In the city, one's friends and acquaintances do not form the closed circle of the ideal-type village. Your city friends will have other friends who are little known, or even unknown to you. The circle of friends is a highly personal rather than social affair; each one of us has his or her own circle of friends and acquaintances, and these may differ quite strongly, even between such close people as husband and wife. Given this situation, the individual has no group to which he may be said to 'belong' since the form of group interaction tends towards superficiality of contact rather than depth. The modern cocktail party is a perfect example of the institutionalisation of shallow acquaintance; indeed the essence of this social inter-action is summed up in the terms used to describe the con-versation—'small-talk' and 'cocktail-chatter'. Gist and Halbert suggest that, 'One has neither the time nor the energy to know intimately all those he meets in the city; therefore he is forced, as a matter of self-protection, to formulate stereotyped con-ceptions of the multitudes whose faces he perceives; they account for much of the reputed coolness and hard-heartedness of the city'.[19] In *Middletown in Transition*, the Lynds postulated that,

> One insensibly becomes a citizen of a wider world as a larger city tends to develop a more metropolitan emphasis . . . Residential areas tend to become more segregated and homo-geneous. Such externals as where one lives become more important as placing one in the larger and less familiar popula-tion . . . and, personal means of placing one in the group, involving considerations of the kind of person one is, yield to

more quickly determinable, shorthand symbols, notably what one owns.

And so on; with any writing on rural-urban contrasts the similarity of views on the form of interaction is apparent. But if reference to Toennies, and Parson's comments on Toennies, is made, it will be noted that Toennies stresses the importance of the 'wills' or attitudes which underline the actions. And since social interaction is based on an interaction of ideas then the manifest actions which differ from rural to urban setting must be traceable to different 'wills'. In this matter R. C. Angell's concept of the 'moral' community would seem to be pertinent. He says that 'the principle of *moral* community is best exemplified in modern city life by small integrated groups which have worked out an integrated way of life. On the larger scale of territorial aggregates it is seldom that one finds a true moral community, because people who are striving to realise common values in one field have divergent orientations in others'.[20] In other words, social interaction is segmentary and not whole.

While pressing this interpretation of the difference in forms of interaction between ruran and urban, the temptation to moralise is at times extremely strong. The superficiality of the cocktail party is an easy target for satire (see Dorothy Parker and a host of other American writers). Yet it must be remembered that the rector's tea party or 'sherry at the manor house', could be just as boring or tedious. We do not wish to make moralising comparisons of the one or the other. The real point at issue is the *depth* of social interaction which is likely to take place in the rural and urban setting. What has been suggested is that, within the smaller rural community interaction is more all-encompassing, whether the individual likes it or not. In the city interaction is more segmentary in many ways, but this does not preclude deep friendships arising in this environment. The essential point is that in the rural area the community is there and all are a part of it: in the city each person has his own group of acquaintances, colleagues, companions and friends, and these groups are personal to the individual, but they are not social entities in any larger sense.

In this chapter we have considered the contrasts that can be made between rural and urban aspects of the concept of community. Using ideal types, and the linking continuum, we have

26

employed Sorokin and Zimmerman's eight criteria of differ- ence. From this basis we may continue, in the next chapter, to consider what insight into rural-urban differences may be gained for this country from published statistics. We may then sum up on the heuretical value of the rural-urban concept.

Chapter Three

RURAL-URBAN COMPARISON:
A QUANTITATIVE APPROACH

INTRODUCTION

SINCE we have described in some detail the qualitative aspects of the differences between rural and urban, it is now worth while considering if any useful information of a quantitative type can be employed to clarify the differences suggested.

This is not an easy task in this country, since rural and urban are not categories that are frequently employed in the collection of social data. The main sources that do give national data, limited though they may be, are the decennial census of population and the Registrar General's annual Statistical Review. In these two sources the actual terms 'rural' and 'urban' are from time to time employed, but the types of data analysed in these categories are unfortunately limited in scope.

A further problem comes in determining just what is meant by the terms 'rural' and 'urban' when they are so used. For the most part it can be taken that, unless it is otherwise stated, rural and urban areas are those so named in local government classification. As the Registrar-General says, ' "urban areas" include boroughs and urban districts as defined under the Local Government Acts, and rural districts are also as defined by those Acts'.[1] Use can also be made of the fact that data may also be presented for the conurbations defined in 1950 for the 1951 census and for urban areas outside conurbations with populations (a) of 100,000 and over, (b) with populations of 50,000 and under 100,000, and (c) with populations under 50,000. If use is made of the Standard Regions employed by the Registrar General for dividing England and Wales into ten large areas, one can make rural-urban contrasts using a variety of census tables. For this purpose criteria must be adopted for deciding if any particular region should be deemed 'rural' or 'urban'. Useful contrasts can be made between 'rural' regions and the census conurbations.

The next problem is that of deciding what contrasts between rural and urban may usefully be attempted. By culling the literature, both American and British, it was possible to draw up a large list of suggested contrasts. Some come from as historical a source as Weber's *Growth of Cities in the 19th Century*, others come from contemporary writers of text-books or journal articles. After checking for overlap and combining where necessary, it was possible to produce a list of statements that could be used as hypotheses. The type of work done in the U.S.A. by Duncan and Reiss,[2] where census tracts were used for direct contrasts between rural and urban, has not been attempted in this country and the field is therefore virgin or barren, according to the way one looks at it. Without detailed tabulations from census data nothing like the American studies could be attempted. What follows, therefore, is, at best, a somewhat scrappy round-up of what can be found in the field of rural and urban data in this country.[3]

THE STARTING POINTS

In the following pages we deal with hypothetical contrasts between rural and urban categories. For convenience, there has been impressed on the categories four major classification types.

1. Population Structure
2. Vital Statistics
3. Health Statistics
4. Social Statistics

Within these main classifications, it is possible to deal in detail with particular aspects of rural-urban contrast.

(1) *Population Structure*

(a) *Sex:* Proposition that there are proportionately more women in urban areas than in rural, and that the proportion of females rises with increase in size. The preponderance of women is especially noticeable after maturity.

The 1951 Census gave the following details:—

Rural-Urban Comparison

Area	1921	1931	1951
England and Wales	1,096	1,088	1,082 .
County Boroughs and London A.C.	1,121	1,118	1,112
M.Bs and U.Ds	1,106	1,093	1,103
All urban areas	1,114	1,107	1,107
All rural areas	1,025	1,017	983

Source: 1951 Census (General Report) Table 39.

The proportionate relationships of females in different age categories in five types of areas may be compared by use of a national index figure of 100 in the following table.

RATIO OF PROPORTIONATE POPULATION IN EACH SECTION
TO THAT OF ENGLAND AND WALES

Females Only

Areas	All Ages	0–4	5–14	15–24	25–34	35–44	45–54	55–64	65+
Conurbations	102	100	98	102	105	105	104	101	96
Urban areas, 100,000+	101	102	102	102	101	99	100	101	99
Urban areas, 50–100,000	101	99	99	100	99	99	101	104	109
Urban areas, under 50,000	100	100	101	99	98	98	100	102	106
Rural Districts	95	100	102	95	93	93	93	93	97

Source: Census 1951 (General Report) Table 42.

As the two tables above clearly show, the urban areas have a preponderance of women over men, a preponderance that is marked in the conurbations between the ages of 25 and 54. The indices of 106 for women aged 65 and over in the urban areas of under 50,000 population and of 109 in areas of 50 to 100,000 population are good indications of the numbers of widowed or single and/or retired women in the smaller 'retirement' resorts. East and West Sussex were, in 1951, the two administrative counties with the highest proportion of women to men in the country. Hove had 41,451 women to 27,984 men, and East-bourne had 33,554 women to 24,247 men.

The conclusion may be drawn that women do predominate in the larger urban areas, particularly in the conurbations, where they are especially dominant in the ages between 25 and 54. But the predominance of women in certain smaller towns should not be overlooked, particularly in places of retirement.

(b) *Age:* Proposition that the age structure of urban areas is more 'top' shaped (i.e. bulges in the middle) because of the number of immigrants in the middle years who swell the urban population to the detriment of the rural population. The urban population, therefore, is more noticeable for a proportionate lack of very young and elderly.

RATIO OF POPULATION
TO THAT OF ENGLAND AND WALES FOR AGE GROUPS
(ENGLAND AND WALES = 100)

Areas	0–4	5–14	15–24	25–34	35–44	45–54	55–64	65+
Conurbations	100	98	96	104	104	103	100	94
Urban areas, 100,000+	102	102	99	101	98	100	101	98
Urban areas, 50–100,000	99	99	97	99	98	100	103	107
Urban areas, under 50,000	100	101	97	97	98	100	102	107
Rural Districts	100	103	113	96	95	95	97	104

Source: Census 1951 (General Report) Table 42.

If the postulate is correct that the middle age groups are over-represented in the towns, we would expect people between 25 and 64 to be over-represented. The index number is well over 100 for conurbations between the ages of 25 and 54, in strong contrast to the rural areas, where it only reaches 96 at most. By contrast the rural areas are at 113 for 15-24s, before slumping to 96 for 25-34s. Urban areas up to 100,000 population show index numbers for 107 for the 65 and over age group, again denoting the particular features of retirement towns. The urban areas of 100,000 plus are very close to the 100 base throughout the age groups.

It may therefore be concluded that the rural areas are disproportionately high for young people 5 to 24, and share with the smaller towns the higher proportions of over 65s, though the towns up to 100,000 population show particularly disproportionately high indices for over 55s. The conurbations demonstrate clearly their attraction for people in the prime of life—the 25 to 54 years age group.

(c) *Occupation:* Proposition that the rural areas are much more agricultural than the towns, the latter being typified by occupations in industry, trade and commerce. It is often claimed that the main difference between rural and urban is that the rural community is concerned with the land, agriculture and farming, whilst the urban community is based occupationally on manufacture, industry and professional and administrative occupations. It is not possible from the 1951 census to give a distinct rural urban contrast, but what can be done is to utilise the data given for various occupational groups for conurbations and standard regions.[4] The following comparisons may then be shown by a consideration of the proportions per 1,000 males occupied in certain occupation orders.

In England and Wales 68 males per 1,000 are occupied in the category 'agriculture, etc.' In none of the six conurbations is the proportion higher than 20 per 1,000 (and that one is West Yorkshire, a rather sprawling conurbation). In the standard regions five have proportions higher than England and Wales. In the Eastern region (159) and the South-Western region (137) the figures are more than twice the national figure; in the other three, North-Midlands (97), South (97) and Wales (95) the figures are about 50 per cent up on the national. It would therefore seem a reasonable exercise to compare the five 'rural' regions with the five non-London conurbations, these being examples of 'urban' regions. The table shows details of these figures.

If it is accepted that the plan of contrasting the five 'agricultural' standard regions with the five non-London conurbations is useful, then we can see from the above table what other principal types of occupations have any rural-urban tendencies.

PROPORTIONS FOR 1,000 MALES IN SELECTED OCCUPATIONS

Areas	Occupations									
	Agriculture etc.	Metal Manufacturing and Engineering	Building and Contracting	Mining	Transport	Personal Service	Clerks Typists	Commercial Finance excluding Clerical	Professional Technical excluding Clerical	Unskilled occupations not elsewhere specified
Eastern Region	159	129	70	1	89	34	58	88	52	63
S. Western Region	137	129	70	14	96	36	50	83	48	62
N. Midlands Region	97	156	56	84	87	26	47	78	40	70
Southern Region	97	138	65	1	92	41	48	83	55	69
Wales	95	135	76	132	103	24	44	73	45	81
England and Wales	68	160	60	42	100	33	61	87	51	80
Conurbations:										
W. Yorkshire	20	176	43	27	83	29	56	97	44	82
Merseyside	13	147	65	3	199	30	75	85	43	101
S. E. Lancashire	12	185	46	12	90	27	66	101	52	106
W. Midlands	9	331	44	8	74	22	54	77	49	120
Tyneside	8	222	58	66	112	25	64	85	48	104

Source: Census 1951, Occupational Tables.

33

Metal manufacture and engineering is clearly *more* of an urban type of occupation that it is a rural one and it is noteworthy that all the regions fall below the national figure, and all the conurbations above it, but it should be borne in mind that in three of the five regions there are more men per 1,000 in this category than there are in agriculture. One would, therefore, be unwise to consider this occupational category as being typically an urban one; it is simply *more* of an urban one.

Building and contracting is a category that shows no very strong urban or rural tendency, although it should be noted that four of the regions lie above the national figure, and four of the conurbations lie below it. The proportions per 1,000 are fairly small, however, and the differences found are not great, so that it would be unwise to attach too much importance to the differences shown.

In mining the distributions follow no other criteria than the locations of the coal-fields, some of which are in predominantly rural areas such as South Wales, whilst others are in the conurbations, such as Tyneside. The divergencies here are so great that the only safe conclusion is that mining is a localised occupation which bears no direct relationship to urban or rural environments.

Transport, again, is an occupation that is conditioned by location, since the port areas of Tyneside and Merseyside show figures well above the national index. No particular value, therefore, comes from this category except to point to the fact that transport, which might, *a priori*, be thought to be an urban occupation is not so when considered in terms of people engaged in it per 1,000.

Personal Service is a category of occupation in which only 33 men per 1,000 are engaged in nationally and the overall proportions are therefore very small for any deductions to be made. It is noticeable that all the conurbations are below the national figure, whilst three of the regions are above it. Also these three regions are the South, the South-Western and the Eastern ones—all regions away from the industrial north, and areas where the wealthy and the retired tend to live.

In clerks and typists, all five of the regions are below the national figure, whilst three of the conurbations are above it. The fact that the West Yorkshire and the West Midlands conurbations fall below the national proportion may perhaps be a function of their manufacturing rather than commercial natures.

In commercial and financial occupations (excluding clerical) there is no discernible trend, since nearly all regions and conurbations are very close to the national figure of 87 per 1,000. The West Yorkshire (97) and the S.E. Lancashire (101) conurbations have the highest figure, but the other three conurbations fall below the national index.

Similarly in professional and technical occupations (excluding clerical) there is no apparent rural or urban allegiance, two regions and one conurbation being above the national proportion, but neither side showing any particular trend.

In the miscellaneous or rag-bag category of 'unskilled occupations not elsewhere specified' it is very noticeable that all but one of the regions fall well below the national figure of 80 per 1,000, and the one region exceeding this (Wales) does so by only one point (81). In the conurbations the West Yorkshire conurbation has 82 per 1,000, but all four others have over 100. It is therefore quite clear that in the unskilled and unidentified elsewhere categories the conurbations have many more than the regions.

In summing up on these selected occupational categories, therefore, we may conclude that agriculture is a good indication of difference between the regions and the conurbations, but the other categories are by no means so clear as criteria of difference. In the British rural (as here defined) regions, there are likely to be as many, if not more, men employed in metal manufacture and engineering as there are in agriculture, calculated on the basis of occupations per 1,000 males. The rural regions, then, have as high a proportion as the conurbations in building and contracting, in transport and in non-manual occupations of clerical, commercial and financial types. Only in unclassified unskilled occupations do the conurbations score much more highly than the regions. From these selected data it would appear to be grossly misleading therefore to think of, for example, the Eastern or the South-Western regions as being *primarily* agricultural. They are areas where agriculture exerts a much greater influence upon the labour force than in, say, the Tyneside or West Midlands conurbations. In the most rural

regions agriculture is still an occupation followed by less than
two men in every ten. It has to be recognised, of course, that
the analysis here used, dealing as it does in such large areas as
the Standard Regions, is very crude and must include large
villages and towns, and even cities, where one would not expect
large proportions of men to be engaged in agriculture. This
limitation must be accepted but it is of value to remember that
in this country even the rural areas are very close to urban centres
and it is not possible for any arbitrarily chosen geographical
area of reasonable size to omit urban centres. Even in the
South-West and the East, the 'isolated' villages are relatively
close to urban centres that might well be designated as large
towns, or even cities, in some classification using number of
population as the basic criterion. To carve out an area that
would have a predominantly agricultural population in this
country would require either a limitation in size to a very small
area, or else the choosing of a very particular shape of larger
area so as deliberately to leave out urban centres.

(*d*) *Nationality:* Proposition that the urban areas contain a far
greater proportion of foreign-born people than do the rural
areas.

The 1951 Census does not give an analysis of place of birth
by urban and rural categories, and so use must be made of the
broader comparison between regions and the conurbations.
The following table gives the possible comparison in proportionate terms for both sexes.

It may also be noted that in the 1951 Census, General Tables,
Table 36 gives details of foreign-born population for major
standard areas and also for 'urban areas in which foreign-born
residents exceed 5,000'. These areas comprise, with numbers,
London Administrative County (137,334), Manchester (10,802),
Birmingham (8,970), Leeds (8,123), Bradford (7,989), Liverpool (6,249) and Nottingham (5,602) in addition to thirteen
London Boroughs (Hackney, Hampstead, Hendon, Isling-
ton, Kensington, Lambeth, Paddington, St. Marylebone,
St. Pancras, Stepney, Wandsworth, Westminster and Willesden).

In considering the details given in the above table of Standard
Regions and Conurbations it is best to consider one sex at a

Rural-Urban Comparison

BIRTHPLACES: PROPORTION PER 10,000 OF EACH SEX
PROPORTIONS PER 10,000 OF THE
POPULATION OF EACH SEX BY PLACE OF BIRTH

Where enumerated	Common-wealth Countries and Colonial Territories etc.		Foreign Countries and at sea		Irish Republic		Birthplace not stated	
	M	F	M	F	M	F	M	F
England and Wales	80	74	167	142	107	109	84	91
Regions:								
Northern	39	31	73	57	39	28	75	75
East and West Ridings	36	29	136	98	66	52	73	77
N. Western	52	34	140	97	126	122	85	89
*N. Midlands	41	36	160	93	75	56	68	73
Midland	55	41	122	78	136	111	92	96
*Eastern	72	74	199	123	84	82	117	126
London and S. Eastern	146	137	251	268	156	189	86	98
*Southern	130	140	186	170	106	116	78	86
*S. Western	92	101	132	122	76	77	87	96
*Wales	40	29	121	72	62	47	66	72
Conurbations								
Greater London	149	132	284	298	179	209	74	87
S.E. Lancashire	48	34	152	127	142	135	62	61
W. Midlands	59	37	88	65	166	134	98	100
W. Yorkshire	39	29	200	143	78	69	82	87
Merseyside	96	37	105	68	161	174	99	101
Tyneside	55	30	82	57	38	29	80	73

* The 'rural' regions.
Source: Census 1951, General Tables, Table 35.

time. The national proportion of men born in Commonwealth or Colonial countries is 80 per 10,000 enumerated and this figure is exceeded by three regions—London and South-Eastern (146), Southern (130) and South-Western (92)—and by two conurbations—Greater London (149) and Merseyside (96). It

37

must be recognised that in addition to being the capital city, London is also a major port, and mariners from the Commonwealth would be enumerated, as they would in Liverpool, where it is noticeable that for women the comparable figure is only 37 per 10,000, well below the national figure of 74. In general, then, the over-representation of Commonwealth and Colonial born men is in the South of the country, and in two of the 'rural' regions.

For men born in foreign countries, the locus shifts a little. In regions, the national figure of 167 is passed by London and South-Eastern (251), Eastern (199)[5] and Southern (186), and in conurbations by Greater London (284) and West Yorkshire (200). Once again two of the 'rural' regions are above the national figure.

Since nationally both men and women born in Eire form a higher proportion of foreign-born than do people from the Commonwealth or Colonies, it is worth looking at their location. The regions with higher proportions of Southern Irish men than the national figure are the North-Western, the Midland and London and South-Eastern, none of which are 'rural' regions. In the conurbations only West Yorkshire and Tyneside are below the national figure, which is well exceeded by all the others. It does, therefore, appear that Southern Irishmen tend not to congregate in the rural areas.

The category of 'birthplace not stated' must be included in the table since the numbers concerned are rather large, and, if attributable to any one other category, could make nonsense of many of the inferences drawn. Since it is obviously not possible to re-allocate these people to the other categories, otherwise this would be done, it is only possible to take heed of them and to speculate on the disproportionately high figure for the Eastern region, where one may wonder if this covers American servicemen and their families.

So far as women are concerned there are no great differences in people from Commonwealth and Colonies, apart from the discrepancy in the Merseyside conurbation already noted. In the Eastern, Southern and South-Western regions there are actually slightly more women than men in proportionate terms, but the differences are not great. In the Foreign Countries category the proportionate figure for women tends to be decidedly smaller than the comparable one for men in most regions and conurbations, with the outstanding exception of the London and South-Eastern Region and the Greater London Conurbation. In both these areas the proportionate figure for women is greater than that for men. In dealing with people from Eire the differences between the sexes are not so strongly marked as in the case of the general Foreign countries, but once again the women's figure is higher than the men's for the London and South-Eastern Region and the Greater London Conurbation, and also in this category, for the Merseyside Conurbation. The Southern Irish women are over the national figure in four regions (only one, the Southern, being a 'rural' one) and in four conurbations. As for the men, the women also show large numbers of 'birthplace not stated'.

Whilst it has been noted that comparison on such a large scale between regions and conurbations must of necessity be fairly crude, it does appear from the Census data that foreign-born people are more likely to be found in urban areas than in rural, but certain caveats must be noted. At the Census enumeration Commonwealth or Colonial people were more likely to be found in a general *area* covering London, the South and the South-East. Foreign-born people showed no very strong dispersion, but the location of American bases may well affect this picture. The Southern Irish are likely to be urbanised, but are under-represented in the West Yorkshire conurbation and very sparse in the Tyneside Conurbation.

This general analysis, therefore, tends to give support to the proposition stated, but the rural-urban picture is distorted by the attraction of the south of England to the foreign-born.

(2) *Vital Statistics*

(a) *Births:* Proposition that the rural birth rate is higher than the urban one.

More recent data than the Census of Population can be used for certain vital statistics, since the Registrar General's Statistical Review for England and Wales gives annual information on vital matters, much of which is analysed in a useful urban-rural form.

Rural-Urban Comparison

The Crude Birth-rate is not a very good basis for comparison, since it compares populations that may contain strikingly different proportions of women of child-bearing age, and as is known, the urban areas have a higher proportion of these than have the rural. The comparability factor, therefore, is calculated to make allowance for this uneven distribution of potential mothers, and also for the proportion of women over the country who may be in psychiatric hospitals, and, therefore,

LIVE BIRTHS

Area	Crude birth-rate per 1,000 home population	Comparability Factor	Ratio of local adjusted birth-rate to national rate
England and Wales	17·2	1·00	1·00
Conurbations	17·3	0·96	0·97
Areas outside conurbations:			
Urban areas, 100,000+	17·2	0·99	0·99
Urban areas, 50–100,000	16·9	1·00	0·98
Urban areas under 50,000	17·2	0·99	0·99
Rural districts	17·0	1·04	1·03

Source: Registrar-General's Statistical Review, 1960, Table 13.

not (to use the official phrase) 'exposed to risk'. The product of the crude birth rate and the comparability factor gives a birth rate standardised for sex and age structure and makes allowance for women in psychiatric institutions, not at risk. The third column in the above table, by using a national index figure of 1, shows how only the rural areas score above 1, whilst conurbations are three points below unity, and the other three urban categories are below the national index. It may, therefore, be concluded that, although the *crude* birth rate is lower than the national one and all but one of the urban categories, when allowance is made for the female population structure, the rural areas come out on top.

(b) *Infant Mortality:* Proposition that infant mortality is greater in urban areas than in rural.

Stillbirths from the following table do not seem to show any rural or urban trend. Infant mortality in England and Wales is, fortunately, relatively low these days, and any differences between areas are small in relation to total births. Nevertheless it can be seen in the above table that the major urban areas

STILLBIRTHS AND DEATHS AT VARIOUS PERIODS
IN THE FIRST YEAR OF LIFE, PER 1,000 LIVE BIRTHS

Area	Still-births	All Infants		Legitimate Infants		Illegitimate Infants	
		Under 4 weeks	Total under 1 year	Under 4 weeks	Total under 1 year	Under 4 weeks	Total under 1 year
England and Wales	20	16	22	15	22	20	26
Conurbations	19	16	23	16	22	20	26
Areas outside conurbations:							
Urban areas, 100,000+	20	16	23	16	23	19	27
Urban areas, 50–100,000	20	15	21	15	21	18	25
Urban areas, under 50,000	21	15	22	15	22	20	26
Rural Districts	19	14	20	14	20	20	27

Source: Registrar-General's Statistical Review, Tables 23 and 24.

do have a slightly higher infant mortality than the category of rural areas for all infants. It is interesting to note, however, that in the rural areas the mortality for illegitimate infants is as high as, and in some cases higher than, the bulk of the urban areas.

(*c*) *Deaths:* Proposition that the death rate is higher in urban areas than in rural ones, and that it increases with size of city.

The undifferentiated death rate can be taken from the annual Registrar-General's figures, and with a comparability factor worked out, rural-urban differences become obtainable.

Rural-Urban Comparison

DEATHS, BASIC RATES

Area	Crude rate per 1,000 home population	Comparability Factor	Ratio of local adjusted death rate to national rate
England and Wales	11·5	1·00	1·00
Conurbations	11·3	1·09	1·07
Areas outside conurbations:			
Urban areas, 100,000+	11·9	1·06	1·10
Urban areas, 50–100,000	11·9	1·00	1·03
Urban areas, Under 50,000	12·0	1·02	1·06
Rural Districts	10·9	1·01	0·96

Source: Registrar-General's Statistical Review, 1960, Table 13.

As the above table indicates, the crude death rate is lower for the rural areas than for any of the urban ones, or the country as a whole. When the crude rate is adjusted by means of the comparability factor, which makes allowances for differences in age and sex and for the distribution of chronic sick in hospitals in various areas, the rural areas emerge with the lowest rate still. Thus the first part of the proposition is substantiated, but the second part, dealing with increasing mortality rates with increase in urban size, is not substantiated. So far as the crude death rate is concerned, the data show a trend quite the reverse of the proposition, when the adjustment is made for comparison there is simply no trend at all. It would seem that the proposition cannot make allowance for the different *sorts* of towns that people die in. In the roughest of hypotheses, one might expect that, the larger the town, the more industry, dirt, smoke, etc., one might get, and the more epidemics, tuberculosis, etc., one might expect. Unfortunately for such sweeping ideas, people tend to die in large numbers in what might be called 'retirement' towns. Even allowing for the weighting of the comparability factor, one could postulate high death rates in such healthy places as the south-coast resorts. A new example will show the problem, towns being especially chosen for their high rates.

42

DEATHS IN SELECTED AREAS

Town		Estimated home population 30th June 1960	Crude rate per 1,000 home population	Comparability Factor	Ratio of local adjusted rate to national rate
England and Wales		—	11·5	1·00	1·00
High Crude Death Rate:					
Bishops Castle, M.B.	Shropshire	1,240	27·4	0·35	0·83
Bodmin, M.B.	Cornwall	6,170	26·7	0·35	0·81
Eye, M.B.	Suffolk	1,580	26·6	0·31	0·72
Woodstock, M.B.	Oxford	1,880	26·6	0·51	1·18
Hay, U.D.	Brecknock	1,410	24·8	0·69	1·49
High Comparability Factors:					
Kirkby, U.D.	Lancashire	51,330	4·7	2·70	1·10
Harlow, U.D.	Essex	49,000	3·9	2·61	0·91
Corby, U.D.	Northants	34,700	5·4	2·54	1·20
Stevenage, U.D.	Herts.	38,430	4·8	2·30	0·96
Crawley, U.D.	Sussex	52,150	5·1	2·15	0·95
High Local to National Ratio:					
Narberth, U.D.	Pembroke	1,030	19·4	0·98	1·65
Kingsbridge, U.D.	Devon	3,100	21·9	0·86	1·64
St. Just, U.D.	Cornwall	3,900	20·8	0·87	1·57
Hetton, U.D.	Durham	18,510	13·3	1·33	1·54
Brierfield, U.D.	Lancashire	6,770	17·9	0·97	1·51

Source: Registrar-General's Statistical Review, 1960, Table 13.

The five places with the highest crude death rates are all very small, even though four of them are classified as municipal boroughs. With such small populations a slight increase in deaths numerically can easily increase the death rate quite appreciably. The interesting point, however, is the fact that these five examples are all places where one might expect to find people living in retirement, and when people are retired they are of an age when death is likely. The Comparability Factor is low in these cases, since the populations are heavily weighted by older people, and, when the adjusted rates are compared with the national one, three of the five are below the national rate, one is slightly above, and only one, Hay, is greatly above.

In the five urban areas chosen for having the highest Comparability Factor index, four are well-known new towns and the fifth, Kirkby in Lancashire, is an overspill district. In all these cases we may expect a young population and therefore a high comparability factor to level up a low crude death rate. The effect of the weighting is to bring the rates much closer to the national index, with the two more Northern towns, Kirkby and Corby, above the national figure.

In the third category of towns, those with the highest index of local adjusted to national rate, the places are mainly small and all but one have crude rates above the national figure. For these four the comparability factor is only just below unity and the local adjusted to national rate is therefore high. In the case of Hetton, Co. Durham, the crude rate is lower than the national, but a comparability factor of 1·33 brings the adjusted local to national index up to 1·54. Hetton is also noticeably larger in population than any of the other four places, and therefore less likely to produce a large death rate just because a few extra people happen to have died in one year (e.g. Narberth's place at the top of the national list arises from a total of only 20 deaths over the whole year whilst Hetton had 247).

Summing up on the question of deaths, it is very difficult simply from the crude and adjusted death rates to make any definite generalisations since urban areas differ so much in *type* as well as simple population category. On the one hand we find new towns with a very young population where we would not expect to have a high death rate because of large numbers of old people; on the other hand we have retirement towns where people go late in life, knowing well that they will die there. Retirement places can be anything between small villages and large towns the size of Eastbourne (58,000) or Worthing (77,000).

A far more striking comparison than the unsuccessful rural-urban one, is a comparison between North and South by regions. In this we find that the South and East of England are below the national figure, with Wales, the Midlands and the North being above.

DEATHS, BY STANDARD REGION

Areas: North to South order	Crude rate per 1,000 home population	Comparability Factor	Ratio of local adjusted death rate to national rate
England and Wales	11·5	1·00	1·00
Northern	11·8	1·14	1·17
North-Western	12·6	1·10	1·21
East and West Ridings	11·7	1·09	1·11
*North Midland	10·8	1·08	1·01
Midland	10·5	1·17	1·07
*Wales	12·4	1·07	1·15
*Eastern	10·4	1·01	0·91
London and South-Eastern	11·4	0·98	0·97
*Southern	10·9	0·99	0·94
*South-Western	12·4	0·91	0·98

* The five 'rural' regions.
Source: Registrar-General's Statistical Review, 1960, Table 13.

It is noticeable in the above table that of the five 'rural' regions three have ratios below unity compared with the national base in the third column, and the North Midlands is only 0·01 above unity. In terms of the Crude Death Rate one sees, however, how the South-Western region is very high, and also has the lowest Comparability Factor of all.

A further interesting comparison can be made by comparing the conurbations with the rest of their surrounding regions. For example, data are given for the Northern Region as a whole, for the Tyneside Conurbation and for the remainder of the Northern Regions. In these cases, it is noticeable that the death rates for the conurbations are greater than for the Region, which are then greater than the remainders of the Regions. In the following table the results are given in this order.

DEATH RATES IN CONURBATIONS

Area	Crude rate per 1,000 home population	Comparability Factor	Ratio of local adjusted death rate to national rate
Tyneside Conurbation	11·8	1·17	1·20
Northern Region	11·8	1·14	1·17
Remainder of Northern Region	11·7	1·16	1·16
West Yorkshire Conurbation	12·7	1·04	1·15
East and West Ridings	11·7	1·09	1·11
Remainder of East and West Ridings	11·0	1·12	1·07
South and East Lancashire Conurbation	12·6	1·12	1·23
Merseyside Conurbation	11·4	1·20	1·19
North-Western Region	12·6	1·10	1·21
Remainder of North-Western Region	13·1	1·04	1·18
West Midlands Conurbation	10·4	1·22	1·10
Midland Region	10·5	1·17	1·07
Remainder of Midland Region	10·6	1·12	1·03
Greater London Conurbation	10·8	1·03	0·97
London and South-Eastern Region	11·4	0·98	0·97
Remainder of London and South-Eastern Region	13·0	0·86	0·97
Wales I (South-East)*	12·2	1·12	1·19
Wales (including Monmouthshire)	12·4	1·07	1·15
(Wales II Remainder)	13·2	0·94	1·08

* Wales I (South East) is not a designated conurbation, but is included here since it contains the main urbanised areas of Wales.

Source: Registrar-General's Statistical Review, 1960, Part I, Table 13.

In this table the Northern Region, East and West Ridings, Midland Region and Wales all show a consistent pattern for adjusted death rate ratios, of conurbation highest, region next, and region minus conurbation (remainder) lowest. In the

North Western Region, the Merseyside Conurbation is 0·02 below the whole Region, and is slightly out of line with the general pattern, and London shows no differences, all three categories being at 0·97, that is, all below the national index. Apart from these few exceptions, the general picture is one of adjusted death rates being higher in the major urban centres of regions than in the remaining parts, and this, in very broad terms, tends to support the original proposition of higher death rates in urban areas than in rural ones.

In concluding on this question of deaths, it would seem best not to accept the proposition without serious reservations. Certainly in terms of crude death rates, the distribution of older people in the south and east, and especially in retirement towns, cuts across any specific rural-urban categorisation. When adjusted rates are considered the 'rural' standard regions come out low in the order, but these are, again, mainly regions in the south and east of the country. When particular examples are considered from the cases of high death rates, no particular rural-urban dichotomy appears. Finally, the analysis by the explicit rural-urban aggregates does not give any trend by sizes of towns, but only a straight difference between the rural districts and all urban ones, no matter what their size. Perhaps the best conclusion is that there *is* something in the rural-urban postulate regarding deaths, but in this country the difference is a complex one, with other factors besides the simple rural-urban one operating.

(*d*) *Violent Deaths:* Proposition that violent deaths are more common in urban areas, especially deaths from accidents and homicide. These deaths are likely to be much greater amongst men than amongst women.

Details are given in the Registrar-General's Statistical Review of deaths arising from motor vehicle accidents, all other accidents and suicides, with analyses by urban and rural areas. Dealing first with deaths from motor vehicle accidents, where the analysis is made by the area of normal residence of the person killed, and not by the place of the accident, it is noticeable that the mortality ratios for women are higher than those for men in the first four, highly urban, categories, and then are lower in the smaller urban, becoming lowest in the rural. For

STANDARDISED MORTALITY RATIOS[6] 1950-3,
AT ALL AGES, BY SEX

Areas	All causes of death		Motor Vehicle accidents		All other accidents		Suicide	
	M	F	M	F	M	F	M	F
Greater London	97	93	79	93	80	92	99	104
All conurbations	104	100	87	106	89	98	104	106
Conurbations, excluding Greater London	111	108	94	108	97	105	108	107
Urban areas, 100,000+	105	102	88	101	93	100	103	120
Urban areas, 50-100,000	100	98	93	89	100	107	107	107
Urban areas, under 50,000	100	102	97	87	106	105	99	98
Rural Districts	90	97	137	108	118	94	89	73

Source: Registrar-General's Decennial Supplement, 1957, Vol. 2, Area Mortality.

men there is a very distinct difference between 'rural districts' and all other urban categories. In the urban areas themselves Greater London has the lowest mortality ratio, but there is no distinct trend showing a clear increase with the other categories. For women there is no such clear rural-urban contrast and there is no trend within the urban categories. The very high mortality ratio for men in the rural districts is a striking feature of these data. In a further table in the Decennial Supplement, where a breakdown by ages is given for death rates per million living for motor vehicle accidents, the rural districts stand out above the other categories for age groups 0-14, 15-44 and 45-64, but not for 65 and over (where they are actually nearly the lowest of all). The main emphasis is in the 15-44 age group where the rural figure is 284 compared with the national figure of 199 per million living; this excess of about 50 per cent is quite outstanding, and there is no obvious explanation for it.

Deaths from all other accidents tend to show an increasing progression as one goes from the conurbations to the rural districts for men but no such pattern for women. For men, however, the rural districts do have the highest standardised mortality ratio for this type of death, again refuting the original proposition.

For suicides both men and women in the rural districts are clearly below all the urban categories, and the original proposition is upheld by this category of death. There is, however, no clear progression amongst the types of urban areas for either sex.

There is no actual category of 'murder' in the Registrar-General's classification of causes of deaths, and criminal statistics published by the Home Office are of no use for rural-urban comparisons. The Registrar-General's nearest category, and one that can be used quite reasonably so far as definition is concerned, is the category of death from 'homicide or operations of war'. If we discount the chances of the latter part in England and Wales in 1960, we have a category for which raw numbers are given for conurbations, urban aggregates and rural districts. A simple index can then be constructed to give deaths per million resident population.

DEATHS FROM HOMICIDE OR OPERATIONS OF WAR

Area	Both sexes		Males only		Females only	
	Number	*Per million total population*	*Number*	*Per million total population*	*Number*	*Per million total population*
England and Wales	289	6·31	180	8·15	109	4·60
Greater London	52	6·33	34	8·80	18	4·13
Conurbations	130	7·70	84	10·50	46	5·17
Urban areas, 100,000+	47	8·01	26	9·23	21	6·88
Urban areas, 50–100,000	23	6·54	17	10·11	6	3·27
Urban areas, under 50,000	52	5·02	32	6·43	20	3·71
Rural Districts	37	4·04	21	4·56	16	3·52

Derived from: Registrar-General's Statistical Review, 1960, Part I, Table 19.

In this table the rural districts as a whole show a distinctly smaller homicide rate than any other areas, and well below the national rate. This is so for both sexes combined as well as for the two sexes separately. When the urban areas themselves are considered, what appears to be a form of progression, with the rate increasing as population size grows, for the 'both sexes' column is not repeated in the two columns for the separate sexes. But it can be said that the highest rates for all three columns come in either the conurbations or the urban areas outside conurbations with over 100,000 population. The Greater London area category was purposely examined to see if it might head the list, but as the rates show, Greater London is not a particularly homicidal area.

Health Statistics

(a) *Epidemiological Diseases:* Proposition that diseases of an epidemiological type are more common in urban areas than in rural ones. In this category it is possible to deal with morbidity and mortality data for certain diseases.

The Registrar-General's Statistical Review gives the numbers of cases of particular diseases which, by law, must be notified during any year, and a rate per 100,000 population for England and Wales is included. It is, therefore, a simple matter to calculate a similar rate for other areas. The six notifiable diseases given below are those with the largest numbers of notifications; the smallest category for the country is acute pneumonia in where there were 14,543 cases. Below this figure, area totals become rather small for further calculations.

The following table demonstrates that there is a straightforward rural-urban difference in notifications for whooping cough, dysentery and respiratory tuberculosis. For scarlet fever, measles and acute pneumonia there are no real differences.

There is a progressive decline in notifications as size of population decreases in the urban aggregates for dysentery and respiratory tuberculosis, but for the other four diseases no clear progression is indicated.

Thus, the best indicators of difference between rural and urban are dysentery and respiratory tuberculosis among the notifiable diseases, but when one considers the types of illnesses that are more usually thought of as 'epidemics'—such as measles, whooping cough, etc.—whooping cough is the only epidemiological disease having a clear rural-urban difference. Turning from morbidity to mortality we find that many infec-

Rural-Urban Comparison

Area	Scarlet Fever	Whooping Cough	Dys-entery	Measles	Acute Pneumonia (Primary and influenzal)	Respira-tory T.B.
England and Wales	70	127	95	348	32	46
Greater London	71	138	111	169	26	57
Conurbations	71	136	113	330	35	54
Urban areas, 100,000+	78	126	111	338	40	53
Urban areas, 50–100,000	75	124	96	325	25	45
Urban areas, under 50,000	66	132	79	425	28	42
Rural Districts	68	106	67	310	27	32

Derived from: Registrar-General's Statistical Review, 1960, Part 1, Table 31, part (b), Final numbers after correction.

tious diseases are rarely the cause of death, and a mortality table using the previous diseases would, in some cases, be useless. Thus, the death rates per million living for England and Wales in 1960 were 1 for dysentery, 0 for diphtheria, 1 for measles, below 1 for scarlet fever, and 1 for whooping cough.

The following table therefore gives details of mortality for respiratory tuberculosis and influenza only of the morbidity categories. It also includes, in addition, details of mortality for pneumonia and bronchitis, as well as for three principal causes of death in this country—malignant neoplasma (cancer), vascular lesion affecting the central nervous system (stroke/thrombosis) and arteriosclerotic heart diseases including coronary disease (normally called 'hardening of the arteries'). As these details show, the rural crude death rate for respiratory tuberculosis is distinctly lower than for any urban areas, although the urban areas show no definite progression within themselves. For influenza, the death rates show no rural-urban difference at all, two quite unlike areas sharing the lowest rate.

In the case of pneumonia the rural districts and the urban areas with the populations under 50,000 share the lowest rates

Rural-Urban Comparison

and there is a progressively higher rate as population increases. The rate for Greater London is outstanding for this particular disease.

For bronchitis ('the Englishman's disease') the rural districts are by far the lowest, and then there is a steady progression as size of urban areas increase, but in this case Greater London is not the highest, being only just above the national rate.

DEATHS FROM CERTAIN CAUSES, PER MILLION POPULATION

Area	Respiratory T.B.	Influenza	Pneumonia	Bronchitis	Malignant Neoplasma	Vascular lesions affecting c.n.s.	Arteriosclerotic heart diseases, including coronary disease
England and Wales	68	24	532	579	2,159	1,666	2,010
Greater London	62	16	697	588	2,360	1,286	2,013
Conurbations	70	21	590	680	2,255	1,504	2,002
Urban areas, 100,000+	88	24	547	624	2,269	1,758	2,139
Urban areas, 50-100,000	69	16	541	570	2,205	1,801	2,070
Urban areas, under 50,000	67	30	473	540	2,134	1,839	2,075
Rural Districts	51	26	479	409	1,920	1,657	1,845

Source: Calculated from Registrar-General's Statistical Review, 1960, Part 1, Table 19.

For malignant neoplasma there is a rough progression from large to small population, although this is not absolutely clear; the fact of the rural districts being lowest is quite clear, however.

Vascular lesions affecting the central nervous system show no rural-urban contrast.

Arteriosclerotic heart disease shows a clear rural-urban contrast, but no progression within the urban categories.

The Registrar-General's decennial supplement, 1951, volume 2, Area Mortality, gives data for the period 1950-53 for both sexes and with standardised mortality ratios. These, in general, tell the same story as the more up to date but cruder figures in the above table. It may, therefore, be concluded that for certain diseases of epidemic type there is a distinct rural-urban contrast.

(*b*) *Mental Diseases:* Proposition that imbecility and feeble-mindedness are greater in urban areas, but that insanity is greater in the rural areas.

The annual reports of the Registrar-General give no useful data on mental ill-health, but a special supplement on 'General Morbidity, Cancer and Mental Health' gives information about admissions to mental hospitals for the years 1950 and 1951. Unfortunately the areas used do not include the conurbations and urban aggregates, and a poorer classification, that of county boroughs, urban districts and rural districts must be used instead. The following are details of mental ill-health.

In the following table, with its 22 columns, the admission rates for urban districts are lower than those for county boroughs in all except two cases: for manic depressive reaction (females) they are higher and for antisocial personality (male) they are equal. The admission rates for rural districts are, in turn, lower than those for urban districts in all but one case, that of epilepsy (male) where they are equal.

The case of Greater London, taken as an example of urbanism, is not very clear. For men the admission rates are higher than those of the county boroughs in only 3 out of 11 cases, although for women Greater London is higher in 7 out of the 11. Since the admission rates for women are generally higher than those for men in the first eight categories, the male/female distinction obviously is of importance and is more significant than the Greater London/County Boroughs are.

There are no figures in the data included in this supplement for feeblemindedness.

The proposition that insanity is greater in rural areas than in urban areas is negated, but the proposition regarding imbecility and feeblemindedness remains untested.

(*c*) *Medical Services:* Proposition that there are more hospitals and doctors *per capita* in urban areas than in rural ones.

The above proposition is a difficult one to test in this country,

MENTAL HOSPITALS:
ADMISSION RATES PER MILLION HOME POPULATION
BY PLACE OF RESIDENCE, DIAGNOSTIC GROUP AND SEX

Area	All Admissions		Schizo-phrenia		Manic-depressive reaction		Psychoses, all forms	
	M	F	M	F	M	F	M	F
Greater London	1184	1740	321	323	237	538	769	1286
County Boroughs	1268	1537	295	250	270	462	815	1102
Urban Districts	1107	1431	240	224	261	472	722	1051
Rural Districts	854	1322	176	204	220	446	583	982

Area	Senile Psychosis		Psycho-neurosis		Anxiety reaction		Hysterical reaction	
	M	F	M	F	M	F	M	F
Greater London	97	223	182	262	87	80	25	61
County Boroughs	122	198	201	247	98	98	26	49
Urban Districts	117	175	186	236	77	75	30	54
Rural Districts	94	159	124	204	52	64	17	45

Area	Antisocial Personality		Behaviour, character and intelligence disorders		Epilepsy	
	M	F	M	F	M	F
Greater London	37	13	99	54	34	30
County Boroughs	27	16	94	56	50	34
Urban Districts	27	10	85	40	33	29
Rural Districts	13	7	60	38	33	20

Source: Registrar-General's Statistical Review for the two years 1950–1: Supplement on General Morbidity, Cancer and Mental Health (1955), Table M.21 (b).

since there are no statistics giving a distinct rural-urban categorisation. So far as hospitals are concerned the country is divided into regional hospital boards which cover every member of the population, and with the attendant ambulance services that can take patients rapidly from home to hospital it can only be said that some people in rural areas may well be *further* from hospitals than people in urban areas (and this, of course, has a very great effect on visiting of patients in hospitals) but it would be entirely false to give any impression of people in rural or urban areas having more facilities or less facilities when all are members of a National Health Service, which makes available specialist services in any part of the country as the need may arise.

The position of general practitioners is different. Every person has the right to register with a general practitioner who will then have a 'list' of registered patients. The original proposition might then be re-phrased to say that 'in urban areas there will be more doctors *per capita* and therefore the practitioners' "lists" will be smaller in urban areas than in rural ones'.

Statistics given by the Ministry of Health show the percentages of patients on lists of various sizes for counties[7] and county boroughs in England, and if the counties are roughly taken as rural aggregates and the county boroughs as urban ones, some crude comparison can be made. Since Wales is predominantly rural it too is included.

PERCENTAGE OF PATIENTS ON LISTS OF VARIOUS SIZES
AT 1ST JULY 1960

Area	Number on lists	% on lists of under 2,500	% on lists of 2,500–2,999	% on lists of over 2,999
England (Counties)	30,400,956	48	25	27
England (County Boroughs)	12,576,079	40	27	33
Wales	2,601,563	65	19	16
Total (England and Wales)	45,678,598	47	25	28

Source: Report of the Ministry of Health for 1960, Part 1, Table F.

As this table shows, Wales and the counties have higher percentages on the lists of under 2,500 patients than have the county boroughs, and conversely the county boroughs have the highest percentage on lists of over 2,999. The proposition is therefore not only rejected but should be reversed. The rural areas, by this count, have a higher proportion of doctors *per capita* than have the towns.

Some examples from the lists of counties and county boroughs help to illustrate the situation. If we discount the Isles of Scilly where all the people are on lists of under 2,500, the county with the highest percentage on lists of under 2,500 is the very rural county of Westmorland, with 96 per cent under 2,500, 4 per cent between 2,500 and 2,999 and no one over 2,999. Counties with 70 per cent or over on lists of under 2,500 patients are Devon and Exeter 84 per cent, Sussex East 77 per cent, Cornwall 75 per cent and Cambridgeshire 70 per cent. County boroughs with high percentages on lists of over 2,999 are mainly industrial centres such as St. Helens 65 per cent, Barnsley 60 per cent, Rotherham 57 per cent and Coventry and Rochdale both with 54 per cent. Towns with very low percentages of over 2,999 are Eastbourne 2 per cent, Burnley and Worcester 8 per cent, Bournemouth 9 per cent and Barrow-in-Furness, Chester and Hastings all with 10 per cent. The appearance once again of 'retirement towns' is noteworthy, although the phenomenon of Burnley with 78 per cent on lists of under 2,500, the highest in this category for county boroughs, is something of a mystery.

Overall, the examples substantiate the reversal of the proposition, which should now be re-stated as—there are more doctors *per capita* in rural areas than in urban ones.

(4) *Social Statistics*

(a) *Marriage and Divorce:* Proposition that there are higher proportions of married and divorced people in urban areas than in rural areas.

The 1951 Census of Population gives data for the marital condition of both sexes per 1,000 population aged 15 and over. Since the categories deal with single people and people who are

MARITAL CONDITION, BY SEX

Area	Marital Condition distribution per 1,000 of each sex aged 15 and over						Number of married women aged 15–44 per 1,000 females of all ages	Females per 1,000 males
	Males			Females				
	Single	Married	Widowed and Divorced	Single	Married	Widowed and Divorced		
England and Wales	265	684	57	248	616	136	270	1,082
Greater London	254	699	47	263	597	140	273	1,131
Conurbations	251	700	49	255	605	140	272	1,119
Urban areas, 100,000+	249	699	52	235	622	143	273	1,097
Urban areas, 50–100,000	248	699	53	248	611	141	267	1,112
Urban areas, under 50,000	252	694	54	242	622	136	267	1,090
Rural Districts	319	631	60	248	631	121	266	983

Source: 1951 Census. General Tables. Table 30.

widowed or divorced as well as the married ones, an overall assessment of the position is possible.

Marriage

As the table on page 57 shows, the proportion of married men in rural districts is, at 631 per thousand, the lowest for any of the areas used, whilst the conurbations, at 700 per thousand, are the highest. It is noteworthy in this factor that there is a rural-urban dichotomy, but no worth-while indication of any trend down the urban size grades. For women the picture is different, with the proportion of married women in rural districts being the highest of any of the categories, at 631 per thousand, whilst Greater London and the conurbations come out as the lowest. It must be recalled, however, that the sex ratio varies considerably between the areas used, and as the final column of the table shows, there are only 983 females per thousand males in the rural districts as against 1,131 in Greater London. From this fact alone it is obvious that women in the rural districts have statistically a much greater likelihood of being married, whilst for the men there is a greater chance of not having found a mate. There is, therefore, a larger proportion of single men (319 per thousand) in the rural districts, this being easily the highest proportion for all the areas. The proportions of single women vary much less than do the men, and the figure is exactly the same for England and Wales, urban areas with populations between 50,000 and 100,000 and for the rural districts at 248 per thousand. It should be remembered, however, that the general age distribution previously considered showed larger proportions of women in the cities, and so it is reasonable to conclude that the levelling up between the areas is caused by migration of women to the towns in search of employment and/or husbands. The penultimate column showing the number of married women aged 15–44 per thousand females of all ages demonstrates that although the rural districts are the lowest area, with 266 per thousand, the differences between areas are very slight. A further analysis of this situation made by the Registrar-General shows the proportions of single, married, widowed and divorced amongst the 15 and over age group compared with the national figure.

Rural-Urban Comparison

Area	Single		Married		Widowed		Divorced	
	M	F	M	F	M	F	M	F
Conurbations	95	103	102	98	94	102	120	115
Urban areas, 100,000+	94	95	102	101	102	105	108	103
Urban areas, 50–100,000	94	100	102	99	104	103	106	108
Urban areas, under 50,000	95	98	101	101	108	101	88	88
Rural Districts	121	100	92	102	100	90	73	79

Source: Census 1951, General Report, Table 45.

As can be seen from this table when the marriage figures are compared with those of the previous table, a proportional figure is merely replaced by an index based upon 100 for England and Wales. The position of the rural districts is unchanged.

Divorce

Unfortunately the above table, although it has the advantage of separating widowed and divorced people, does not give a figure for Greater London. Nevertheless, it is very clear that for both men and women the proportions divorced are considerably lower in the rural districts than in any of the urban areas. It is also noteworthy that the urban areas with populations under 50,000 are clearly distinct from the larger urban areas. The conurbations then stand out clearly from the other urban areas. Whilst this analysis would appear to be very satisfactory from the point of view of the proposition, it should be noted that the census data are based upon the places of residence of people enumerated on the census day. If there is any movement of people who normally live in rural areas or small towns to larger towns or conurbations when they become divorced this will be masked by the census, which does *not* enumerate the place of residence when the divorce took place. It would therefore be wise to bear in mind the limitations of the data and to note that the proposition states 'that there are higher proportions of divorced people in urban areas than in rural ones'; there is nothing said about the incidence of divorce itself which would require special enumeration.

(*b*) *Education:* Proposition that educational facilities are better in urban areas than in rural areas.

This proposition is similar to the proposition on medical services, in that educational opportunities in this country are, in theory, not affected by a person's residence, wherever it may be. However, there are differences from hospital services in that public education (as contrasted with fee-paying schools) is organised through counties and county boroughs which are far more numerous than hospital regions and analyses of ratios of children in grammar schools show wide variations about the country.

For rural-urban comparisons the 1951 census can be used to show the percentage of males and females of various ages who at enumeration were still in full-time attendance at some type of educational establishment.

PERCENTAGE OF PERSONS IN FULL-TIME ATTENDANCE
AT AN EDUCATIONAL ESTABLISHMENT

Males

Area	Age last birthday					
	15	16	17	18	19	20–24
England and Wales	34	19	10	6	5	4
Conurbations	34	18	9	9	8	4
Urban areas, 100,000+	32	16	8	7	6	3
Urban areas, 50–100,000	34	19	10	8	5	4
Urban areas, under 50,000	35	20	11	7	5	4
Rural Districts	33	19	11	3	2	3

Females

Area	Age last birthday					
	15	16	17	18	19	20–24
England and Wales	34	19	10	6	5	2
Conurbations	34	18	9	8	5	2
Urban areas, 100,000+	29	15	8	6	5	1
Urban areas, 50–100,000	33	18	9	5	5	2
Urban areas, under 50,000	35	20	11	5	6	2
Rural Districts	36	22	12	2	6	2

Source: Census 1951. General Report, Table 54.

As the above two-part table shows, the rural districts are no different from any others for the ages of 15, 16 and 17, but when the age of 18 is reached there is a drop for both males and females which is repeated at 19 for males. The interpretations of these data are very tricky, however, and it would be foolish to conclude that these small differences are very important. Since the census enumeration is of people where they are actually found on the census night it follows that large proportions of students at training colleges and universities, not to mention the public and boarding schools, will be enumerated according to their place of residence on Sunday, 8th April, 1951. This date is not one where one would expect many students to be in residence, since it falls after Easter (Good Friday—23rd March) but sufficient students could be in residence at various rural places to have some effect on the resultant enumeration.[8]

Other classifications of people by terminal education age according to standard regions and the individual conurbations tend to show a higher school-leaving age of people enumerated in the South compared with the North. Once again, this may not reflect the opportunities for education in the North, but merely the fact that people with higher education tend to move to the South.

Therefore, although the census data show the places of enumeration of people with varying ages at which they ended their education, nothing in the way of a decision on the original proposition can be made.

(*c*) *Voting Behaviour:* Proposition that voting in local government elections is greater in urban areas than in rural areas.

It should be borne in mind, before analysing voting figures, that there are many instances of unopposed candidates in local government elections, and it could be a corollary of the proposition 'that there will be fewer uncontested seats in urban areas than in rural ones'. The data given annually by the Registrar-General can be used for certain analyses. This is given for England and Wales and also separately for England and for Wales. It is noticeable that interest in local contested elections is generally higher in Wales than in England, although the proportions of councillors returned unopposed is much higher for Welsh county boroughs, municipal boroughs and urban districts, although identical with England for rural districts. There is no apparent explanation for this.

LOCAL GOVERNMENT ELECTIONS

Area	*Number of councillors returned unopposed*	*% of councillors returned unopposed*	*Number of councillors returned at contested elections*	*% of electors voting at contested elections*
England and Wales:	2,853	38·0	4,651	38·0
County Boroughs	165	13·0	1,107	35·4
Municipal Boroughs and Urban Districts	1,543	32·7	3,175	40·4
Rural Districts	1,145	75·6	369	37·5
England (excluding Monmouthshire)	2,594	37·0	4,416	37·8
County Boroughs	153	12·5	1,070	35·2
Municipal Boroughs and Urban Districts	1,327	30·8	2,987	40·1
Rural Districts	1,114	75·6	359	37·3
Wales (including Monmouthshire)	259	52·4	235	44·6
County Boroughs	12	24·5	37	40·8
Municipal Boroughs and Urban Districts	216	53·5	188	48·2
Rural Districts	31	75·6	10	59·3

Source: Registrar-General's Statistical Review, 1960, Part 2, Table V.

The above table demonstrates very clearly the very high proportion (75·6 per cent) of councillors in rural districts who are returned unopposed. Indeed the figure is so high compared with the other types of areas that one might consider that the electorate system has virtually broken down in the rural districts, so great must the apathy be. Even for one-third of councillors (more than half in Wales) in the municipal boroughs and urban districts to gain their seats by default is telling enough. Only in the English county boroughs, with only one-eighth of the seats uncontested could one consider that the concept of an elective system is truly in operation.

Certainly for local elections the proposition is strikingly upheld for the aspect of *contesting* seats. For actual voting where
seats are contested, the Welsh show more interest than the
English. In England there are no rural-urban differences, but
for Wales the interest shown by voting increases with the
decline of the size of area, with the rural districts having by far
the highest percentage poll. In Wales, therefore, the proposition
is reversed.

(*d*) *Other Propositions:* With the lack of data on certain propositions about social phenomena it is not possible to test a number
of hypotheses. These can, therefore, only be recorded in
propositional form and left untested until official circles decide
to make analyses by rural-urban methods or else field studies
give sufficient data for wider generalisations.

1. *Religion*
   Proposition that (*a*) there are more church members and
   communicants in urban areas than in rural ones; (*b*) there
   are more buildings in proportion to members in rural areas;
   (*c*) there are more Roman Catholics and Jews in urban areas.
2. *Crime*
   Proposition that there is more crime against property in
   urban areas, but more crime against the person in rural
   areas.
3. *Housing*
   Proposition that (*a*) there is more house-ownership in urban
   areas; (*b*) that there is more overcrowding in urban areas.
4. *Tax Payers*
   Proposition that there are proportionately more very
   highly taxed people in urban areas.
5. *Public Houses*
   Proposition that there are more public houses in proportion
   to population in urban areas.

No doubt the reader could add many items to this list; the
above have merely been taken from the existing literature on
rural-urban differences. The prime difficulty in producing data
on a national scale lies in the fact that only a certain amount of
information is analysed by the official statistics according to
categories that can be used for rural-urban contrasts. Such
annual publications as the reports of the Ministry of Education
and the Home Office Criminal Statistics are of no use at all

and to work from basic sources such as the local annual reports of education committees or watch committees would be a gigantic task for any small research group without official status. It is, therefore, not possible to go beyond the limits of the present national data, and with the limitations imposed by them the present survey must be incomplete.

CONCLUSIONS

It would be cumbersome to attempt to summarise the findings given in this chapter, since each section has already been dealt with in as succinct a manner as the data allow. As has been seen, most propositions have been upheld, but a number have not, and some have been reversed.

Two reasons may be advanced for the variety of results to the propositions.

Firstly, many of the propositions are, inevitably, derived from American sources and cultural and geographical differences between the U.S.A. and Britain are likely to lead to differences in rural-urban matters.

Secondly, the propositions are not always related to the present day. For example, Weber's magnificent study dates from the end of the nineteenth century, since when things have changed. Sorokin and Zimmerman's comprehensive study is now over thirty years out of date. In *this* country at *this* time there is very little that can be used other than broad, often unsubstantiated generalisations.

It is, therefore, important to recognise the special position of Britain (or rather, for these specific researches, England and Wales) at the present time, and especially to note the situation of a developing country in the post-war period. It is unfortunate that so many of the data used are already ten or eleven years old at the time of writing, but to wait for the results of the 1961 Census of Population would delay the book even more.

As for English-American differences, in land alone the two countries are fantastically different. The U.S.A., with an area of $3\frac{1}{2}$ million square miles is a vast continent with differences of climate, landscape and vegetation almost unbelievable to natives of this country with its 93,000 square miles and only slight variations. In rural-urban terms, therefore, we must expect on *a priori* grounds that the contrasts between town and country will be greater in the U.S.A. than in England. England is a *very* urbanised country, as Wibberley makes plain.

> Of the 50 million people living in Great Britain, only about 3 million live in isolated dwellings scattered through the countryside. The remainder live in small or large settlements . . . The people who are living in the villages and the hamlets of lowland Britain are living at the relatively lavish density of 100 acres for each 1,000 persons as compared with only just over 20 acres for the same number of people in the middle of London. Anyone who believes that large areas of land under urban uses are a serious waste of land should be glad that most people allow themselves to be crowded together in cities and large towns rather than insisting on living in smaller villages and market towns. More than one-half of the population of England and Wales live in or near the fourteen chief urban centres.[9]

Yet with the tremendous number of people compressed into such a small country as this, 80·6 per cent of England and Wales is still used as agricultural land, and 6·4 per cent is still woodland. Urban development takes only 9·7 per cent (3,600,000 acres) of the total land area of 37,130,000 acres. The general picture in England, therefore, is of many people clustered together in urban centres, with a large proportion of the land still agricultural or woodland. It must, however, be noted that the urban centres are generally close to each other; Liverpool is only 35 miles from Manchester, which is only 38 miles from Sheffield, which is only 33 miles from Leeds. Such clearly different urban centres within such short distances of each other compare strangely with American cities such as Los Angeles, which is now said to be about 50 miles in diameter and largely composed of undifferentiated suburban sprawl.

The population structure of the two countries differs greatly also, since the U.S.A. is peopled very much more by immigrants than is Britain. The ethnic or racial areas of American towns, or even the strongly national rural areas, are by no means as evident in this country. Admittedly many towns and cities today have established or growing coloured quarters inhabited by Negroes or Asiatics, but there is nothing remotely comparable with the highly institutionalised system of the U.S.A. and there is no similarity whatsoever with the position in the Southern States of the U.S.A.

As for transport, in Britain roughly one family in three has a car; in the U.S.A. the proportion is more like five out of six. With certain exceptions, which amount to only a very small proportion indeed of the total mileage, most roads in Britain are not suitable for what is called a 'motor age'. The roads therefore tend to act as deterrents to any long or even medium distance travel except in a few cases. The Duke of Bedford may advertise Woburn Abbey as 'just a trip along the M.1', but this is directed to travellers from Birmingham to London. Travellers from Sheffield who were attracted to Chatsworth by an advertisement of 'just a quick spin along the A.621' would find themselves in a narrow, two-lane twisting and undulating moorland road, where any overtaking is a chancy business. Thus, whilst the increasing ownership of motor cars in Britain is inducing people to go out more into the countryside, the British road system is acting as an effective deterrent to such acts. It would probably be true to say that few people in Liverpool would, without serious thought, consider 'popping over' to Manchester for the odd afternoon. The road, even though it is mostly a modern one, is not such that it positively attracts people to travel for pleasure. Transport in Britain then, with the added new threat of the closure of many railway branch lines, cannot be said to be 'opening up' the country. For most urbanites, their lives are very urban.

With regard to the second point about the propositions—that they are not always relevant to the present day—there are several instances where the analyses show little rural-urban difference, and it may be considered that, in Britain today, a certain standardisation has replaced what may have been past differences. For example, the fact of a person living in a town or in a village in this Welfare State should not affect the provision of health facilities or educational facilities. In fact, the data showed rural dwellers to be rather better served for general practitioners and no rural-urban difference in education was discoverable. The differences in population structure are still to be found, since cities attract the young, and especially unmarried women. Occupational differences are apparent, but the fact that agriculture is still a minority occupation even in

66

rural areas was noted. In the realm of vital statistics and in health the stereotype of the robust, even bucolic, countryman and the grey-faced, coughing urbanite was hardly upheld in such clear distinction. Differences there certainly were, but never so great as to make rural and urban like different faces of a coin; rather there were shades of difference of a common pattern.

What did come from the data was a distinct pointer towards the importance of types of area, irrespective of rural or urban. Thus, several times, such places as Eastbourne and Worthing cropped up at extreme positions in the analyses. The importance of the *sort* of town that one was dealing with became much more important than size of population. Enlarging upon this, one saw how Greater London must often be seen as quite separate from the other conurbations, most of which are in the industrial north or midlands. The differentiation between north and south was often more real than the differentiation between rural and urban. One saw how the South-East was completely different from the North-East, and that the South coast 'retirement' towns were completely different from industrial towns of similar size in the North.

These data fit in well with the differences between towns made in Moser and Scott's fascinating analysis of 157 towns in England and Wales, with populations in 1951 of 50,000 or more.[10] Ranging from Harrogate with a population of 50,000, right up to London Administrative County with 3,348,000, the analysis covered all except three of the County Boroughs in England and Wales, 64 municipal boroughs, 12 urban districts and London A.C.

The object which Moser and Scott set themselves was to 'see to what extent one can discern a systematic pattern for all, or groups of, towns both in the common and contrasting elements'. Working largely from 1951 Census and other registrar-general's statistics, the authors used a multivariate technique known as component analysis and produced four major 'components' which were derived from what might be called groups of correlations between 60 variables. These four major components were (*a*) social class, (*b*) population change between 1931 and 1951, (*c*) population change between 1951 and 1958, and (*d*) overcrowding. The first two components were used for

67

principal analyses and Scott and Moser were able to produce an empirical typology of towns from the statistical data. Whilst London A.C. and Huyton with Roby (near Liverpool) were not amenable to classification with other towns, the other 155 were placed in three main groups, (*a*) mainly resorts, administrative and commercial towns, (*b*) mainly industrial towns and (*c*) suburbs and suburban towns, and sub-categories gave fourteen groups in all.

In a regional analysis the 157 towns were divided into four regions, (*a*) North, (*b*) Midlands and Wales, (*c*) London and South-East and (*d*) South and South-West. Analysis of the variables used in population structure and change, households and housing, economic character, social class, health and education, once again drew attention to differences between north and south, and to the constant appearance at extremes of such exclusive suburbs as Coulsdon and Purley, and Epsom and Ewell, and the retirement towns such as Worthing, Eastbourne, Hove and Bournemouth.

Moser and Scott's analysis is a most valuable step in the application of quantitative methods to urban sociology and, as they themselves state, should be only the first step in further studies of this kind.

In the analysis made in this chapter, coupled with the urban analysis of Moser and Scott, it would seem that a north and south dimension has forced itself upon the rural-urban one. At times this has blurred the primary object of the exercise, but in doing this it has added interest to the way in which rural and urban should be considered in Britain. When, in subsequent chapters, attention is given especially to urban affairs the importance of *types* of urban centres will not be overlooked.

Chapter Four

URBAN SOCIETY

WHAT IS URBANISM?

IN the last two chapters we have considered the traditional approach to urbanism, using the rural-urban continuum concept for a comparative analysis of the two forms of community. In the descriptive analysis eight headings were used for pointing to sociological differences; in the quantitative analysis four main categories of data were employed.

It is now necessary to consider, from the information so far gained, what factors stand out that make urbanism, as such, a special concept worthy of particular study. Most of the more technically advanced, and many of the developing, societies in the world are becoming more urbanised. When we read that the U.S.A. is becoming more urbanised, the mental image that presents itself is usually one of growing cities, more people living in urban areas compared with rural ones, and a rather ill-defined idea of 'town-life' becoming more important.

It is important to bear in mind that, with the development of mass communications, some people consider that we are almost leaving the form of urban society and moving towards a mass society, in which any rural-urban differences are subsidiary to, and of less importance than, the similarities which run throughout the society as a whole, irrespective of whether people live in towns or villages. With the development of the mass media for communication and entertainment, and with the mobility that is made available by increased personal and public transport, the rural-urban differences may, by some, be claimed to be of little importance in the overall pattern of people's social lives.

We have, therefore, various points of view to be considered in the analysis of the concept of urbanism in modern-day society.

The rural-urban continuum concept has come under fire, of

late, from a number of people, and in Dewey's analysis it is pointed out that the actual components used by various writers for analytical purposes show little agreement on basic criteria. Dewey therefore concludes that although it is possible to point to differences that are real, these differences are not such as to make the rural-urban continuum an important conceptual tool today. Wibberley sums up the problem neatly in these words,

> In the middle of the twentieth century we are uncertain as to what is really meant by the term 'rural community', and whether there are now any significant differences between rural and urban people in the life they live, in their hopes and aspirations and in the attitudes and mores . . . The dominant cause of recent changes in the structure and functions of rural society has been the breakdown of self-sufficiency in country areas through the phenomenal growth of material and personal mobility. In highly developed countries, a common culture is arising between town and countryside—a culture that is neither urban nor rural . . . The problem for most European countries is to achieve an environment, even in their thinly populated rural areas, where persons with urbanised minds can live and work happily.[1]

Hoffsommer makes the point that 'Historically, most rural-urban differences have been derived from studies of relatively static peasant societies or from the frontier situation or its succeeding aftermath in American life',[2] and he then quotes Nelson[3] as saying, 'The best one can do is to recognise that the extremes of rural and urban societies are identifiable and to admit that there is a transition zone between the extremes in which social life partakes of the nature of both urban and rural communities'.

Even the extremes, however, are today being challenged as models for analysis. Stewart points out that 'the functional distinction between urban and rural areas is the distinction between spatially extensive industries and occupations, mainly agriculture, and spatially intensive industries and occupations . . . The day may not be far off when some agricultural specialities will become so space intensive that in function and even location they may properly be regarded as urban'.[4] With broiler houses for chickens firmly established in Britain, and with experiments now being carried out with broiler calves, which will never see the light of day, but will live all their lives under artificial conditions in the sheds so resembling Nazi concentration camps, the above quotation is particularly apposite.

We see then that with current developments of both technological and social kinds the value of the rural-urban dichotomy and the linking continuum is being seriously challenged as a rather out-dated tool which might have been of value when the American frontier was still being opened up, or when in England few village-dwellers ever went beyond the nearest market town. But today, with changing conditions, it seems to be losing, if it has not already lost, its value as an analytical tool.

However, it would be foolish to write off this concept simply for the sake of being modern in outlook and as this chapter develops it will be shown that urbanism can still be usefully analysed by using rural-urban contrast. The main point though, will be to look more closely at those features which, are peculiarly urban, and for this purpose it is valuable to use Louis Wirth as a starting point.

Wirth wrote that

> the degree to which the contemporary world may be said to be 'urban' is not fully or accurately measured by the proportion of the total population living in cities. The influences which cities exert upon the social life of man are greater than the ratio of the urban population would indicate; for the city is not only increasingly the dwelling place and the workshop of modern man, but it is the initiating and controlling centre of economic, political and cultural life that has drawn the most remote communities of the world into its orbit and woven diverse areas, peoples and activities into a cosmos. [5]

If we accept Wirth's statement then we accept that population and density figures alone will not give us a satisfactory description of the social content of urbanism; as Wirth pointed out urbanism is 'a way of life'.

We may consider urbanism in three ways. Firstly, we may consider the relationship between people and the physical environment, the urban ecologist's way of looking at things. Secondly, we can consider those aspects of social organisation for which urban society is noteworthy. And thirdly, we may consider the way of thinking which typifies urban life. Wirth expresses these ideas as (1) a physical structure comprising a population base, a technology and an ecological order, (2) a system of social organisation involving a characteristic social structure and a typical pattern of social relationships, (3) a set of attitudes and ideas and a constellation of personalities engaging in typical forms of collective behaviour and subject to characteristic mechanisms of social control. These follow closely on the three forms of community (ecological, cultural and political) suggested by Park and Burgess. Ecology, social organisation and the ethos of the community then should be the distinguishing criteria for our analysis of what makes urban society what it is.

THE ECOLOGICAL APPROACH

As we all know, even the most 'unplanned' town or city does not grow in a completely random fashion. Although development may not be controlled from above by means of a 'master plan', as in new towns, the influences from as it were below influence the siting of industry, commerce, distribution, residential areas, and so on. In Western societies it is common to find certain types of urban areas which are apparent to the most unsociological appraisal. Every town has its centre with certain main services located within a particular district: every town has its residential areas of varying types—the millionaires' row down to the slums.

One of the particular things that happens, then, with urban development is specialisation and delimitation of urban areas. Within the small village there are too few shops, offices or industries to allow for such divisions. One may recognise the main street or the cross-roads by the post office as the village centre but it would be grandiose to label this the main business centre. One may recognise that a particular terrace of cottages is very old and decrepit and sadly lacking in sanitary amenities, charming though it may be in appearance, but one does not refer to these ten or a dozen cottages as the slum district. The home of the village hussy is not labelled the vice area. We are therefore brought to the need for recognition of the importance of scale in the rural-urban continuum. As villages grow into larger villages, towns and cities, specialisation of areas is a common event, but there is nothing magical in this. Scale alone permits the specialisation being recognised. Accepting then that the small town may show many of the ecological features in miniature of the large city we recognise that the city demonstrates what is essentially a development, not a radical change.

The question of scale is an important one, since with increase in size there comes an important change in the relationship between the individual and the environment and in a larger analysis between the sections of the environment and groups of people. A considerable amount of work on the various types of urban areas was done by the Chicago school of sociologists in the 1920's and 30's, and it was largely from their efforts that it became a part of sociological practice to consider cities according to the concepts of the 'natural area'. Burgess's concentric zone theory, in which he used Chicago as a model, was a rough approximation to a bulls-eye pattern of city growth, even though the American pattern of building on the 'block' system actually produced a gridiron street network. Burgess proposed five principal rings of development which were:

1. The central business district, where such amenities as department stores, large restaurants, theatres and cinemas, along with the main offices and banks were located. This area caters especially for people travelling in for work, business and leisure, and is not characterised by permanent residents.
2. The zone of transition, an area immediately adjacent to the central business district where older private houses are being taken over for offices, light industry or sub-dividing for residential accommodation. The immigrant areas, vice areas and generally unstable social groups, rather than settled families, characterise this zone.
3. The zone of working men's homes. This area is of older houses largely populated by the working class families. Amenities may be lacking, but socially the areas are fairly stable and characterised by normal family life.
4. The residential zone, the essentially middle class zone of newer and more spacious dwellings: in this country, essentially suburbia.
5. The commuters' zone, beyond the built-up area of the city and probably within an hour's travel to the city for work and leisure. Much of the commuters' zone is thus still green fields,

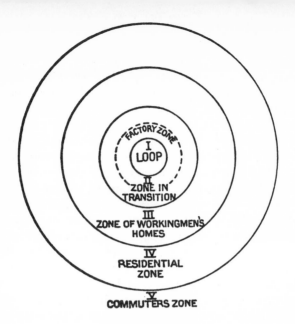

URBAN AREAS

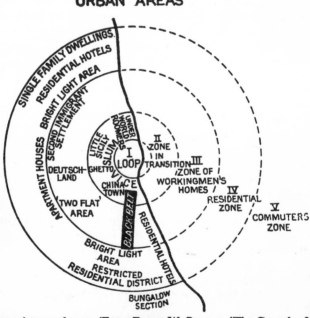

Burgess's zone theory. (From Ernest W. Burgess, 'The Growth of the City', in R. E. Park, E. W. Burgess, and R. D. McKenzie (eds.), *The City, Chicago*, 1925, pp. 51–3. By permission of the University of Chicago Press.)

74

but the original villages may now be greatly enlarged by new middle and upper class housing and are, in fact, primarily dormitories for the city.

It should be appreciated that Burgess's theory was a great simplification of the pattern of urban growth at a particular time in history in a particular country. The application of his generalisation to American cities other than Chicago in the 1930's showed that many actual areas were exceptions to the general theory, and it is obvious from the pattern put forward that a transitional zone cannot stay transitional for ever.

In 1939 Homer Hoyt put forward what he claimed was a modification of Burgess's zone theory which allowed for a greater degree of change, and was thus more dynamic than the original. Burgess's theory paid little attention to the importance of roads and railways as lines of urban development, and certainly industry was given very little prominence. Hoyt's sector theory was valuable in drawing attention to the expansion of cities in wedge-like fashion. Thus, upper class residential areas tend to be on one side of a town, rather than in a ring all round the centre. Similarly, industry tends to have its side of the town and to expand along transport routes. Once again, the theory was based on a circular concept, whereas American towns are built in grid pattern, but the generalisation made by Hoyt was a refinement upon Burgess's original and not a rejection of it.

Other American studies attempted generalisation of urban ecology, notably Firey, who drew attention to the importance of the perpetuation of high-class areas in Boston which should have been down-graded by the effects of transition, and Harris and Ullman who put forward a multiple nuclei theory which drew attention to the importance of certain 'growing points' within urban areas which led to gradual coalescence of functional areas.

All these theories[6] are concerned with city growth and its effect upon social living and it is therefore necessary to consider how they could be applied in Britain.

Taking as the main concept Burgess's concentric zone theory, it is wise first of all to exclude the major conurbations, especially Greater London, because here we have cases where towns have grown and joined up with each other into amorphous masses that cannot properly be called cities. The concentric zone theory is probably best applied to towns and cities where there is still one main centre that can be used as a focal point.

Around the central business district there should then be the transitional zone, the zone of working men's homes, the residential zone and the commuters' zone. This theory has been applied to three towns and cities fairly well known to me and comments on them may be used to show the agreements and exceptions.

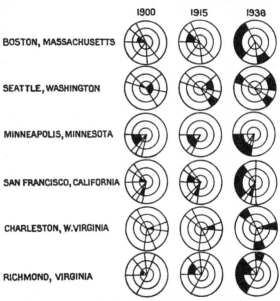

Hoyt's sector hypothesis. Shifts in location of fashionable residential areas in six American cities from 1900 to 1936. Fashionable residential areas indicated by solid black. (From Homer Hoyt, *The Structure and Growth of Residential Neighbourhoods in American Cities*, p. 115. By permission of Homer Hoyt, Washington.)

The cities, in rising size of population, are Huddersfield (128,000), Nottingham (313,000) and Sheffield (499,000).

In all three cities there is an easily recognisable central business district where there are to be found the principal departmental stores, offices, local government headquarters, banks, cinemas, theatres and shops of the more expensive and less frequently visited kind. In Huddersfield and Nottingham it is simple to decide where the centre of the city is, since Huddersfield has a major cross-roads with a small square, and Nottingham has a large square that is a famous feature of the city. Sheffield is more difficult, since it has no clear focus of cross-roads or square that is undeniably the centre, but a relatively small area, ultimately to become a recognised 'civic circle' in the heart of the city.

Given the agreed centre-points of the three cities, the various types of specialised parts can be picked out. For example, in Sheffield there is a warren of solicitors' and accountants' offices in streets near the Cathedral; in Nottingham there are many near the Shire Hall and in Huddersfield many are near the Market Square.

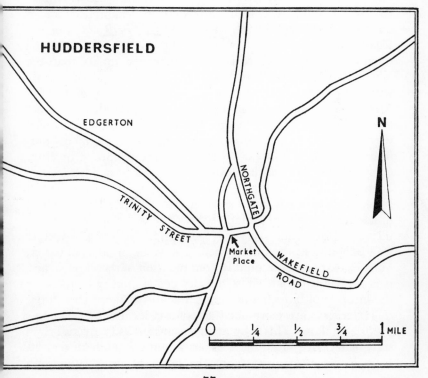

Whilst there is a tendency for some minor specialisations within the central districts, the three cities by no means show uniformity in everything. Huddersfield, the smallest, is predominantly one main street with off-shoots of varying importance going off at right angles, and with one or two further important streets lying parallel to the main one. Nottingham, with a certain focus on the central square, is much more circular in general pattern. Sheffield, the largest, can hardly be said to have one neat shopping centre, since the principal market is at one end of the central district and the famous 'Moor' shopping street is at the other. There is, thus, even a duplication of Woolworth's, Marks & Spencer and British Home Stores within the main centre itself. It is also worthy to note that all three cities have important shopping centres with shops selling durable goods such as furniture and clothing along roads radiating from the centre. In Huddersfield this is to be seen least developed, although the Wakefield Road is a case. In Nottingham, Arkwright Street is an example, and in Sheffield there are several, such as Infirmary Road, London Road and Spital Hill. Noticeably these extensions from the town are usually shops and stores of cheaper quality than the city centre ones and tend, therefore, to be associated mainly with roads that lead to the more working class areas of the city. Along roads leading to the higher class suburbs there is sometimes a row or group of shops that aims at a better clientele, with the more expensive types of women's shops, men's outfitters, furnishers and car salesrooms. (Trinity Street in Huddersfield, Derby Road in Nottingham and Division Street and West Street in Sheffield.) From these extensions of the central business district it can be seen that social class has an effect upon the location of certain types of shops which are by no means of the local, everyday type, and which might just as well be found in the centre itself. The value of land, however, must be taken into account in consideration of these shops, and it is noteworthy that whilst the city centre proper tends to be the location of branches of national chains of shops and stores, the extensions are more likely to contain locally-owned, single proprietor shops. This is by no means meant as an overall rigid statement, since successful local shops, and non-chain department stores even, operate in the heart of these cities, and national firms (especially, for example, furniture companies) see the advantages of having branches on the extension roads. But with the large financial investment that is now a part of all city centre development, it requires tremendous resources for a small local entrepreneur to compete for central sites. A very good example of this type of thing was demonstrated in Nottingham in 1960, when a somewhat old-fashioned iron-monger's shop close to the city centre was sold. The sale price of £87,000 worked out at nearly £700 per square yard, and was said, in the press, to be a national record at the time. The purchasers were a firm of army surplus and working clothes retailers.

A further current development that is very noticeable is the way in which city centres are now being built upwards. In all three of the cities here noted the skyline has risen quite appreciably in the last few years and the older three- or four-storey office buildings, often with shops at ground-floor level, are today being slowly replaced by modern buildings of eight or more floors. Some of these new buildings are what might be called 'single purpose', such as the one in Sheffield built solely for Coles Department Store (a branch of the John Lewis Partnership) with its own multi-storey car park; others are 'multi-purpose' such as Norwich Union House in the centre of Nottingham, with shops at ground-floor level, and with more than one firm in the floors above. Yet another example may be found in Sheffield where a whole new building with shops at ground-floor level and offices above was recently offered to let as a speculative venture by a building company. These types of development, which can, of course, be seen on a huge scale in London, are having the effect of offering much more in the way of office facilities in the city centre, and this increases the use-density of the central business district. It also emphasises that this district is no longer intended for the small shopkeeper with limited capital; his place is now further out.

As one moves from the central business district itself, which in all three cities is really only a small area in relation to the city as a whole, the next zone, according to Burgess's general theory is the transitional zone, or as it is sometimes called in other terminology, a zone of deterioration, or twilight zone. The main point being made, whatever the terminology used, is that

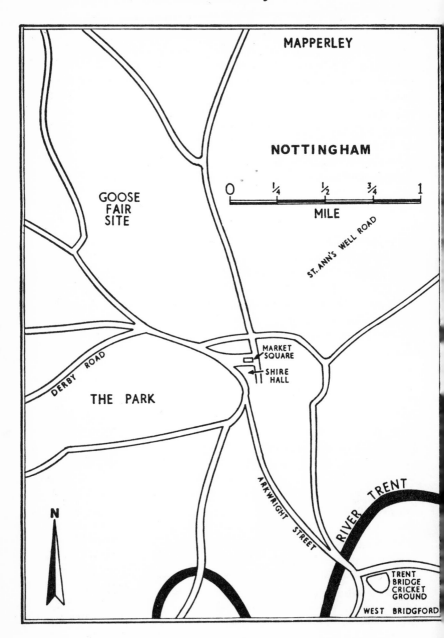

here is a zone where the land-use is changing. What were originally domestic premises are tending to become taken over by industries, offices, and, in other cases where domestic use continues, the houses become split up into flats and rooms. The dynamic situation implied in the use of the concept of 'transition' makes this zone an interesting one, but the changing aspect of the land-use means that in this aspect of the zone theory a re-formulation will have to be made sometimes when the transition has occurred.

At the present time, in the three cities being considered here, the examples of transition are best seen on the sides of the city which lead to the more middle class residential areas. At this point, therefore, it is appropriate to point to an omission in Burgess's theory, in that hardly any attention is given in the basic concentric pattern to the incidence of industrial areas. Whatever the pattern may be in America, in this country it is usual in any town or city to find that there is a concentration of industry in a particular part. Where, as in Sheffield, there are obvious economic advantages to be gained from firms whose work is complementary to each other being near to each other, it would be surprising, for example, if the manufacturers of cutlery were far from the manufacturers of cutlery caskets. Accessibility to transport, especially to railways, also is of importance, and the historical factors of accessibility to water power, and water transport (by way of barges) have their effects upon location of industry. In many ways it is very obvious that industry does not just locate itself in a random pattern about the city, but neither does it locate itself in a ring around the central business district. Industry and the older working class areas are normally found close together. The middle and upper class suburbs, whatever their age, are rarely found intermixed with industry. In this division there is nothing that has not been demonstrated by economic and social historians many a time. The factories are located according to power and transport facilities. The workers' houses are built close to them to allow speedy access to work in days before transport is developed. The middle classes, having transport, or not working in the industrial zones, live further away from the smoke and dirt, usually on the windward side. Sheffield is probably one of the best examples of this in the country. The

Sheffield 'Black Belt' which begins on the edge of the central business district goes in a north-easterly direction straight to Rotherham, the boundary between the two towns being of no significance industrially at all. Around this vast area of steel works and engineering works are to be found many of the

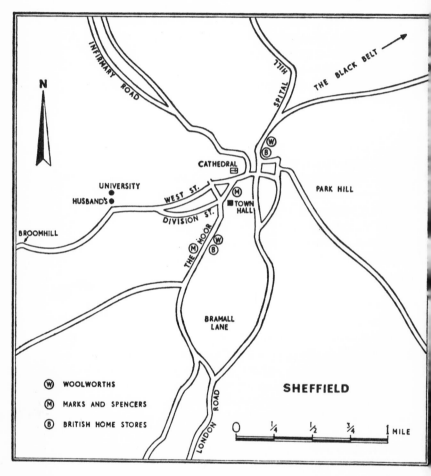

poorest quality houses remaining in the city; street upon street of small terraced houses. Moving in an arc on both sides of this, to north and east, are to be found older houses of better quality (the larger bye-law type with semi-detached villas) and the older council estates. Moving yet further around the circle the areas become more middle class, so that on the south-west side of the city centre, there are the most desirable suburbs in the city, all placed with easy access to the Peak District and Derbyshire, and all to the windward of the Black Belt, since the prevailing wind is from the west. The extreme hilliness of Sheffield results in numerous exceptions to this general plan, with streets of terrace houses in the middle-distance range of middle-class suburbs, but it is worthy of note that an area described by John Betjeman as being one of the finest suburbs in England is less than three miles as the crow flies from the heart of the Black Belt, but this three miles is almost exactly on the other side of the city centre from the industry.

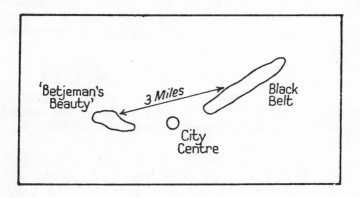

In many ways, therefore, Sheffield shows a division of the city that cuts across the centre, rather than radiating out in concentric circles. This has many important effects, and at this stage their importance on the transitional zone must be noted. From observations made outside the present examples, it would seem that most towns have a recognisable transitional area, but whether it is correct to think of it as a *circular* zone is debatable. It is common to find that the parts of the city which were the *original* middle-class housing areas when the town grew in the nineteenth century are now undergoing radical change. This change probably began early in the twentieth century when family size declined, when domestic servants grew fewer, and particularly when horse and carriage gave way to internal combustion engine and electric trams. The movement further out of the prosperous classes left areas of well-built large houses, sometimes with intermingled streets of smaller terraced houses where their attendant working class people lived. Such an area of this type near the site of the Nottingham Goose Fair is sometimes referred to as 'streaky bacon' because of the alignment of 'fat' and 'lean' streets. The houses vacated by single families have seen a variety of uses since their owners left them. Many of those nearest to the city centre became offices, branches of banks, consulting rooms, hairdressers and so on. At the points closest to the centre it is usual for most houses to become offices. A little further out there are still many offices, but they become more the smaller type of business with Friendly Societies, Trade Unions and hire-purchase branches mixed in. At this stage, too, the business-place-cum-house such as is used by dentists, osteopaths and chiropodists is more common, and the area is a mixture of houses which are purely business places (although it is not uncommon to have resident caretakers in a flat made from the old attics), houses which are homes of people carrying on businesses or professions on the ground floor, and houses which still remain in use for domestic living only. Of these latter category a variety of types are to be found. Some houses are still one-family homes, but the families vary enormously in type. Since the actual value of the houses is not as high as in the outer suburbs quite substantial houses may be bought relatively cheaply, and this may appeal to people who are more concerned with having a good *house* than with the desirability of the *neighbourhood*. Such people may live close to an aged widow who is still struggling to maintain a house that she has lived in for fifty years or more, and who has not been able to buy a more suitable bungalow in the outer suburbs because of their inflated prices, or who may simply hang on because it is too difficult to contemplate the upheaval of moving from a life-time's associations. Next door, perhaps, there may be a similar house run very efficiently by a more active and younger widow who fills her rooms with lodgers and maintains the house in perfect fashion. Yet again, and especially where 99-year leases may be running out, a house may be let out in as many rooms as possible, with little attempt being made to provide separate washing or cooking facilities, and single people, couples, or even families with no better accommodation within their reach, may crowd into the property, which itself may be left to deteriorate by the landlord. In such housing, coloured immigrants faced with tremendous accommodation problems may be expected to find a home.

In this sort of area, then, there is no lack of variety, and one may find a sectarian chapel, an architect's office, a student lodging house, the home of a decayed gentlewoman and a house of doubtful repute all close together. But this pattern is not repeated in a ring-fashion all around the city, because the old, substantial merchants' or businessmen's houses of the nineteenth century were not built all round the centre. Their counterparts on the working class arcs are smaller houses of the older bye-law type, usually in long terraces fronting straight onto the pavement (or with gardens so small as to be ridiculous) and with yards at the back, private or shared. In these areas family life is still to be found in the one-house-one-family pattern, and these are houses that, when sold, may be bought by coloured immigrants. This type of area is also one where the population structure tends to be loaded towards old-age. In a survey in Sheffield in 1956 in such an area 300 households were visited; 31 were one person only and 64 consisted of man and wife only. Thus in 95 cases (32 per cent) there were no 'children' of any age in the households. Households of the stereotyped family pattern, that is man, wife, and unmarried child or children no matter what their age, comprised only 134 cases, or 45 per cent. Only 40 households had children under school age, and 111 households had children in school, the two categories not being mutually exclusive. In general this area, which is around the famous Bramall Lane football and cricket site, is being vacated by the younger families who, when they can, are going to the new council estates, and the people who are staying are the older people without young children. This particular area is not one that has become a focus for coloured people, but in the Attercliffe area of similar housing many coloured people are to be found and it was in this latter area that Mosley intended to hold a public meeting in 1962, to the dismay of the local population. In the event, when a lesser official addressed a small crowd he was verbally thrashed by a Sheffield woman who was herself married to a coloured man.

In Nottingham, the St. Ann's Well area was the scene of unpleasant race disturbances in 1960.

In the inner ring of older terraced houses described above, the policy of urban renewal is now beginning to take place. In Huddersfield in the Northgate area a great expanse of old terrace slums was flattened and a completely new road approach was devised. In this area multi-storey council flats (named after Anita Lonsbrough, the Olympic swimmer) were built. In Sheffield several new areas of building, notably the prize-winning Park Hill flats, have completely changed the skyline.

The transitional zone is today in Britain a zone of great interest, particularly to the town planners who are concerned with the problems of renewing land that may be described as socially worn out as well as physically blighted. The movement of population from the inner slums to the outer council estates that began in the 1920's led to a great depletion of population in the inner ring that is now being dealt with by slum clearance which replaces the old two-storey terraces by exciting varieties of houses, maisonettes and flats in all shapes and sizes of blocks. In Sheffield particularly, with a hilly terrain, the opportunity has been seized by the City Architects' department for the building of urban housing that led the *Daily Telegraph* architectural correspondent to call it the most exciting building in the whole country. The problem of renewal in these areas then is one that can be fascinating and stimulating when the city corporation itself, with great financial resources behind it, tackles the job. The present result is that the *future* in these parts of the transitional zone looks better for the slum areas than it does for the ex-middle class ones. The better quality old houses are often far from slums, but they are old and they are not always well maintained. But renewal in these parts is not likely to attract the city council's attention, and the result is a patchwork of renewal. Large firms may replace their converted houses by new office blocks. An excellent example is that of the firm of Husband's in Sheffield, the engineers who built Jodrell Bank observatory. Their original office in what was once a fine stone-built house of Georgian style was demolished to make way for a new 'custom-built' office block of nine storeys. Nearby university departments in converted houses

will eventually move to a new twenty-storey Arts Block. But in
the rest of this area there is the mixture as before—houses
converted to offices and sectarian chapels, flats, rooms, boarding
houses and so on. Whatever the eventual outcome, these old
middle class types of areas are unlikely to achieve the homogeneity of style and function that is planned on a large scale by
the city council itself. Jane Jacobs would probably consider this
a good thing anyway.[7]

The third zone in Burgess's classification, the zone of
working men's houses, is likely to be found in large quantity in
any town since the working classes outnumber the middle
classes by three or four to one whatever system is used. What
needs to be considered is whether the working men's houses are
found in a concentric ring between the transitional and
suburban ones.

It is probably true to say in any town that, apart from
private estates such as The Park in Nottingham, no older
middle class area is without working class streets. Edgerton in
Huddersfield, Mapperley in Nottingham and Broomhill in
Sheffield all have their terraces of small houses. Unlike the
mews cottages in London, these have not become fashionable
because of their central location and convenience; most are
still occupied by respectable working class people. It would
therefore be possible in practically any town to walk round the
city in a circle at a distance of, say, a mile or a mile and a half
from the centre and constantly find oneself in ordinary streets
of terraced houses occupied by ordinary working class families.
In some areas the streets like these would be a small minority,
in others they would be the norm. Thus, a ring there would be,
but of very uneven thickness and, in the middle class areas
quite insufficient in quantity to be called a *zone* of working
men's houses. The general zone, if zone it really is, would be
better described as one in which the housing is of an older type,
though usually of substantial type and out of date rather than
badly built. Amenities, such as gardens, may be lacking or
small in size, but few houses would be on the condemned
registers. As one went round the city, size and quality would
increase as one tended towards the middle class sector, but
there would still be smaller houses even in the areas where
large ones predominated. The courts and back-to-back houses

still to be found in the poorer areas are unlikely in this zone.

As one moves further out from the city centre in Burgess's categories, the next ring is the one called the Residential Zone. This term is intended to convey the idea of better standards of housing than that of the Working Men's homes. In this country the idea would be conveyed in estate agents' advertisements referring to 'residential areas' of varying degrees of excellence, ranging from the not-very-good 'highly popular' to the reasonably good 'most desirable in the city'. The zones' boundaries can also be drawn by using the terms of the estate agents when they refer to 'older type' houses and 'modern'. Roughly speaking, this division is made according to the houses built before and after the First World War. Thus a house built in 1919 would qualify as modern. (To distinguish the more modern the term 'post-war' is often employed for houses built after 1945.) With a little experience of estate agents' terminology and phrases it is not difficult to recognise the type of houses they describe, in spite of their euphemisms and jargon. A major distinction between older and modern houses comes with the presence or absence of such 'older' indications as sash windows, attics and cellars. Inside the houses the older ones have higher ceilings, often with moulding, wood fire-places and high mantelpieces, black ovens in the kitchens and picture-rails round most rooms. The doors are all panelled and skirting boards and door surrounds are wide and have numerous curvy pieces to them. The original toilet fixtures are a water-closet with high tank (rather than the 'low-level suite'), a wash-basin on iron brackets rather than a pedestal, and a bath that is on claw-foot legs rather than being panelled. In the kitchens the original sinks are of white porcelain with wooden draining-boards, or even may be shallow ones in brown.

Looking first at the area which extends beyond the original middle class houses, the general result is to find houses of the 1920's and 1930's in what may be called the established suburbs. Of course, quality varies enormously, as do size and amenities, but the most noticeable feature is that here is a zone where the semi-detached house really comes into its own, with the customary small front garden, slightly larger back one, and garage usually added on later if space has permitted. Type of finish and roofing may vary greatly according to locality in the country and local materials, but the residential zone here described is the place of the conventional three-bedroomed house that, in the hands of the small private builder, has hardly changed at all in any fundamental way for forty years.

In the circle that goes round the city variations are to be found. In the middle class areas the houses are likely to be of larger size and better quality. Two living rooms and three bedrooms, with a separate kitchen and the lavatory separate from the bathroom will set the highest standard of amenity. As the quality declines one living room with a living-kitchen and only two bedrooms will become more prevalent. In this general ring, too, there will be found the earlier council estates, perhaps built in the 1920's when the original post-war slum clearance schemes were begun. In these now aging areas the quality of building is usually good, but the size is relatively small and it is common to find only one living room and a fairly small kitchen; sometimes the bathroom is on the ground floor leading from the kitchen. The older council houses can be picked out because of their being built in estates larger than any private builders of the times attempted. The particular points that mark them out are the shopping centres, children's playgrounds and other amenities that went with the planning. Grass verges and deliberate tree planting are also useful pointers. The council estates are rarely found on the middle-class side of the city, partly because of land values, partly because of the need to build houses near of access to the work of the inhabitants. In many cases it is found that the original re-housed slum dwellers moved out along their own radials from the city centre; only a few examples of council blocks of flats built in the 1930's are to be found.

With subsequent growth of the cities it is noticeable that movement was outward, using up more open land, until relatively recently. Thus in most towns, and very noticeably in the three chosen ones, the immediate post-war (i.e. post 1945) development was on the edges of the already developed areas; bombed sites were more likely to be used for temporary prefabricated bungalows than for high density building. It is, of course, necessary to remember that in these years the need for housing was tremendous, and technological development in high-storey building was by no means as well developed as now. A new ring of housing, therefore, developed on the outskirts of the cities, ranging in quality and type according to the builders and the developers. In the middle class areas, with the small private builders, the mixture was very much as before, although planning legislation controlled to some extent the densities, styles and materials used. In the private houses ceilings became lower, picture rails disappeared, fireplaces were all-tiled, and bathrooms became low-suited, but from the outside it is not now always easy to distinguish a pre-1939 house from an immediate post-1945 one. In the municipally built council estates, opportunities were sometimes seized by the enterprising city architects and planners. Even in very early post-war developments, such as the Greenhill area in Sheffield, street layouts based on the Radburn principles were used and houses, maisonettes, flats and point-blocks were brought together in such a way as to produce a residential area that could make the visitor wonder if this really was England that he was in. (And this phrase is intended to be complimentary to the designers.) In very few places indeed in any of the three cities under review are there any purpose-built blocks of flats for middle-class tenants at all, and the few that there are (such as Stumperlowe Mansions in Sheffield) may be well laid out as a unit in themselves, but they are not part of any overall local plan. The situation is, then, one where the *co-ordinated* layout of the post-war residential area is incomparably better in the municipally planned and owned council estates than in the haphazard development of the private builders. Even where private firms have built on a relatively large scale the result is merely housing, not residential planning. For example, the private builders are limited almost wholly to three- and four-bedroomed bungalows or houses; two-bedroom houses are few, and single bedroom flats almost non-existent.

A further distinguishing point is the development of amenities with houses. In the council areas spaces are set aside for schools, shops, churches, playgrounds and so on, and development usually takes place reasonably well in keeping with the housing. In privately developed areas open space is at a premium and schools and playgrounds (if any of the latter) lag far behind. A good example of lack of public open space may be taken from the case of Crosspool, a middle class residential suburb of Sheffield. Here the residents discovered that so many fields had been sold to builders that only one, belonging to a chapel, was left. The city council declined to buy it for a playground and so the local residents formed a special association to raise the money to buy the field in straight competition against builders. With help from philanthropists, trusts and Ministry of Education grants they finally succeeded in 1961.

The extension of the residential zones here described has been limited in some places only by the city boundary, or, as in Sheffield, by reaching up to specially protected green belts. Extensions of the town or city boundaries have brought about further extensions, such as at Clifton in Nottingham, and new developments sanctioned by the Local Government Boundary Commission may enable Nottingham and Sheffield to engulf important areas at present outside their boundaries.

With this gradual spread, there comes a linking up with smaller established communities. In some ways this has already happened in Nottingham where such places as West Bridgford and Beeston can be said, in some ways, to be suburbs of Nottingham already, and merely Urban Districts independent of the city through historical accident. In Sheffield, itself sometimes called 'the largest village in England', the villages of Dore and Totley were outside the city until 1935; today they are merely middle class suburbs completely engulfed in urban development. This type of development, spreading building over a wide area of land, has resulted in the final zone in Burgesss plan, what he called the 'commuters' zone' being hard to define today in British cities.

Few cities in this country outside London have people who can really claim to be commuters in anything like the American sense. Although daily travel into London from Brighton (53 miles) may approximate to American commuting standards, there is no evidence that any business-men working in Leeds travel daily to and from Preston (56 miles) although Harrogate (16 miles) is quite popular. From Stoke-on-Trent to Sheffield (47 miles) or from Hereford to Birmingham (52 miles) would both fall within the London to Brighton distance, but neither are well-known commuting routes. The true spirit of commuting derives from long distance travel over routes where the transport system, be it road or rail, is geared to the idea. Thus the 'Southport Line' which brings in large numbers of commuters each day into Liverpool, is a recognised rail route. The road into Leeds from Harrogate is thronged with Jaguars and Humbers. These types of commuting represent, in Britain, the nearest equivalent to the London and American systems of working in a large city and 'living' (i.e. having one's home and family) in another distinct town. The essential feature of this type is that the commuter need not feel at all that he is a citizen of the large city other that in those economic functions which concern his work. He has another complete community in which he 'belongs', and to which he can turn for his ordinary amusements, leisure activities and family life. The city may be useful for occasional expeditions for shopping, for theatres and so on, but the commuting residents of Harrogate and, to a lesser extent, Southport, may feel quite content to live most of their domestic lives in these towns.

In contrast to this town-to-city form of commuting, there is the more normal type of daily travel which takes place between villages and towns or cities. This type of travel is, of course, likely to be over much shorter distances and can result in the commuters also using the towns for much of their lives other than merely work. For the person who lives in a small village five to ten miles from the urban workplace the town itself may be the principal focus for evening entertainment, for the purchase of house equipment and even day-to-day provisions. Children may be transported daily to a town preparatory school before being sent away to boarding school. Friendships, with their ensuing home visits, may stem from urban interests and associations. What is left for the village is likely to comprise attendance at the local church (if attendance at all), limited day-to-day shopping for staple foods and household requisites and a limited amount of informal neighbouring with some of the villagers.

It is, of course, almost impossible to generalise about the commuters' villages, since they vary so enormously in size, location and social structure, but in two Nottinghamshire villages, close to each other and about eight miles from the city, great differences arose in the social composition. In one village there were very few middle class people at all, and commuting was restricted almost wholly to young women going into offices in the city. In the other village many more houses had been taken over by middle class commuters and there was an appreciable number of male commuters. In the former village, where middle class leadership was absent, the associational social life was negligible. In the latter village, the church, annual gala, cricket club and so on, thrived from the efforts of the commuting classes, who had, in effect 'taken over' much of the village. Yet, this did not mean solely that the commuters were restricted to the village life, since, with their own transport, they could also visit the city, and friends elsewhere, for social occasions. In general, it added up to a wider and more active social life outside (and bringing people into) the home on the part of the middle class commuters than the working classes. With the increase in the number of two-car families in the middle classes the extension of social activities over a wide field must be expected. Even in 1954, when I carried out a survey of West Bridgford which, although a separate Urban District, was virtually a suburb of Nottingham and contiguous to it, in the highest class of housing area one in six of the households sampled had two cars and the proportion today must be considerably higher. These people compared with lower social classes had fewer suggestions for needed recreational facilities in West Bridgford itself. Nearly half of the housewives had their groceries and their meat delivered from Nottingham, and over two-thirds shopped regularly in the town. Only fourteen out of a sample sixty housewives felt the need for any additional shops near at hand but an adjacent council estate gave a figure of 52 out of 60. In enumerating clubs and associations of which they were members, the husbands and wives in this residential area tended to have fewer memberships in West Bridgford than people in lower social class areas, but they led easily when it came to enumerating memberships outside West Bridgford. Thus, although these people were not commuters in the sense of the village dwellers discussed above, they did show a breadth of interests and associations that marked them off from the lower social classes in the suburb. It is also noteworthy that these people lived on the edge of the built-up area, so close to a small village that some houses were actually in the village ecclesiastical parish, and for church attendance the predominant Anglican movement was to the village rather than the parish church in the suburb centre.

With the British love of compromise (or perhaps trying to get the best of both worlds) the attraction of the rural residence and urban work is very apparent, and it can only be expected that the tendency towards living on the outskirts or in the 'villages' around a city will continue to attract large numbers of people of various types—both country lovers and status seekers. Within this general trend there is a tendency for people of high income and/or status to move out from the towns themselves and to seek thereby for a dual status. Perhaps it is, as Anthony Sampson suggests, a part of the Englishman's basic desire to become a landed aristocrat. If one cannot own Chatsworth itself, at least one can live near to it and pretend to be a country squire, entertaining one's city-based friends in place of the Prime Minister. But whatever the basic reason may be, with the ownership of *transport* these people are not lost to the town or city. Even if the Member of Parliament for Hallamshire Division of Sheffield lives in Derbyshire he is still a *Sheffield* business executive and a prominent Sheffield figure.

An interesting side-light on commuting is a slight reverse action that is very common in Sheffield and by no means uncommon in Huddersfield and Nottingham. This is the practice of dining out in the evenings in the countryside public houses. In the reasonably accessible Derbyshire area there are a good number of hotels, pubs and what once were called 'road-houses' which cater particularly for evening meals, usually of good quality in comfortable, even luxurious, surroundings, at a good price. For the urban dweller, therefore, it is a regular practice to take guests from the town to the country for evening meals. This practice is so common in West and South Yorkshire that the *Yorkshire Post* carries an occasional advertisement page headed 'Dining in the Ridings' in which hoteliers, predominantly rural, advertise their wares. When one looks at this phenomenon it is slightly strange for people to enjoy driving along unlit moorland roads in the pitch-darkness of a winter's night just for the pleasure of eating out in 'the country'. For drinking out in the country, the road from Baslow to Sheffield has such a reputation on Saturday nights that a few years ago municipal bus drivers on the late services on this route named it the 'suicide run' and were threatening to strike.

There can be no doubt that the commuters' zone has its place in the British scale of urban life today. The tremendous development of the private car has opened up the possibility of living a rural *and* urban life for many well-to-do people. Certainly there may be some problems of education for the pre-boarding school age child, but even this can be overcome with a powerful car, and if there is any railway line nearby, the commuter always has a second string to his bow if snow or ice should make the roads impassable. It is, however, a part of the British national character that we accept being snow-bound as part of our tradition, so no one ever really worries about this unless starvation faces us.

SUMMING UP THE CONCENTRIC ZONE THEORY

It is hardly worthwhile pursuing a discussion as to whether or not Burgess's Concentric Zone Theory is applicable in Britain, since it is sufficiently justifiable in use if it helps us to understand the distribution of various types of social areas in the urban environment. Burgess's theory never did, and never was intended to, fit all cities exactly; it was a rough guide of a valuable sort, and with this we should be satisfied. There is no doubt that the Sector Theory adds more detailed knowledge and the Multiple Nuclei Theory enables us to go into further detail but, as a starting point for understanding, Burgess's scheme will do good work, because it gives us a starting point for some analyses of the British urban setting.

It would be foolhardy to try to generalise at a high level for all British towns and cities, from the small to the vast, the industrial to the recreational, the plains to the hills. And with all the great social differences that are possible, a typology of cities is obviously of great value, as was shown in the previous reference to Scott and Moser's work on British towns and cities. But for the ecological approach it can be said that British cities do appear to show a fairly general pattern of a conventional centre, a transitional zone at some stage of redevelopment, a working men's zone and the residential and commuters' zones. The pattern is certainly *not* a simple bulls-eye one, since industry is almost certain to have strong social effects upon the residential areas and their location, but one can see a general pattern and not just a jumble.

Other things being equal one may expect something that could be viewed understandingly from the following general plan.

Given a prevailing wind from the *West*

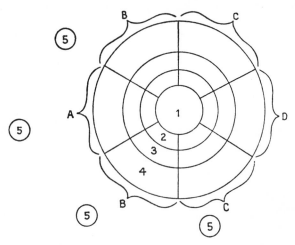

1 = The City Centre. 2 = Transitional Zone. 3 = Zone of Small Terrace Houses in Sectors C and D; Larger Bye-Law Houses in Sector B; Large Old Houses in Sector A. 4 = Post-1918 residential areas, with post-1945 development mainly on periphery. 5 = Commuting distance 'villages'.
A = The Middle Class sector. B = The Lower middle class sector.
C = The Working class sector (and main municipal housing areas).
D = Industry and lowest working class areas.

It is not claimed in any way that the above diagram depicts any town or city in this country. But if, by applying it to a city a better understanding of the ecological problems is gained, then the outline is justified.

THE SOCIAL STRUCTURE OF THE CITY

For any consideration of the social structure of the urban area to be of any use it must be shown that there is *something*

96

special about urban social structure that makes it recognisably and significantly different from the social structure of our society as a whole. It is no use simply giving a generalised picture of the country as would perhaps suit a set of lectures on 'The Social Structure of Modern Britain', and then claiming that because over 80 per cent of the population is urbanised then no more need be said. To repeat Wirth's proposition, 'Urbanism as a characteristic mode of life may be approached empirically from three interrelated perspectives', and one of these three is the perspective which considers urbanism 'as a system of social organisation involving a characteristic social structure, a series of social institutions and a typical pattern of social relationships'. Examples of these distinctive features are suggested; 'the substitution of secondary for primary contacts, the weakening of bonds of kinship, and the declining social significance of the family, the disappearance of the neighbourhood, and the undermining of the traditional basis of social solidarity'. In case one should doubt these claims, Wirth states that they are phenomena which can be 'substantially verified through objective indices'. The low and declining urban reproduction rates are adduced as evidence that the city is not conducive to the traditional type of family life, including the rearing of children and the maintenance of the home as the focus of a whole round of vital activities. Other factors illustrating the decline of the urban family are the transfer of industrial, recreational and educational activities to agencies outside the home, the employment of married women and mothers, the existence of lodgers in the household, postponement of marriage, larger proportions of single and unattached people, smaller families and more families without children than in the country, emancipation of the family from the larger kin group, individual and diverging interests within the family in vocational, educational, religious, recreational and political life—the list goes on. Indeed, the reader, after little more than a page of this catalogue is so bombarded with what the family does *not* do or have in urban society, that he may wonder whatever it has got at all. It is also noteworthy that most of the statements made are comparative ones, rather than absolute statements. There is an implied, or over-stated, comparison with rural areas which is merely repeating or adding to the types of hypotheses dealt with previously. In some cases, in Britain, the objective indices can be (and have been) tested for validity. There *are* differences in the population structures of rural and urban districts, as we have seen. But whether some of the inferential statements made above are really valid when they are looked at in terms of sociological structure is a matter for question.

Wirth charges the city with 'undermining the traditional basis of social solidarity', and in this statement there is really a historical element so important that any comparison of *present* urban with *present* rural would be valueless. What Wirth is really saying is that the *development over time* of the city has brought about a change from the *old* bases of social solidarity. These charges, to him, are importantly shown in the *substitution* of secondary for primary contacts, weakening of kinship bonds, decline of the family and disappearance of neighbourhood. Yet are these trends really trends ascribable to the city itself, or are they a part of the general development of socity in the nineteenth and twentieth centuries? Indeed, are these hypotheses valid ones anyway? Has there been a substitution of secondary for primary contacts?; have the bonds of kinship weakened?; has the neighbourhood disappeared? Perhaps these things have not happened anyway. Wirth argues that, 'Characteristically, urbanites meet one another in highly segmental roles. They are, to be sure, dependent upon more people for the satisfaction of their life-needs than are rural people and thus are associated with a greater number of organised groups, but they are less dependent upon particular persons, and their dependence upon others is confined to a highly fractionalised aspect of the others' round of activity'. While one might agree with the general line of argument, it could also be argued that Wirth is giving a particular slant to the case which makes it appear that the urbanite loses *altogether* his primary contacts, simply through living in the city. This seems to ignore the fact that the more complex social and population structure of the city gives wider opportunities for social contacts of all ages. It is true that in a small isolated community one's contacts may all be within a very narrow circle of people, and therefore many people will stand in a variety of roles to each other, each person knowing the others in a multi-dimensional way. But this does not necessarily mean that the urban person who, for example, would only know his postman in that one role (and not as a member of the village church, football club and local hunt) does not have primary contacts just the same. The urbanite and ruralite can surely both have primary contacts with relatives, family, friends, neighbours and so on. MacIver and Page define the primary group as 'that in which a small number of persons meet "face to face" for companionship, mutual aid, the discussion of some question that concerns them all, or the discovery and execution of some common policy'.[8] As examples, there are given—'the play group, the group of friends, the gossip group, the partnership, the local brotherhood, the study group, the local gang, the tribal council'. Whilst MacIver and Page do say that 'in primary group life one's relations with the others are always, to some extent, *personal*', they go on to describe secondary relations as being those involving categoric or 'rational' attitudes, e.g. buyer and seller, voter and candidate, official and citizen, teacher and student, practitioner and client.

If we accept MacIver and Page's views on the primary relationship and group, we can see that many relationships within the rural community are, in fact, of a secondary nature. The housewife and the village store-keeper, the village policeman and the householder, the teacher and the school-child and the local doctor and his patient are in a secondary relationship.

On the other hand, play groups, gossip groups, study groups, local gangs all exist in the most urban of environments, and 'We contrast, then, the type of relationship between friends or between lovers or within cliques of gangs or families with the type that permeates the large-scale groups'. All these sorts of primary groups and relationships exist in urban settings, and it is misleading to suggest that they do not. To say, as Wirth does, that 'the contacts of the city may indeed be face to face but they are nevertheless impersonal, superficial, transitory and segmental' is to ignore completely the whole range of highly personal and intimate relationships which exist within the marriage bonds, the parent-child relation, deep friendship and so on which exist in any sort of environment—rural or urban. There is obviously a confusion in the application of the idea of secondary relationships supplanting primary ones when the analysis of urban life is made in this way. What is really meant is that, in a small community everyone stands in a face-to-face relationship to everyone else, and this results in people knowing each other in a 'whole' way, rather than a segmental way. The village postman *is* known in a variety of roles and statuses and these, added together by everyone who knows him, result in him being evaluated more thoroughly as a man than could possibly be so if the recipients of the mail knew him only from his occasional words over the delivery of a parcel or registered letter. But this 'multi-dimensional' relationship need not necessarily be a deep one; the actual social relationship between postman and recipient of mail is still essentially a secondary one determined by the vast organisation of the General Post Office and British taxpayers. No relationship of mail recipient with postman can be so deep or intimate as that between husband and wife (unless it be the postman's wife we think of) and marriage is just as popular in urban areas as in rural ones.

It is, therefore, very doubtful whether the idea of the *substitution* of secondary for primary contacts in the urban setting is completely valid. Rather it should be said that the size of the group enlarges the possibilities for social contacts of every kind, and when this occurs the individual interacts with many more people in single-role situations. Whilst this may make for a more superficial or impersonal relationship with shop assistants, policemen, postmen and so on, it does not deny the individual the possibility of many deep personal relationships with spouses, children, kinsfolk, friends, cronies, gang-mates and so on. Indeed, if the small face-to-face informal groups suggested by MacIver do characterise primary relationships, then it can be said that the city enlarges these contacts.

It is obviously appropriate here to consider the particular case of the bonds of kinship which Wirth says are weakened by by the urban environment.

> Low and declining urban-reproduction rates suggest that the city is not conducive to the traditional type of family life, including the rearing of children and the maintenance of the home as the locus of a whole round of vital activities. The transfer of industrial, educational and recreative activities to specialized institutions outside the home has deprived the family of some of its most characteristic historical functions.

It is then suggested that urban families are likely to have more mothers employed outside the home, more lodgers, later marriage, and that there will be greater proportions of single and unattached people, as well as smaller families and more childless families than in the country.

Accepting that the data that can be obtained for England and Wales do support some of these statements, it must be borne in mind that the actual differences are by no means so great. The proportions of one-person households in town or country does not exceed 10 per cent in more than a few cases; childless marriages in the city are not the norm, and the size of family is not so different as to be apparent to the ordinary citizen. The danger is one of making differences in minority proportions appear to be differences of vast proportions. Working wives are certainly very common in the towns,[9] but in these days it would be surprising if analysis did not show a fair proportion in rural areas too. Lodgers may be more common in towns than in villages, but lodgers are not the norm in the urban household.

When Wirth's assertion is looked at critically the *causal* relationships between the various factors and the putative decline in the urban family are by no means clear, and need challenging. The transfer of industrial, educational and recreational activities from the home is a feature common to the whole of our society—not merely the urban sector. The home as 'the locus of a whole round of vital activities' is a vague, somewhat Mumfordian phrase, which can mean anything the reader wishes it to mean, but it can just as well be argued that the overall changes of our society have had an equal effect on both rural and urban families, and that the historical process of our whole society must be considered. Indeed, it is interesting to note that in the particular case of the family one British sociologist[10] has been driven to devote a whole book to refuting unsupported statements about the 'decline of the family in contemporary society', and in this interesting work the idea of 'decline' is vigorously refuted.

It is, however, apparent that there is a system of social organisation, with a characteristic social structure and a typical pattern of relationships, which can be called urban. The social structure is based essentially upon large numbers of people, so large that certainly it is impossible for everyone to know everyone else, or even recognise everyone else. One of the characteristics, surely, of an urban community is that one is always seeing people one has never seen before. In this situation then, the interactional pattern is a pattern of segmental relationships between *strangers*. In his work, travel, shopping, recreation, religion and so on, the urbanite is coming up against a steady stream of new faces; he is acting in a segmental role with many people whom he has never seen before. Now the relationship between shopkeeper and customer in the village store is essentially a contractual (i.e. secondary) one, but it is filled out with a padding of other factors because of the multi-role knowledge of shopkeeper and customer about each other. This makes for a more 'personal' relationship and the whole commercial transaction becomes more 'human' and less impersonal. A similar sort of situation is seen in the suburban shopping centre where a counter-service 'corner' shop may be a place of commerce and personal chit-chat. (For example, at my own local baker's shop, the woman behind the counter greets every regular customer by his or her name, and is always ready with the appropriate question about the person's health, children, spouse, and so on. The effect is very impressive to the newcomer.) The antithesis is the large city centre self-service store where every attempt is made to reduce human contact, and where, because of the scale of the enterprise and the vast numbers of customers from all parts of the city, nothing beyond the purely contractual relationship is possible— or even desired by either side to the contract. Yet such shopping facilities are greatly used by urbanites, and their utility is obviously appreciated as is demonstrated by their very great success.

If the village was really typified by the general store and the urban area by the self-service store, or even supermarket, then the sort of contrast made by Wirth would perhaps be partly valid. But the essential point is that the city does not stop having the local general stores simply because there are city centre self-service facilities. Although the local shops are *not* the same thing as the *one* village store, I suggest that the principal feature of the urban area is that of *variety*. This means that the social relationships of the urban structure encompass a far greater range than those of the rural one, and are *not limited* to its multi-role relationship. To use a simple analogy, a child who has only two toys will have to play with those toys or play with nothing, and, given the desire for toys, the child will come to know them well. If he has a large number of toys there will be a variety of choice for any particular game, and the same doll will not have to be used again and again. But it is noticeable that no matter how many dolls a child may have, there are always one or two which are the favourites, and tend to be played with more than the others. In this way, the urban individual has breadth of choice, but also has the ability to have special friends, companions and so on. Indeed, if one uses value-laden words, the deep, personal relationships of the small community could equally well be called 'parochial', 'stifling' or 'narrow'.

There would seem then to be no reason to vilify the urban environment for a loss of traditional ways or historical functions of the family, if urban development has afforded wider opportunities for social interaction. The urban environment offers variety and choice in social experience in addition to the customary relationships of home, family and extended kinship. In putting forward this alternative view of the urban social structure, I do not mean to ignore the accepted problems of the urban area. For example, it is accepted that suicide is a particularly urban phenomenon, and that the loneliness of the crowd is a desperate state of affairs. But to say that 'the superficiality, the anonymity and the transitory character of urban social relations make intelligible . . . the sophistication and the rationality generally ascribed to city-dwellers' is certainly not to describe the families of Young and Willmott in Bethnal Green or Kerr in Liverpool or even Willmott in deepest Dagenham. Wirth would argue that in the urban setting the individual 'gains, on the one hand, a certain degree of emancipation or freedom from the personal and emotional controls of intimate groups', but, 'he loses, on the other hand, the spontaneous self-expression, the morale, and the sense of participation that comes with living in an interacted society'. Whilst one can see what Wirth means by gains, the losses are far less clear, particularly when he implies that the urban society is not integrated. The city is not integrated at a personal face-to-face level for all the inhabitants, but then this can only occur anyway for very small villages, and stops even at the size of the market town. What is obviously true is what the Lynds suggest, that with increasing size, acquaintance and association become more selective. This results in a proliferation of groups rather than just the one and thus the structure of the community becomes more complex, more difficult to understand, harder to organise and more 'optional' in that people can opt in or out of various social activities. At this stage it becomes difficult for some people who would like to establish relationships to do so, and so the opting in, particularly for strangers to a town, may become a difficult process of adjustment. However, it is here that the width of experience of the town acts as an alternative for the urbanite. Although the morale and sense of participation that Wirth speaks of may be lost because the community as a whole cannot express this at face-to-face level, the society itself affords the individual an almost limitless choice of self-expression in the voluntary activities made possible by the very size of the population. *In addition to* the family, the local kin and the neighbours (who can all be amicable people, even in cities) there are the other social activities of cultural, sporting and recreational types which make the urban setting a place of constant opportunities for meeting new people and widening the individual experience. This experience need not always be at a high intellectual or cultural level either, since few people live in such rarified atmospheres. The ability of the town teenager to go to six different dance halls, a speedway, an ice rink, an all-in wrestling hall and two football league grounds is a breadth of available experience afforded, on the spot, to no village youth in this country. That people do like the social structure of the city is demonstrated by the continuous movement of people to cities. The other face of the coin is seen in the disappointments found by many people in the new towns, which they find lacking in amenities and facilities. This does not mean a lack of schools, good houses or even boy scout and girl guide groups. What appears to be missing is the decent-sized dance hall, the coffee bars, the skating rinks, the streets and streets of shops for window-gazing and the variety that the city offers.[11] I feel that this is, in essence, the sort of thing that Jane Jacobs is getting at when she places so much emphasis on the street and the shop-keepers in her own locale in New York. She has undoubtedly shaken many town planners to their very core because she frankly likes living with a lot of other people in a busy area where there is bustle and noise and plenty going on all the time. This is not what Lewis Mumford likes, it would seem to have been less than popular with Louis Wirth, it would certainly never have commended itself to Ebenezer Howard, but it *does* appear to suit large numbers of ordinary people who are blissfully unaware of the superficiality, anonymity and transitory character of their relationships and just go on enjoying life all the same.

THE URBAN ETHOS

In his discussion of the rural-urban continuum Richard Dewey states that Louis Wirth describes an urban personality as one which

> is featured by reserve, blasé outlook, indifference, sophistication and cosmopolitanism, rationality; relativistic perspectives; tolerant, competitive, self-aggrandizing and exploitative attitudes; feelings of friction, irritation and nervous tension bred by frustration; acceptance of instability and insecurity; tolerance of eccentricity and novelty and approval of efficiency and inventions, and marked degrees of personal disorganization.[12]

Giving also a similar list for social organisation, Dewey says that all these concepts serve 'only to emphasize the amorphous nature of currently used definitions of urbanism'. There would appear to be hardly any sort of feeling or attitude that is not encompassed by this great list of suggested aspects of urban personality. Whether it can be truly said that these traits are specifically urban ones is a matter for conjecture, for they may apply to urban environments or they may equally be traits of an industrialised society itself.

The city has always been regarded as the place of innovation, and such adjectives as 'sophisticated' and 'blasé' do, at first glance, seem to be more appropriate to the urban setting than the rural and yet, if for the urban place one were to use

Huddersfield (population 128,000) as the example, and for the rural, Forest Row in Sussex (population 3,258) it would not be merely the fact, probably unknown to anyone without looking up the reference, that Forest Row has more A.A. starred hotels than Huddersfield, which would make the comparison less obvious than it seems. Huddersfield is northern, provincial, industrial and all that is evoked by the word 'Yorkshire'. Forest Row is close to East Grinstead and was deliberately chosen because it featured in an *Observer* article in the 'Commuter Country' series. With the given location and description of the two places the words sophisticated or blasé would perhaps be better changed round and applied, in this case to the rural spot, 'set in some of the best Home Counties countryside' according to the article.

This contrast is a particularly interesting one to make because it draws attention to the fact that population size, population density and general size of place is not necessarily linked with all the phrases used by Wirth to describe the urban ethos. If this is so, the urban 'personality' is something which derives more from the *social* environment and structure, than the physical, or even demographic. One can be reserved, blasé, indifferent, sophisticated, cosmopolitan, rational, etc. etc., in the heart of the Home Counties just as much as, if not more than, in urban Huddersfield. Yet, whilst recognising the ease with which it is possible to make the urban characteristics fit the rural, it is also apparent that as *total* social structures, Huddersfield and Forest Row are poles apart. It is in the complex social structure which goes with the population of 128,000, the varied industries, schools, transport, shops and services that all go together to make up Huddersfield, that one sees a social organisation based upon very different ideas from that of Forest Row. Huddersfield is a total community of many facets; Forest Row is, as the *Observer* says, 'commuter country' and, therefore, satellite to London.

Perhaps in England the real distinction that should be made in considering the urban ethos, is the distinction between London and 'the rest', so often described as 'the provinces'. Between the capital and the provinces, taking the latter term to refer to those parts of the country other than the capital, there exists a relationship very akin to that which is applied to the urban and non-urban personality classification. 'Provincial' is an adjective which includes such ideas as 'unpolished' and 'narrow'; it is an adjective applied very often in a deliberately derogatory sense to all places outside the orbit of the capital. It may be suggested that to live in the Home Counties is to attach oneself psychologically to London, and so to avoid the stigma of provincialism, even though this may mean accepting that one's place of reference thereby becomes an amorphous area of several hundred square miles.

What Wirth is suggesting in his aspects of urban personality is an outlook on life which is related to the individual rather than the group. Reserve, indifference, rationality, self-aggrandisement, and so on are all terms which place an emphasis on individual achievement and interest rather than on that of any given group. It is argued that the complexity of the large urban community makes it impossible for the individual to think meaningfully of the *whole* group of people as one unit and, as a reaction to this, he tends to think more and more of himself. Along with status symbols, conspicuous consumption and the rest, the individual then relates himself to other people by means of symbols of achievement rather than by personal assessment. It is a short step then to desiring the symbols for their status value in an impersonal way, that is, in seeing the symbols virtually as ends in themselves because of one's conditioning.

Robert Lynd made the interesting point that

> Individuals can and do live comfortably in our large cities with no formal ties between themselves and the structures of the culture save the money ties between them and their jobs. One may or may not elect to exercise one's political right to vote, one may or may not own property, money, or belong with anybody else to anything; but one must tie into the structure to the extent of getting money regularly. The culture puts an extreme reliance upon this money nexus between the individual and his job to hold the culture together.[13]

At the basic level of interaction, the economic values are the prime determinants of the social values. As Lynd says, one must get money regularly. It should be added to this that one should get money regularly in a socially approved fashion, but in the wider community social approval would appear to be given to practically all means that are not illegal, and even some illegal ones are only mildly condemned. Seen from the viewpoint of economic achievement by any legal means the urban ethos would then favour an emphasis upon individualism, and could be used to put most other attitudes into a reasonably coherent framework. If it is recognised that both historically and contemporaneously the city is essentially an economic unit of people, then it must not be a matter of surprise if economic values tend to dominate the people of the city. Trade, commerce and industry are economic activities of the city and their ethos must dominate all others. It would then follow that what is good for trade, commerce or industry is good for other aspects of living. If industry needs innovation then innovation as a value is a good thing; if trade is based upon a contractual relationship then contractual relationships are good things. Many value judgments of more utopian thinkers may be opposed to such a materialistic way of life, but it is irrefutable that modern societies *are* materialistic. The American National Resources Committee noted that 'cities have traditionally been regarded as the home of inventions and revolutions. They secularise the sacred beliefs, practices and institutions; they democratise knowledge, fashions and tastes, and, consequently, generate wants and stimulate unrest'.[14] In such a social climate production and consumption are the key activities, and it is worth noting that one of the most successful voluntary movements in Britain in recent years has been the Consumers' Association, with a membership of 230,070[15] (far more successful in the interest it has aroused than its stable-mate the Advisory Centre for Education).

In the organic solidarity of the urban community is to be seen the solidarity of a community depending for its continuance upon change, progress, innovation and a general state of flux. The urban ethos, then, must be attuned to movement and change, and must be ready to accept this as a socially acceptable thing. Conservation and preservation, except in such artificial enclaves as museums and parks, are the very antithesis of the urban outlook where 'renewal' and 'development' are the key words.

If it is accepted that a social life based upon an approval of change requires a particular type of outlook, then the suggested words of Wirth—tolerant, competitive, self-aggrandising and exploitative—would seem more appropriate to urban than rural communities.

The size and complexity of urban groups must also entail a different type of social control from the rural one. As was stated in the discussion on rural-urban differences, the change is from the rural personal control to a more diffuse and less personal one, often changing in places to a control by specialists (e.g. police, social services, etc.). The *total* community of a large city cannot act to bring a deviant into line, as could be done by reaction to a village scandal, and the control of the urban locality is different in kind from that of the village in that it is a much more haphazard control deriving from the relationships of the urban neighbourhood. It must therefore be accepted that tolerance of or avoidance of eccentric behaviour is much more likely in the city than the countryside. The eccentric person who, for example, dresses oddly and acts in a peculiar way may be accepted or rejected by the village according to the actual reasons for, and understanding of, his eccentricity. Many a village loon is cherished by the villagers who understand his whole background. In the city, however, the eccentric is tolerated in an impersonal way; that is to say that he is permitted his eccentricities because of the lack of involvement of his fellow urbanites with him and, probably, their lack of knowledge of his case. The result may be the continuance of the eccentricity in both places, but for different reasons. If, however, the eccentricity is deemed to be socially undesirable, then it is in the village that positive action may be expected, whereas in the town a general turning of backs would be more common.

The live-and-let-live attitude of the urban grouping is a function of the size and complexity of the urban social structure, but it must be remembered that the urban scene is not one of complete licence or anomie. The economic values of the town and city are clearly expressed in many social attributes and activities. As numerous writers have pointed out, place of residence in the city is an important factor. Reimer says 'the city dweller's "address" tells not only where he lives, but where he belongs in the social scale . . . home ownership is, after all, one of the most conspicuous forms of conspicuous consumption'.[16] Along with residence there may be the use of leisure and the membership of voluntary clubs and organisations, the ownership of a motor car along with its size and type and period of renewal, the education of children according to type of school and system of education used—public or private. All these facets of life are useful indications which enable the urbanite to demonstrate to the rest of his fellow citizens 'what' he is, even if he cannot establish clearly 'who' he is. Indeed, it is interesting that in trying to 'place' a newcomer to the urban locality we are more likely to ask 'what' he is rather than 'who', since the former refers to his achieved status, especially in occupation, whilst the latter refers to his ascribed status, mainly through kinship, which may well be meaningless in a mobile society.

Through the visual symbols of status the urban dweller is able to place his fellow urbanites *to some extent* in the complex structure, and the business-man's bowler hat and furled umbrella are as useful as the gas-meter reader's peaked cap and blue macintosh in this respect. Instant recognition makes for rapid adjustment between individuals and groups, and this is necessary in a complex environment.

The so-called superficiality of the city cannot be avoided if one lives with many thousands of other people in a complex society. But it does not follow that the *whole* outlook of urban dwellers is superficial. Rather it should be said that the urban ethos is, on the large scale, one which accommodates itself to large numbers of necessarily transitory social contacts, and which makes use of symbols of rank, achievement, status and so on so as to keep the machinery going. On the smaller, more personal, scale the city dweller does have codes of social control which operate in social groupings of class, neighbourhood, church, political organisation and so on, as well as the obvious unit of the family and household. It is, therefore, more correct to think of the urbanite as a person with a multiplicity of roles and statuses living at various levels in a complex community of great size with many sub-divisions; indeed, in a heterogeneous community. The village dweller is, by contrast, a dweller in what is largely a single community where all the roles and statuses fit into one comprehensible pattern and where one code of rules, complex though they may be, will fit everyone.

One of the problems of urban living is that of learning the sets of rules that govern the various aspects of one's life. To take one single example, the codes of behaviour expected of people in various voluntary associations differ, so that the conduct expected of a person in, say, a tennis club may be quite different from that of the same person in a political party. As a tennis player the one person may be known as a gay-hearted member; at the political club, with a totally different set of people, he may be a very serious-minded politician. It is in accepting that a person can live separate parts of his life in different groups that the urban ethos has its basic function. It means that the emphasis is upon associational rather than communal roles and upon a permissive atmosphere within which the urban dweller so often may *choose* whether or not to be associated with certain activities and groups. Only in certain situations and places do the 'oughts' and 'ought nots' apply. In the suburban neighbourhood one 'ought' to care for one's garden, one 'ought not' to let one's children play in the road. In a less refined area these two rules might not apply. Over the whole area of the city, then, it would be difficult to find one set of rules that apply. In one area one ought not to live with a woman who is not one's wife, in another area one ought not to poke one's nose into other people's affairs.

In summing up the urban ethos then, it might be said that with a social structure of great complexity, much of which is derived from basically economic relationships, many of the attitudes of the urban dweller are of a *laissez-aller* nature. Yet it would be misleading to suggest that urban life is wholly sophisticated, blasé and impersonal. The lives of the working classes, who form the bulk of the urban population are far from this, and these people live lives which are often strongly conditioned by values derived from family and locality groups.

It should also be noted that the urban personality is not a factor that can be ascribed without qualifications to all urban places. It was noted in dealing with rural-urban quantitative differences that there are towns and cities of very different population structure, and this, along with location, industrial background and so on have great influence upon the 'feel' of a town. It has been said of Huddersfield (albeit without support-ing evidence) that it has more Rolls-Royce cars per head of population than any other town in the country.[17] This would fit in well with the 'where there's muck there's money' remark so often aimed at anywhere north of the Wash. Certainly, from my own experience of Huddersfield it is a very money-conscious town. Nottingham is a very clean, prosperous and tradition-conscious town which at times almost has an air of complacency. In cultural activities it has a fine record, and it is reputed to have the prettiest girls in England. These sort of ideas give Nottingham an air of well-being. Sheffield, for a city of half a million population, is very isolated and its industry is very dirty though immensely important. For all its size, Sheffield still has the air of a small town, particularly in its politics and its local press. Sheffield people tend to be defensive about their home town, about the dirt of the industrial area, and there is a parochialism that is astonishing in so large a city. Not being a regional centre in the way that Leeds is, Sheffield tends to be inward-looking—or else outward-looking in a defensive way. With its recent developments in housing and planning Sheffield now has many features of which it can be justifiably proud, yet the pride is still a prickly sort of pride and is not borne with any assurance. These generalised, and possibly contro-versial, descriptions of the feel of three towns could probably be repeated with infinite variations by all people who have lived in different urban settings. All have their own particular sort of atmosphere and no town is quite like another.

Thus, with all the generalisations that may be made about urban personalities, it is important to recognise the differences that exist, and it is without doubt a necessary step that needs to be taken in increasing urban understanding for more research to be done on urban contrasts so as to develop the ideas tried out in the quantitative analysis of Scott and Moser.

URBANISM AS A CONCEPT

In this chapter we have used a three-prong analysis of the concept of urbanism, and the analysis in each case has shown that it is by no means easy to generalise about the urban setting in sociological terms without being led into generalisations that need qualification as soon as they are made. Yet it has also been seen that the city and the town do have features of sociological importance. Certainly the ecological approach helps greatly in understanding the social causes and effects of urban development and its ensuing social segregation. In the social structure and social ethos of urban places we found forms of interaction and attitudes that are discernible in a general way.

Of course, no town or city can be just like any other one. Even the new towns, built as they are to a drawing board specification, show differences from each other, and, it is expected, will gradually develop their own particular personalities.

What is perhaps one of the most important factors in the analysis of urbanism is the distinction that must be made between the overall social structure and the social structure as seen and felt by the individual. It would be over-ambitious and not a little jargonish to call these macrocosmic and microcosmic viewpoints, but such terms are popular with some social scientists and may make the point to them. Towns are highly complex social groupings and, whilst every individual is affected in some way and to some degree by the whole structure of the city (as indeed he is affected by the structure of the whole country and even the international structure), his day-to-day life is usually lived at a much more local and personal level so far as his general consciousness of social interaction is concerned. Thus, for example, a university lecturer in Sheffield lives in a city of half a million population where the main industries are steel, engineering and cutlery. The social structure of his place of work is influenced by local industry, and metallurgy and engineering are two important faculties of his university. The location of the industrial zone affects the place where his home and family are, being away as far as possible from the dust and pollution of the 'black belt'. The form of education that his children receive is, at the secondary level, determined by the policies of the socialist controlled city council who determine the ways in which the rates are spent. But all these things are at a level at least one step removed from the day-to-day conscious living of the hypothetical lecturer. He lives more consciously with his colleagues at work, his family at home, his neighbours in the locality and his friends wherever they may be found in clubs, associations and so on. This is to say that, whilst he is one part of a complex social structure of half a million people whose interdependence is almost wholly based upon secondary relationships, he is also a person with face-to-face personal relationships with a much more limited number of people in a limited range of activities. Some of the groups may have overlap of membership—perhaps a colleague at work is also a member of the same church—but all the relationships, no matter how separated they may be, are of a reasonably personal type.

It is therefore necessary to consider the human-personal aspects of urban life (the microcosmic) as well as the wider secondary ones (the macrocosmic) if a *full* understanding of urbanism is to be gained. The next two chapters will look at the large-scale and the more personal-scale problems from two particular viewpoints. The larger-scale problem can be usefully studied by looking at the attempts that have been made in this country to control the development of the urban centres through town planning. The more personal aspects can then be seen by a consideration of the concept of the neighbourhood in the urban environment.

Chapter Five

THE CONTROL
OF URBAN DEVELOPMENT

THE historical background to the development of control over
urban growth has been well described by Ashworth in *The
Genesis of Modern British Town Planning* in which he covers,
in detail, the nineteenth century and the twentieth century up
to 1947. Faced with the problems which arose from a rapidly
increasing population in a society which was becoming industrialised and urbanised at an unforeseen rate, the Victorians
produced both interesting ideas and interesting people.

In the study of social problems arising from industrialisation
and urbanisation, there were produced royal commissions and
expert reports which carried great weight and resulted in
important legislation. In a time before the popular press,
wireless or television had made their impact, these government
publications undoubtedly made a great impact in their own
right. At the end of the nineteenth century the classic surveys
of Booth and Rowntree, both independent social surveyors,
dealt with the conditions of the working classes in an objective
and analytical fashion. The point is made, therefore, that in the
nineteenth century there arose a genuine desire to find out how
matters stood. In the presentation of factual data many
nineteenth-century reports of commissions and committees
compare favourably with those of the present day, and it is
well-nigh incontrovertible that the status of these reports in the
public mind was higher than it is in the present day, when a
plethora of royal commission and committee reports lies
mouldering on governmental shelves.

Yet it would be wildly mistaken to think of the nineteenth
century as a time when problems were spotted, studied and
immediately remedied. The urban and industrial development

raised problems that got quite out of hand at times, and even in what we today might consider to be 'obvious' matters, such as public health, enormous walls of prejudice had to be battered down before social action could be undertaken.

The nineteenth century was a time of such vast change in this country that it would take a library of books to do full justice to the problems that developed. We can here only pick out certain factors that may help in understanding the social changes that took place and eventually gave us the urban society we have today. Obviously one could go back into the eighteenth century or even before for a full picture, but we will take an arbitrary date of 1801, this being the year of the first population census. As Ashworth points out, in England,

> in 1801, as for long before and ever since, London, which had a population of 864,845, was dominant. Manchester-and-Salford together, Liverpool, Birmingham, Bristol and Leeds were between 50,000 and 100,000, and there were in England and Wales eight other towns with populations between 25,000 and 50,000; these were, in order of magnitude, Plymouth-Devonport-Stonehouse (counted as one), Norwich, Portsmouth, Sheffield, Rochdale, Nottingham, Newcastle-on-Tyne and Bath.[1]

These population figures, dealing with our major cities 160 years ago, when the total population of England and Wales was only 8,893,000, should be read again slowly lest their importance is overlooked. One hundred and sixty years may seem a long time in an age where scientific developments in nuclear energy or space travel are measured in months, but, allowing for increased longevity, 160 years could easily span the lifetime of an old man alive today and his grandfather; it would not be impossible to find a person today who had known a person born before 1800. In the span of human history, then, this period is minute. Yet over the period, the population of England and Wales rose from under 9 million to nearly 45 million and this country changed from a rural-agricultural society to an urban-industrial society.

In 1801, Manchester, Liverpool and Birmingham were below the present-day populations of such places as Ealing, Wallasey, Northampton, Walsall, Huddersfield and St. Helens. Sheffield, Nottingham, Newcastle, etc., were below the present size of Bedford, Bromley, Crosby, Wood Green, Gosport, Oldbury and Keighley. It must be admitted that some of the present-day towns used for comparison (all of them at least municipal boroughs in the 1951 census, from which the populations were derived) do not ring as familiarly upon the ear as do the older names.

By 1841, London's population had risen to nearly 2 million and Manchester (with Salford) and Liverpool were over the quarter million mark. From five towns in 1801 with populations between 50,000 and 100,000, the number had risen to thirty-five in 1841.

Between 1841 and 1861, as Ashworth shows, Birkenhead's population rose from 11,563 to 51,649, and Cardiff's from 10,077 to 32,954. The general rise in the latter half of the nineteenth century is perhaps best demonstrated by an index table.[2]

POPULATION FIGURES, RELATING TO ENGLAND
AND WALES, EXPRESSED AS INDEX NUMBERS,
WITH 1851 AS BASE YEAR

Year	London	84 Great Towns	14 Typical Rural Counties	Rest of England and Wales
1851	100	100	100	100
1861	119	122	99·6	109
1871	138	148	99·7	121
1881	162	183	94·4	136
1891	179	217	95·7	150
1901	192	254	95·5	169

A further point of great importance is made by Ashworth when he points out that by 1881 'the main centres of population were thoroughly established and what were the largest towns have continued to be so, though not all of them by any means continued to attract much additional population'[3] It is a point of the greatest importance that this country has seen very little in the growth of new towns since the late nineteenth century. Since 1945 a small number of planned new towns have been developed, but their populations are still small, and some have not overcome the magnetic attraction of London. New local government districts have come into prominence, but many, when examined closely, turn out to be suburban growths of existing cities. Probably the only real case of a new town developing in its own right (i.e. as opposed to government decree) is the steel town of Scunthorpe in Lincolnshire.

The nineteenth century, then, gave us our basic distribution of towns and cities, and the geographical centres of population have changed relatively little since then. Whilst the 'drift' of population to the Midlands and South has been a phenomenon of the twentieth century, there have been no 'ghost towns' left in the North, and even Jarrow, which was supposedly 'killed' by the slump of the 1920's and 1930's, is still alive today.

The overall picture of the development of the British urban-industrial society during the nineteenth and twentieth centuries is one of increasing population, developing industry and technology and a rapid growth of dwelling places. It is interesting to note that of all the industries that benefited from technological improvements and inventions, the building industry was the one which lagged most behind. The position today, therefore, is that most cities have a core of decaying dwellings near the city centre that are slums or near-slums, and the slum clearance schemes of pre- and post-war have not yet eradicated them, nor will do so for some years. The inner ring of the town, then, is based on a road plan laid down many years ago, and only in exceptional circumstances (such as wholesale bombing during the 1939–45 war, as at Coventry) has there been any real attempt to get away from this haphazard and un-planned centre structure. Where new steel-framed panel-walled office blocks are today taking the places of the Victorian-Gothic offices, the street plan is rarely affected in any major way. Civic centres and inner ring roads of the town plans of the 1940's and early 1950's have rarely come about without great modifications forced on the planners by harsh economic reality.

Going further out from the city centre one then comes across the earlier suburban developments which were becoming noticeable in the 1880's when such areas as Leyton and Willesden increased their populations by over 100 per cent between the censuses of 1881 and 1891. The early suburbs show the discrimination which has since developed in the class structures of our towns by way of residential areas. Often to the west of the industrial area, and well away from it, we have the middle class suburbs characterised by large Georgian or Victorian houses, at one time occupied by prosperous merchants and manufacturers. Nearer the industry we get the acres of 'bye-law' houses, built to the requisite sanitary standards of the time, but today inadequate in bathrooms, garages and general facilities for modern living. It should be noted that houses of all types of this vintage were built in terraces, and very fine architectural specimens are to be found all over the country, although many today are in a state of decay. Also worthy of note is the fact that, even amongst the largest houses, large gardens were not necessarily to be found. Indeed, many large houses had no gardens worth mentioning, although public parks may be found close by in many cases. With all their drawbacks, and they were many, the houses of this time, taken as a whole, were town houses built for town people. The lack of control over industrial nuisances, the slow development of sanitary measures and above all the development of transport, private and public, led to a movement from the town centres on the part of the well-to-do. As early as 1841 it was noted in Dundee that 'the newly-opened railways offer facilities for uniting the business of the town with family residence in the country, and threaten, ere many years, to convert Dundee into one great workshop, with the families of its workmen fully detached from the notice or sympathy of the families of any upper class'.[4]

Yet, with the movement outwards beginning, the second half of the nineteenth century was a great time for the founding of urban institutions, and a walk through the older parts of practically any town will bring to light churches, chapels, schools and associational buildings founded in these times.

Of course the problems that developed from this rapid growth and development were ones that could not be eradicated without wholesale demolition, and for all its gradually increasing standards of living this country has never had adequate housing for its population. As Ashworth so rightly points out,

the difficulties were aggravated because an industrial town was usually not developed in the first place as an industrial town. It was perhaps a village or a local market suddenly invaded by

factories and then engulfed by a rapid flood of cheap building
. . . the standard was set by places which were characterised
by successive graftings of something newer and different on to
something older. The tenacity of what had already been
created, however faulty it was subsequently recognised to be,
made it difficult to re-shape a town once it was firmly rooted.[5]

In the further development of the towns, therefore, it became
common practice to leave the centre and the inner ring of
residential property to their own devices, and to concentrate on
the newer, outer ring. Here we find that the desire for space,
grass, gardens and all that go to make up low density housing
come into their own. 'By 1914, apart from Letchworth Garden
City and early schemes such as Bournville and Port Sunlight,
at least fifty-two schemes for garden suburbs were completed or
in progress.'[6] Fifty-two schemes is a number that cannot be
ignored, even if some of them may have been somewhat hopeful
in their ideas of 'garden' from what one may see of them today;
even the most ordinary council estate of the 1930's would
probably equal these early versions in density, gardens, open
spaces, grass verges and so on. The important thing is that the
whole movement (unorganised though it was in the main part)
demonstrated a general desire of so many people, *not* to want to
go back to the country itself, but to bring into the towns some
of the believed advantages of the country. It must be stressed
that there was not just one movement—from the countryside
into the towns—but two movements going on together—
movement from the country to the towns and from the town
centres to the outer ring of development.

The migration from the countryside to the town was
chronicled in this country by P. Anderson Graham, who,
writing in 1892, said, 'The movement is confined to no one
locality but is to be observed in every agricultural district that
lies remote from the town. Nor does it seem to spring from any
clear and well defined cause for discontent on the part of the
peasantry. If they have low wages, as in Wiltshire, they leave;
but if they have high wages, as in Northumberland, they leave
also'.[7] Graham ascribes the rural exodus to a number of factors
besides the obvious one of the hoped-for advancement open to
the town-dweller. He remarks on the breakdown of the rural
isolation brought about by the railways and even the bicycle.

He tells how the charabanc trip to the nearby town had opened the eyes of the country-dweller to the delights of the music-hall and the city taverns: how the popular newspaper (he quotes *The Weekly Budget*) had instructed the country-dweller in the delights of divorce cases and sensational news-stories. Both economic and social changes had brought about the migratory process. A few years later, A. F. Weber, writing in 1899, said that, 'The rise of the suburbs it is which furnishes the solid basis of hope that the evils of city life, so far as they result from overcrowding, may be in large part removed. If concentration of population seems destined to continue, it will be a modified concentration which offers the advantages of both city and country life.'[8]

The plan to combat all the problems was, of course, put forward by Ebenezer Howard in 1898 when he brought out his pioneering work *Tomorrow*.[9] One of the most illuminating parts of Howard's book was his diagram of 'The Three Magnets', which showed how the people were drawn towards three types of 'magnet', the town, the country and what is called 'town-country'. Since the diagram is not easy to read, being over-laid by line drawings of horseshoe magnets, it is reproduced here in an easier format.

TOWN

CLOSING OUT OF NATURE, SOCIAL OPPORTUNITY
ISOLATION OF CROWDS, PLACES OF AMUSEMENT
DISTANCE FROM WORK, HIGH MONEY WAGES
HIGH RENTS AND PRICES, CHANCES OF EMPLOYMENT
EXCESSIVE HOURS, ARMY OF UNEMPLOYED
FOGS AND DROUGHTS, COSTLY DRAINAGE
FOUL AIR, MURKY SKY, WELL-LIT STREETS
SLUMS AND GIN PALACES, PALATIAL EDIFICES

COUNTRY

LACK OF SOCIETY, BEAUTY OF NATURE
HANDS OUT OF WORK, LAND LYING IDLE
TRESPASSERS BEWARE, WOOD, MEADOW, FOREST
LONG-HOURS-LOW-WAGES, FRESH AIR, LOW RENTS
LACK OF DRAINAGE, ABUNDANCE OF WATER
LACK OF AMUSEMENT, BRIGHT SUNSHINE
NO PUBLIC SPIRIT, NEED FOR REFORM
CROWDED DWELLINGS, DESERTED VILLAGES

TOWN—COUNTRY
BEAUTY OF NATURE, SOCIAL OPPORTUNITY
FIELDS AND PARKS OF EASY ACCESS
LOW RENTS, HIGH WAGES
LOW RATES, PLENTY TO DO
LOW PRICES, NO SWEATING
FIELD FOR ENTERPRISE, FLOW OF CAPITAL
PURE AIR AND WATER, GOOD DRAINAGE
BRIGHT HOMES AND GARDENS, NO SMOKE, NO SLUMS
FREEDOM, CO-OPERATION

It is noteworthy that in the 1946 edition of Howard's book F. J. Osborn in his long preface writes of Howard's outlook, 'in which there was no proletarian resentment or class bitterness, and not a trace of nostalgic anti-urbanism, anti-industrialism, or back-to-the-land-ism'.[10] In the same book, in his introductory essay 'The Garden Idea and Modern Planning', Lewis Mumford says of Howard that he was not attempting to break down

> the distinction of town and country and turning them into an amorphous suburban mass . . . For the Garden City, as conceived by Howard, is not a loose indefinite sprawl of individual houses with immense open spaces over the whole landscape: it is rather a compact, rigorously confined urban grouping . . . It may be argued that Howard's town-density is greater than would be generally acceptable (today); he cannot be accused of being an advocate of urban sprawl.[11]

Further, and the point is emphasised by being printed in italics, 'The Garden City, as Howard defined it, is not a suburb but the antithesis of a suburb: not a mere rural retreat, but a more integrated foundation for an effective urban life'.[12]

If one may be guided by Osborn's notes on terminology, 'A Garden City is a Town designed for healthy living and industry; of a size that makes possible a full measure of social life, but not larger; surrounded by a rural belt; the whole of the land being in public ownership or held in trust for the community'.[13] Osborn seems to have a genuine grievance in the various ways that the term 'Garden City' has been applied to all sorts of low-density suburbs, overgrown villages and so on. It is basically a part of Howard's plan that the Garden City should deal with economic and industrial matters as a part of the social unit of the town. Indeed, when one reads his short book (only 110 pages without introductions) the bulk of it is given to essentially practical matters of finance and administration. Debentures, rents, ground rents and administrative costs gain more space than neighbourhood activities or community centres. Indeed, although Howard divides up his 'ideal-type' layout into six wards, he hardly mentions at all the type of *local* amenities that these neighbourhoods should have. Shops appear to be of interest to him only when they are in the 'Crystal Palace' ring. Each sixth of the town will have a four-acre site for schools, playgrounds and gardens on 'Grand Avenue' (which is 420 feet wide) but no details are given. Churches will have sites set apart for them in this area to be financed 'out of the funds of the worshippers and their friends'. The only mention at all of local shops, as distinct from central ones, is of 'a store or depot in each ward' in which the discussion is principally dealing with the sale of local agricultural produce to the town.

When one looks again, then, at the town and country magnets, it becomes clearer that many of the ills of both town and country will be dealt with by the building of a *new* town (which *ipso facto* will not have old slums) that will give better lives for the inhabitants because it will be run in a more economical fashion. There seems to be built in with the plan an assumption that there need be no unemployment and no sweating, that wages will be high and that there will be a ready flow of capital. Just how this is to be established and maintained within the whole of the national economy is not quite as clear as it might be. Perhaps the two last-named benefits of TOWN-COUNTRY, freedom and co-operation, are intended to provide the answer. One interesting point of Howard's plan is that the TOWN-COUNTRY in the form of the Garden City will offer 'plenty to do' as against the country's 'lack of amusement' and the town's 'places of amusement' which appear to be vitiated by the accompanying 'slums and gin palaces'. In the town centre there will be the library, the theatre, the concert hall and the museum and art gallery, set out around 5½ acres of garden and themselves surrounded by 145 acres of public park. Running all round this is the 'Crystal

Palace' containing the main shops for which 'the joy of deliberation and selection' are appropriate, and also acting as a Winter
Garden—'the whole forming a permanent exhibition of a most
attractive character, whilst its circular form brings it near to
every dweller in the town—the furthest removed inhabitant
being within 600 yards'.[14] The odd thing about Howard's plan
is that, although he is willing himself to have public houses in
the town, the whole plan reads rather as if all the population
will be genteel middle class. The whole concept of a town
centre which contains only six buildings (hospital, library,
theatre, concert hall, town hall and museum-art-gallery) set in
an open space of 150 acres, and a quarter of a mile from the
nearest shops and houses seems, if not anti-urban, then non-
urban to say the least. The 'Crystal Palace' concept of the
shopping arcade gives, not a shopping centre, but a shopping
ring of just over a quarter-mile radius and getting on for
$1\frac{1}{2}$ miles circumference. It does seem then that the Crystal
Palace is designed for extremely leisurely 'deliberation and
selection', and is more suited for the winter promenade than
for most shopping expeditions of the average family.

In general, therefore, whilst Howard's plans for the financial
and administrative parts of the Garden City concept were
impressive in their down-to-earth details, his ideas of the
Garden City as a place where people of all classes in the 1890's
would live seems to be somewhat out of touch with reality.
Although poverty at this time was widespread, and drunken-
ness was a common phenomenon, Howard seemed to be able
to ignore these aspects of working class life almost entirely. One
must also consider, in passing, what would have been the up-
keep and repair costs of his 'Crystal Palace' if young people
were as attracted by glass in his town as they always appear to
have been since glass was invented.

Howard's contribution, then, was an important one, but
whilst his general ideas on the containment of urban sprawl,
the preservation of agricultural land and the treating of urban
and rural as one problem were without doubt years ahead of
his time, one must be more cautious about claims that
'Howard's prize contribution was to outline the nature of a
balanced community and to show what steps were necessary,
in an ill-organised and disoriented society, to bring it into

existence'.[15] Howard stressed how very much his diagrams were 'diagram only: plan cannot be drawn until site selected', but the whole basis of the plan seems out of touch with reality. It is not surprising, therefore, to find that 'when Messrs. Unwin & Parker came to design Letchworth itself, they perhaps leaned over backwards in their effort to avoid mechanical stereotypes, in order not to duplicate Howard's diagrammatic city'.[16] Certainly one would agree with Mumford's statement that 'Howard's greatness did not lie in the field of technical planning', if this is to refer to civic design and the actual planning of a town for social units of a population size below 30,000. The plans for breakdown into 5,000 population wards are rudimentary and the description of the essentially *urban* life of the Garden City is not easily found. Indeed, the revolutionary proposals for the layout of the Garden City have never been implemented, although the administrative and financial proposals were used. Letchworth and Welwyn were both built in the form of fairly conventional, normal towns and the schemes that Howard had for an environment of a startlingly new sort were never attempted.

It is important to note how the turn of the century saw two principles going side by side so far as the approach to urban problems was concerned. One line of thought derived from the sanitarian approach of such men as Chadwick, Southwood Smith and Charles Kingsley, and the other from the more Utopian approach of such people as Owen, Buckingham, Salt and Howard, with Cadbury and Lever operating in the twentieth century.

In a number of ways these two main lines of approach have characterised subsequent developments in the twentieth century. The main preoccupation of the government has always been with the problems of controlling, improving and renewing the already-developed areas, whilst the 'private enterprise' interest has been more with the development of totally new areas. This is a logical form of division of interest, since no private individual, no matter how wealthy, can hope to own the centre of a town or city in the twentieth century; only a local or central authority could hope to deal with the overall problems involved in such areas. The interest of private individuals and associations has, therefore, tended to be directed more towards undeveloped areas, and in Letchworth and Welwyn this country has seen two 'private-enterprise' towns built, to say nothing of the many 'garden suburbs' and planned area developments which stretch right up to the contemporary work of Span Developments and the like.

It would therefore seem fair to say that much of the interest in the human and personal aspects of urban development has been directed towards new development, mainly on a fairly small scale. The macrocosmic problems of urban control, redevelopment and so on, had of necessity to be tackled through Parliamentary institutions and the pressure group system. Howard's ideas for the Garden City were probably more important than the plans for 'company' towns, because he envisaged the development of new towns on a business footing which avoided the industrial paternalism of practically all the others. It could be fairly said that Howard's plan for the Garden City was the only one which went into sufficient *economic* detail to make it qualify at all for consideration in the macrocosmic class of planning ideas. If we remember that Howard was a man who lived in a time of free enterprise *par excellence* his *administrative* ideas for the Garden City were more interesting (and certainly more carefully worked out) than his actual civic design for social living. The ideas behind Saltaire, Port Sunlight and Bournville were, at this level, less interesting, since they were basically feudal villages translated into the nineteenth and twentieth centuries, with the paternal industrialist replacing the lord of the manor.

Letchworth and Welwyn are therefore important because these two towns were the concrete instances in the earlier part of the twentieth century of large scale attempts to create planned environments for living. Since neither of them ever attempted to incorporate within them the 'Crystal Palace' ring it is rather on the economic than the civic side of things that they are of interest. These towns were built as a result of idealism plus economic realism, and for all their limitations they must be recognised as genuine examples of what could be done at a time when town planning and town development at governmental level was practically non-existent. But economically the two garden cities could never hope to attain the ideals of the three-magnets scheme put forward by Howard, simply because no one town, or even two, could ever hope to change the social system of a whole country. It must be remembered that Howard was an idealist within the social structure of his time. He was not motivated by particular religious or economic theories of the extreme type which sometimes lead people to set up what are called 'Utopian' communities. Howard was a man of his time, as were many Victorian reformers, and he had no wish to overthrow the social system of his time, or to run away from it and found his own little society. By accepting the general structure within which he hoped to create the garden cities, Howard inevitably had to accept an economic structure which he could not hope to change very much at all.

The high rents and prices, excessive hours and slums and gin palaces of the town magnet, the hands out of work, long hours—low wages, and crowded dwellings of the country magnet could only be remedied to a small degree by the building of the essentially private-enterprise garden cities. In effect, what Howard's plan required was a total renewal of the whole urban environment on garden city lines, which in its turn implied a reversal of many of the current economic and social trends of his day. Had Howard been able to work by government decree he might have been able to deal with some of the problems of both the town and the country magnets, but his garden cities could never be more than partial solutions whilst industrial and agricultural policies were left out of the scheme of things.

But state action in the early twentieth century was, as yet, only slight. The nineteenth century had seen ameliorative legislation to deal with problems of bad housing and, allied with these, the problems of the poor, the working classes (though the two were often the same people) and public health in general. The still-present memorials to this period are the many streets of bye-law housing, defined by Kelsall as 'that type of housing, generally of a monotonous terrace character, which kept *exactly* to the local bye-laws first authorized by the Public Health Act of 1875'.[17]

The fragmentary nature of the nineteenth-century legislation, dealing with individual problems as they arose, continued well into the twentieth century, and indeed still does continue, but a landmark in control of the urban environment was reached when the first town planning act came into force with the Housing, Town Planning etc. Act of 1909 (9 Edw.VII,c.44). Ashworth devotes a whole chapter of his book to this Act and its origins and explains very clearly its significance, 'Town Planning was . . . not altogether a leap in the dark, but could be represented as a logical extension, in accordance with changing aims and conditions, of early legislation concerned with housing and public health'.[18] The increasing population and the continuing urbanisation of that population had given rise to various worries. Ashworth records the concern expressed about the poor physical condition of so many town dwellers brought to light by medical examinations of men at the time of the Boer War. There was also a concern about loss of amenities, especially open space, in the towns, as more and more land was swallowed up by housing development. The continued growth of the towns made it apparent that *control* over development was necessary if urban growth were not to get completely out of hand. Controls over housing and sanitary standards alone could not cope with these wider problems.

Yet with all the concern that was felt about urban spread the prevailing belief at the time was still in the capacity of the new suburbs to deal with the major problems. The new act, which was greatly influenced by the developments of the garden suburbs (especially Hampstead), dealt only with schemes for land which was in the course of development or appeared likely to be used for building purposes. Land which had already been developed could only be included in a town-planning scheme in special circumstances. Compulsory purchase of land was still limited by the conditions prevailing for the provision of working class housing. As Ashworth comments, 'Statutory town planning immediately after 1909 was a mild, uncertain affair. Town planning for all was a novelty which might be gingerly tried, but there was every deterrent to prevent any body from indulging in it to excess'.[19] Since the whole Act was permissive, rather than mandatory, and since even when the option was taken up the restrictions on action were tremendous, it is not surprising that action was fairly slow by more recent standards. By 1915, seventy-four local authorities had been authorised to prepare 105 schemes, covering 16,571 acres.[20]

Encouraged by the success of the 1909 Act, Liverpool University founded its School of Civic Design in 1909, and in 1913 the Town Planning Institute held its first meeting. In the Institute the influence of architects was very strong, largely because of the power and prestige of the Royal Institute of British Architects, compared with the Institution of Civil Engineers and the Surveyors' Institution. This dominance has continued right through to the present day and is illustrated by current advertisements asking for 'architect-planners', who are people with qualifications in both professions, for posts of responsibility.

The emphasis at this time was then upon an acceptance of the increasing geographical size of towns, a belief in the value of suburban expansion, so long as it was at 'garden suburb' densities, and a faith in the ability of aesthetically acceptable housing to solve most urban problems.

The problem was, of course, that Howard's original garden *city* ideas had become hopelessly muddled up with garden *suburb* ideas, the latter being principally concerned with adding new low-density housing areas to present towns so as to relieve the pressure on the central areas. Patrick Geddes, with his emphasis on surveys of the origins and needs of the *whole* town or city, did not make the headway that many hoped for, perhaps in many ways because he was not skilled in communicating his ideas simply. But other critics of the time who spoke and wrote against the garden suburb ideas, such as C. B. Purdom and Trystan Edwards, were not able to restrain this type of development. Town Planning, such as it was, up to the 1914–18 war was still primarily concerned with the new, the suburban and the aesthetic. It was all so relatively small in scale and limited in outlook that 'town planning' is a rather grandiose term to apply. Even the powers that did exist were scattered between government departments, and planning as a co-ordinated activity, covering housing, communications, location for industry, and so on, was not thought of except by a few visionaries.

After the 1914–18 war a new housing and town planning act of 1919 brought in a compulsory requirement for all boroughs and urban districts with populations exceeding 20,000 to prepare town planning schemes by 1926. But a later act, of 1923, extended the time limit to 1929 and when many authorities failed to comply no action was taken. The 1919 Act did bring developed land into the orbit of town schemes and joint committees to cover neighbouring authorities were permitted so long as their functions were advisory only. But the emphasis still was upon land being developed rather than any overall plan for a town or city as an entity, and even the Town and Country Planning Act of 1932, which allowed local authorities to prepare plans for any type of land, had surprisingly little effect.

In these years after the First World War however there were signs of an increasing understanding of the need for greater scale in planning and for a policy of development which would consider the need for completely new towns. The New Towns Group, formed in 1918, pressed for a national policy of building new towns about the country by the state authority, and set the pace itself by the building of Welwyn.

Also in this period the first real signs of serious activity became apparent in the field of national planning policy. 'Emphasis was passing from the design of residential estates to the more general problem of the allocation of land among various uses. Planning was beginning to be seen less in terms merely of visual appearance, health and amenity, and more in terms of social and economic functions'.[21] This statement is illustrated by the fact that by 1930, eighty joint planning committees had been established, representing over 1,000 local authorities. In this period the idea of *regional* planning begins to come to the fore, and town planning becomes a very different matter from the mere designing of council houses.

The industrial problems of the times could not but have their effect upon the thinking of people interested in town planning, and it is therefore impossible to draw any hard and fast lines between surveys and reports on housing and unemployment during the years of depression, and surveys and reports which claim directly to be concerned with planning as such. All the many studies of the problems of the 20's and early 30's were grist to the mill of the person engaged in town planning. Industry could no longer be divorced from housing, and neither could be considered without communications; by now sanitation had ceased to be a major factor in itself, but was included in housing. Concern was, however, being expressed at the results of urban dispersal and the problems of costs and time involved in travel to work. It was in M'Gonigle and Kirby's famous study that attention was drawn to the disastrous combination of higher rents and increased fares for people re-housed from the slums, so that the authors commented,

> The outskirts of our industrial towns are rapidly developing into municipal and private housing estates, and thousands of working-class families have been transferred from the centres of our towns and cities to the outskirts, but the works and factories have not (at any rate in the North of England) followed the workers to the neighbourhood of their new homes. For families displaced from insanitary dwellings by slum clearance schemes the alternative accommodation offered by the Local Authority constitutes, usually, the only houses available . . . Some families accept unwillingly, because they realise that their transfer to a suburb will add a sum, which may amount to half a crown a week, to their unavoidable expenditure. It is not uncommon to find people continuing to reside in unsatisfactory houses in the vicinity of their work rather than incur the additional expense of travelling costs from a suburb where housing conditions are vastly superior.[22]

This type of finding, so very pertinent at a time of unemployment, was beginning to put the final nails in the coffin for the urban expansion theme, and made in a human way the point which was not so easy to appreciate when discussion took place on regional themes. Terence Young's study of Becontree and Dagenham (1934) and Ruth Durant's study of Watling (1939) were both social studies that caused doubt to be expressed about the value of the vast new London estates.

With the growing disillusionment about the suburbs as the panacea for all urban evils, there grew up the belief in larger scale planning and the planned development of new towns as more realistic ways of tackling urban planning problems. Housing unrelated to work was unrealistic, as was industry unrelated to resources, products and their transport. In time the idea gradually gained strength that 'town' planning was concerned with all the institutions of society and was not merely a drawing-board exercise in the lay-out of three-bedroomed semi-detached houses in straight roads, cul-de-sacs and crescents.

The phenomenal growth of transportation in the period (Ashworth quotes an increase of 181 per cent in annual passenger miles travelled in Great Britain between 1903 and 1933) and the movement of population from north to south were two factors which were serious enough to require planning consideration on a scale that could in realistic terms only be at a national level. Certainly the magnetic attraction of the South, and particularly the London area, showed a strength beyond anything conceived of in abstract terms by Ebenezer Howard. The problem was a national problem, no matter from what angle it was viewed. The 'special areas', or 'depressed areas' as they were better known, were only a part of a general problem which included the ever increasing sprawl of London and the ribbon developments and suburban agglomerations of every town and city in the country.

The setting up of the Royal Commission on the Distribution of the Industrial Population (the Barlow Commission) was an inevitable outcome of the post-1918 development of the country. A report in 1935 of a departmental Committee of the Ministry of Health on Garden Cities and Satellite Towns had recommended a national approach to the distribution of industry and population, and that pressure, if not compulsion, should be brought to bear by means of a central planning board, but no effects of this report were worthy of note. The Barlow Report,[23] being published in 1940, a time of war, was recognised (perhaps by hindsight but nevertheless recognised) as the first real step towards a realisation of the need for planning as a national exercise on a mandatory basis. Briefly the Report stated:

1. That the nation should no longer tolerate a drift of urban development which created depressed regions in some parts of the country and over-swollen cities in other parts.
2. That pre-war planning under the town and country planning acts was ineffective, largely because it was permissive, negative and lacking in co-ordination.
3. That most great cities were too congested and needed rebuilding on more open lines, with excess industry and

population being offered better accommodation in decentralised situations.

4. That rural amenities must be protected by green belts round and between towns.
5. That to provide for decentralisation and new industries, new towns and trading estates should be built, and selected existing towns (some in depressed areas) should be assisted in extension or revival.
6. That local community activities should be more actively promoted in housing and planning.
7. That the best land should be preserved for agriculture and scattered development discouraged. National Park areas and coastal areas should be preserved from ordinary building development.
8. That there should be more diversification of industry in different parts of Britain.
9. That regional consciousness and administration should be fostered.
10. That, to attain all these ends, a powerful central planning machinery was required.

The Barlow Report was a key document in the development of planning ideas for several reasons. Firstly, it looked at the basic problems of the towns and saw that planning was an economic function in the allocation of land for particular purposes. Planning, in this way, was something far beyond the mere skills of the architect or engineer, and required the expertise of the economist, geographer, demographer and even the sociologist. Secondly, and inevitably following from the first, planning could never be successfully done on a piecemeal basis; co-ordination of knowledge and plans was essential if planning was to benefit the nation as an entity. Thirdly, it was made clear that any success depended upon power being given to the planners to carry out their plans—planning had to be a mandatory activity with strong legal sanctions to back it up.

Obviously activity at the level and scope envisaged by the Barlow Report would raise tremendous problems over the use of land, its ownership, acquisition, development and so on. It was therefore absolutely essential for the economic aspects to be looked at in detail, and for this purpose the Expert Committee on Compensation and Betterment[24] was set up to analyse the payment of compensation and recovery of betterment in respect of public control of the land and to recommend what steps should be taken to prevent the work of reconstruction being prejudiced by economic and legislative factors. Whilst the committee's recommendations were very technical, a brief summary of them would include the principle of the state holding the rights of development of nearly all land, with powers of compulsory purchase where deemed necessary, and fair compensation to be paid to existing owners in all appropriate cases, the value of the land being assessed by the rating authorities every five years.

The third report of this period, that of the Committee on Land Utilisation in Rural Areas (the Scott Committee)[25], considered problems of building and other development in rural areas consistent with the maintenance of agriculture, and particularly the location of industry, the well-being of rural communities and the preservation of rural activities. One of the important recommendations was for a survey of land classification, services, parks, etc. In general the Scott Report preferred industry to make use first of urban sites and then of existing or new small towns rather than villages or open country. The committee was, by its terms of reference, preservative rather than initiatory, but its importance is in the way in which the problems of the countryside were now being included with the problems of the towns in the overall problem of the nation.

The bomb damage of the war years, with all its attendant misery in deaths and injuries, did have one small benefit in bringing home to the nation both the needs and the opportunities for post-war reconstruction when the war was over. Once it was tacitly agreed amongst those concerned that Britain was going to be victorious, thought was given to the preparation of plans for both rebuilding the blitzed areas and renewing the blighted ones. By the end of 1945 plans had been published for Birmingham, Chelmsford, Chester, Coventry, Glasgow, Greater London, Manchester, Merseyside, Norwich, Oxford, Plymouth, Sheffield, Southampton, Teignmouth and Wolverhampton.[26] Not all of these were the final plans by any means; indeed Dale's 1944 plan for Oxford was ominously entitled 'Towards a Plan for Oxford City', but they all demonstrate a wave of enthusiasm that began before the war ended.

In 1943 two acts were passed, one setting up a separate Ministry of Town and Country Planning, the other, the Town and Country Planning (Interim Development) Act, which gave stronger powers of development control over land, irrespective of whether or not a local authority had prepared a scheme for it. Then in 1944 the Town and Country Planning Act gave powers to enforce comprehensive redevelopment of areas of 'bad lay-out and obsolete development' or areas of war damage. There were stronger powers to acquire land for such purposes as open spaces, or securing a proper balance between the different forms of development in a district, and controls were established for the prices to be paid to expropriated land and property. But, to refer back to Ashworth, 'Nevertheless there was no fundamental remodelling of town planning law during the Second World War. At its conclusion the main operative acts were still the Town and Country Planning Acts of 1932, which had not been a conspicuous success up to 1939. Since then, the most important administrative change had been in the nature of central control.'[27]

But at this point of time one reorganisation took place which would seem to have gone against the general stream of central control. Control over the location of industry was made a part of the duties of the Board of Trade, whilst the control over the location of population was a function of the Ministry of Town and Country Planning, who also were entrusted with responsibility for the new towns through the new towns development corporations.[28]

At this point a short digression on the subject of new towns is appropriate since recent developments have brought them into the limelight.

The first group of new towns to be begun after the 1939–45 war comprised fourteen begun between 1945 and 1950. In the counties around London, these were Basildon, Bracknell, Crawley, Harlow, Hatfield, Hemel Hempstead, Stevenage and Welwyn. Beyond the London 'ring' were Corby in Northamptonshire, Cwmbran, between Newport and Pontypool, and Newton Aycliffe and Peterlee in County Durham. In Scotland there were East Kilbride and Glenrothes. The London ring of new towns were, obviously, designed to draw both employment and homes from the ever-growing London conurbation. East Kilbride was to do a similar task for Glasgow. Peterlee and Glenrothes were to be centres of diversified industry in mining areas. Corby, Cwmbran and Newton Aycliffe were each to bring a better planned community to areas with established industrial settlements.

In several cases, such as Welwyn for example, the 'new' towns were to incorporate quite substantial villages or towns; in other cases, such as Peterlee, there was no obvious centre for development. But whatever the existing population, whether in a small town, a number of villages, or practically non-existent as in some cases, the general plans for these new towns tended to follow what is now called the 'open' pattern of planning, and most of them were originally intended to be fairly small by more recent standards. For example, Bracknell, which already had 5,000 population before the new town was started, was originally to be 25,000 when complete. But later revision in 1961 put this up to 54,000. A figure of 50,000 was originally suggested for Basildon, but this was subsequently raised to 80,000 and later still to just over 100,000. In the late 1940's and early 1950's, when the new towns were getting under way, maximum populations of 20,000 were not uncommon as suggested optimum figures. Today only a few of the early new towns remain so low, and 50,000 or 60,000 is much more commonplace, with Basildon now envisaged as the largest town eventually with, as said, just over 100,000.

It should be noted that new towns' populations grow in two ways. Firstly there is the population growth due to immigration of new inhabitants. As many of these people are young married couples, a balanced age structure is not anticipated in the early years. With a high birth rate and low death rate the new towns will then have fairly rapid population growth, and this 'natural increase' can be gauged so as to estimate the final target population for the town. Thus two figures may be considered—the immigration total and the natural increase total. As Osborn and Whittick[29] show, the difference between the two can be as great as 20,000 for Basildon (86,000 to 106,000) and as small as 3,000 for Hatfield (26,000 to 29,000).

For what are today commonly called the 'Mark I' new towns, a fairly general pattern is discernible. They were originally intended to be small towns, populated by young families, and laid out on open lines with conventional two-storey houses arranged in neighbourhoods with low population densities. Green belts around the towns were to be secured and within the towns, parks and open spaces would be generously provided. The preservation of woodlands and streams leading almost into (and in some cases right into) the town centres is not uncommon. In Hemel Hempstead attractive water gardens are situated very close to the main shopping centre. In all, these new towns were strongly influenced by the Garden City movement and Osborn and Whittick in their book on new towns leave the reader in no doubt as to their belief that the Garden City movement, and its formal organisation, the Town and Country Planning Association, had a great deal to do with the adoption of the open planning approach. Certainly the immediate post-war period was one when low densities were generally approved and when the neighbourhood unit concept was almost wholly accepted by planners. But gradually experience with the growing new towns; knowledge gained from social research and the phenomenal growth of car ownership all combined to bring about a reappraisal of the new town concept. Complaints of 'new town blues', especially by the growing generation of young people, were given wide, and at times perhaps undue, prominence in the popular press and other mass media. After the early years of settling into their new homes and getting the young families under way, parents and children seemed to find the new towns dull places. The amusements were limited by the size of the towns, and neighbourhood centres did not seem to attract the participants that had been hoped for. It is interesting to note that the busy neighbourhood activities that had been expected by the planners and community centre people rarely came anywhere near expectation. In his comments on the social life of the new towns Whittick notes several times the activities of amateur theatrical groups, and does not always seem to recognise what a very small minority of the population this type of socially sanctioned exhibitionism attracts. But even he notes that 'adequate facilities must be provided in the town centre, so that the few people from each neighbourhood interested in certain pursuits can come together and form societies large enough to ensure a vigorous and successful life. The town as a whole could ensure the success of much that a neighbourhood could not.'[30] What the proponents of the do-it-yourself entertainment obviously need is some form of statistical analysis to show what likely population is necessary to make a drama group, a handicrafts club, and so on, a viable proposition. If these organisations were economic, business propositions, undoubtedly some research or expertise could be called upon; it is unlikely that chain stores, brewery firms and dance hall circuits are without some measurement of the needed population for success of their ventures. It has been suggested, for example, that a population of between 40,000 and 45,000 is needed before Cumbernauld is likely to attract a cinema to the town.[31] Assessments like this would perhaps show how realistic are the hopes for voluntary associations.

With the disappointments with social developments came also the greatly increased mobility of the population brought about by car-ownership. Licensed private cars, which had stood at 1,944,000 in 1938 were up to 2,258,000 by 1950 and were at 5,526,000 by 1960. (By August 1963 the 7 million mark was passed.)[32]

With this transport revolution, which has now become a major issue in the whole of town planning, there came about a serious re-thinking of new town design, and whilst the plans for Hook, in Hampshire, were actually published for sale, but the town not built, Cumbernauld, in Dunbarton, gained the honour of being known as the first of the 'Mark II' new towns. Cumbernauld was not designated until 1956, and was intended originally to accommodate 50,000 people. However, provision has been made for extending it to 70,000, and this is very likely. The bulk of the immigrant population will come from Glasgow, only fourteen miles to the south-west. The town is situated close to the main Glasgow-Stirling road and the site of 4,150 acres is mainly on a hill top. It is intended that the town shall be compact, and of urban character, with a complete separation of pedestrians and motor traffic. There will be green open spaces on the town perimeter, but very little within the town itself. Residential areas will have no roads which run through them, but an elaborate network of cul-de-sacs will feed into the main internal road system, whilst pedestrian ways from the houses will feed into the network of footpaths leading around

the town and into the centre. On the main traffic roads there
will be no pavements, and pedestrian walks and roads will
cross each other by means of under-passes and bridges. All the
main traffic junctions are at two levels so as to avoid cross-
roads. In general, the residential areas are so laid out that car
movement to the main roads is in the opposite direction from
pedestrian movement to the main footpaths. Although the road
pattern for the town has been based on a projection of an
average of one car to each family in 20 years' time very few
houses actually have garages alongside the house, and blocks of
garages set apart from the houses are the common pattern, with
an obvious advantage in pedestrian/car segregation. There are
plans in the town centre for 3,000 short-term and 2,000 long-
term parkers. Although the residential areas are not built up
in high flats, the densities are relatively high (80 persons per
acre is common) because of concentrated use of space. Terrace
houses with small frontages, few private gardens, no large open
spaces and saving on road space by careful planning all contribute to packing a lot into a small area. With this, land-
scaping is an important part of the housing development and
£40 per house is allowed for this. The resulting concentration
means that two-thirds of the population will be within a third
of a mile of the town centre, and three-quarters will be within
half a mile. Also, no house will be much more than 300 yards
from a bus stop.

The town centre itself is a thin rectangle of about two-thirds
of a mile long, approached by road or pedestrian way at several
points, and the ground level is given over wholly to vehicular
traffic. Thus shops, offices, amusements and so on are at first
floor level, reached by bridges, ramps and escalators, and the
main shopping centre becomes completely pedestrian. In effect,
the town centre will be one huge 'building' of shops and offices
(plus some housing) all built above road level. Shopping itself
will be almost completely concentrated in the centre, with only
local 'corner shops' in the residential areas at one shop to every
3 or 4,000 houses. Industry will be located to the north and
south of the town; primary schools will be within the residential
areas, but secondary schools, playing fields and parks will be
on the periphery. Thus for main shopping, leisure and recreation, Cumbernauld will be a single unit, and no neighbourhood

divisions are intended. A problem arises in the provision of commercial leisure activities, and that is that the development corporation has no say in the provision of commercial amenities, although space can be set aside for them. As has been stated, a population of 40–50,000 would probably be needed to make a new cinema an economic proposition. It is hoped that a bowling alley may be opened eventually, but such commercial propositions can only come from private enterprise being willing to invest in the town. Obviously, then, a larger population makes for a more likely investment. Now that the Mark I new towns are growing to larger sizes, dance halls, bowling alleys and the like are being opened, to supply local needs. Perhaps the general lesson to be learned from the new towns is that they have no magical powers to provide for the recreational and leisure needs of the general population. More people spend their leisure in public houses, cinemas and dance halls than in amateur dramatics, basket-work and hand-loom weaving. The former can be measured by their economic success or their absence. The latter often appear to be in a category of activities which some people think ought to be subsidised by the many for the few.

The details given above of Cumbernauld are, it is hoped, of some interest as an example of a 'new look' in new towns. Further new towns are under way at Skelmersdale (near Liverpool), Livingston (near Edinburgh) and Dawley (in the West Midlands). Others are under constant consideration. Whatever the actual form taken by the forthcoming new towns, their function is likely to be primarily to relieve the pressure on the present large conurbations. The need is to make them attractive to both industry and would-be residents. For this they must be well sited for industrial services and viable in social terms as living communities. At present many new towns lack a solid middle class; the policy of concentrating on fairly small rented houses or flats has not attracted managerial people to them, but has rather led to them increasing the populations of nearby 'unspoilt' villages. The Mark I new towns seem to have lacked excitement and stimulation as plans for modern living. Time will tell if the Mark II variety is any improvement.

Having considered the implications of the 1946 New Towns Act, we may now turn to the other major piece of immediate post-war legislation which determined the course of planning in the early days of peace. The 1947 Town and Country Planning Act laid several basic principles, amongst which were the following:

1. Restrictive control was replaced by a new system of flexible and constantly revised development plans, the first plans being due on 1st July 1951, with revisions every five years. Planning authorities were reduced from 1,441 to 145 county and county borough councils, with joint committees for adjacent areas encouraged.

2. With a few exceptions, alteration in the use of land from its present use was prohibited unless the permission of the planning authority had been granted. Thus a person could own land, but not develop it without permission; green belts could be protected from building sites and office blocks could not be changed to factories.

3. The value of land was frozen, any increase in its value by reason of development going to the state.

4. The Central Land Board was set up to levy development charges and to compensate for loss of development value from a fund of £30 million.

5. Local authorities were given greater powers to undertake development themselves, assisted by powers of compulsory purchase and financial grants for 'blitz' and 'blight' areas.

At this stage, with the 1946 New Towns Act and the 1947 Town and Country Planning Act, the state was armed with its two main weapons for tackling the problems of planning. In the course of experience in the 1920's and 1930's, helped along by the incentives of the war years, the state had come to take over more powers of control and initiation. Planning had become mandatory and large-scale. Furthermore it had become dynamic, positive and economically based. It had been realised that 'town and country' planning was only realistic when it was worked out on comprehensive and co-ordinated lines, embracing national needs in a number of social and economic fields. At this level, town and country planning really becomes national development planning, and the line between urbanism as such and an urbanised industrial society is over-stepped. This is a very significant point for consideration, since it ties in with the parts of the previous chapter where it is stated that, at the larger scale of urban living, the economic basis of relationships is the most important.

In an interesting article, Foley points out that if conurbation growth is to be controlled then there must be control of density of population, of green belts, of employment concentration, of congestion, of community and so on. 'This view can be effectively carried through only if regional and national planning are vigorously fostered as fully complementary to town planning in its more restricted sense.'[33]

Foley suggests that 'town planning's main task is to reconcile competing claims for the use of limited land so as to provide a consistent, balanced and orderly arrangement of land uses',[34] but it is a matter of debate as to whether the control over the location of industry, or the overall development of the major road system, can be left out of town planning if an overall arrangement of the physical environment is to be really effective. But if this is to be done while industrial location is the preserve of the Board of Trade and major roads of the Ministry of Transport, then obviously a high degree of co-operation and co-ordination is required at government departmental level. The problem obviously arises of where town and country planning merges into overall governmental planning for the nation. It could be argued that the closing of railway lines is an action that affects the physical environment very greatly since the communications of an area are affected. But against this it can be argued that for the planning body to control the distribution of railway communications would be to put powers of a never-ending variety into the hands of the town planners and they would therefore soon become the directors of all national development policy. Obviously town planners cannot claim ubiquitous planning capabilities, and it is therefore probably wiser for their powers to be limited to the more obvious functions of general physical layout, zoning of areas and population forecasts.[35] This may, at times, result in limitations on planning and even reversals of policy. The plans made by the local planning authorities will be liable to great change from actions taken by other organisations, and the development plans laid down on the bases of what might be called 'natural development' forecasts may be tremendously affected by novel situations. A good example of this is the case of Minehead,[36] a small holiday resort in Somerset, where the statutory development plans covered what appeared to be the general trends of population change, obvious improvements in the physical amenities, etc. Then the privately made plans for a Butlin's Holiday Camp completely altered the situation and, now that the camp has been approved, built and opened, have brought about a radical change in the whole social composition of Minehead.

Obviously local planning authories cannot prepare town plans for any eventuality, especially those arising from the plans of private developers and speculators. What they can do, and usually do, is to lay down general principles which may be taken as fairly clear guides to the desirable ways in which development may take place. Unless this country is to be controlled in such detail that private enterprise will be abolished and every new development made by the state, then planning must be so organised as to be able to work with the plans of private people who are willing to invest money in new enterprises.

But one thing that local authorities can do, and are encouraged to do by the Town Development Act of 1952, is to get together in plans for the development of smaller towns by the 'exporting' of population from the larger ones. This Act, therefore, helps smaller towns to absorb population from larger ones which consider they have grown too much already. The workings of the Act are well described by Self as follows.

At least three local authorities are involved in every project of town development—the local authority on the spot, the county council over it, and the city authority having surplus population to transfer. It is the first of these authorities which would normally be responsible for the main business of town development, such as the provision of houses, sewerage, water supplies, lighting and cleansing, and possibly shops and factories. The county council would subsequently provide schools, clinics and other social services. But the authorities immediately responsible have not in most cases the resources, staff or experience to undertake what for them may be very large schemes of development . . . The Act tries to meet this problem by providing that any of the three or more local authorities concerned can carry out the actual work of town development and all of them, and the government as well, may contribute to its cost. The government has added the proviso that, whoever does the development, the houses and other assets shall be handed over as soon as may be to the local council on the spot . . . to make sure that the expanded town has genuine local roots and does not function as a housing annexe to some distant city.[37]

This scheme was obviously one of great importance to London since it provided a further opportunity for attempts to contain the further growth of the great wen. Probably the best known applications of the Act have been at Thetford in Norfolk and Haverhill in Suffolk, but Bletchley and Swindon have also agreed on co-operating schemes. In the West Midlands, too, the Act has been of value in attempts to get towns to 'hop' rather than merely swell, and several proposals for town expansion north of Birmingham were made by the Staffordshire authorities.

The Town Development Act thus goes some way towards the action needed to deal with problems which have got beyond the capabilities of any single local authority, and in the government participation (one might even think of 'marriage broking') there is the obvious chance for tying together areas which can help themselves by helping others. But, as Self points out, the Act has its limitations, particularly in so far as financing of the scheme is concerned. 'The Act's weakness was that it left all the details of town development, and the apportionment of the cost, to be settled by agreement of the various authorities, and provided no means of making any authority play its proper part . . . The only real incentive to local government co-operation provided by the Act is the prospect of governmental financial assistance'.[38]

The outcome is therefore that two local authorities will strike a bargain which they hope will be of mutual benefit, the one in importing people, the other in exporting them, and the government comes in to give some financial help to the agreed project. This is planning of a very piecemeal nature in so far as the country as a whole is concerned. There is no direct order from the government to any local authorities to import or export, and 'shot-gun marriages' are strictly *ultra vires*. One is almost led to think of the local authorities in terms of 'states rights' in their powers to accept or decline overtures made to them by other authorities; the 'federal' power has no over-ruling say in the matter. This means that the towns which get together for co-operative schemes are not chosen by any overall planning authority for their particular needs or appropriateness as far as national policy is concerned. Indeed, one concludes from this particular type of planning scheme that the national need is merely the sum of these individual needs and not any concept beyond this simple addition. Of course, the Ministry of Housing and Local Government, through its officials, can undoubtedly do a great deal to encourage and discourage in particular instances, but there is no manifest overall plan for the entire country.

The instances of planning in this fashion seem to demonstrate a form of arrangement which typifies ways of doing things in contemporary Britain. It would appear to be policy that if one or two authorities get together, with a certain amount of government help, to solve their problems, then this is an acceptable way of dealing with population problems. This coupled with the direct government sponsorship of the New Towns, should then be sufficient to deal with the growing conurbations, especially those of London and the West Midlands.

Regional planning as such is therefore not really a part of the British planning system, and national planning, in terms of an overall development plan for the whole country, does not exist. The Ministry of Housing and Local Government acts as a prodder, a broker, a helper, an adviser and a prohibiter, but it would be wrong to think of it as the highest level plan-initiating body for the planning of this country. It must co-operate with other ministries—amongst the obvious being the Board of Trade and the Ministry of Transport—but it cannot dictate policy to them. This dispersion of powers may then be said to reflect the beliefs of the particular party in governmental power at this time (and at the time of writing it is the Conservative Party). Under another government policies might well be different, particularly with respect to the ownership of land and rights to develop. But whatever party may actually hold governmental office the British system of local government is unlikely to be upset overnight and thus the essential feature of town planning through the established bodies of county councils and county boroughs is unlikely to be radically altered in the foreseeable future. Regional planning bodies with executive powers are not likely to supersede the established local bodies.

The conclusion to be drawn from this analysis of the development of legislative action on urban development is that in Britain town planning is an interesting mixture of positive and negative features. It is positive in the fact that the whole country is divided into local government planning areas of county boroughs and county councils who have development under continuous review. It is positive in the policy for the deliberate creation of new towns. It is positive in encouraging co-ordinated plans for the transfer of population from overgrown towns to growing ones. But it is still largely negative in that no planning has attempted to do other than encourage industrial location; direction of industrial location has been avoided at all costs, as has directed movement of population. These are features of possible planning which may be inferred to be un-British and beyond the bounds of this type of democratic society. Building of certain types may be prohibited in certain zones of a town so as to prevent industrial development in residential areas, but no official body can make a firm build a factory or a builder build a house. Given the zoning, the activity for the zone will follow as and when interested parties decide to go ahead. Perhaps the term 'negative' is over-strong for the prohibitions that prevent uncontrolled building and land-usage. The rules and regulations are mainly protective to the amenities of areas and are aimed at preventing the worst excesses. But there is a lack of positiveness in the type of approach which allocates land for shops in a new residential suburb but which takes no concern in the types of shops which ensue from traders renting premises. A new estate could have seven chemists and no grocer and still be perfectly all right so far as land-use regulations were concerned. This lack of positive enforcement of detailed plans seems to be in keeping with the British tradition of guidance or encouragement rather than direct decree. In a society which places emphasis upon freedom of action, private enterprise and individual choice it would perhaps be surprising to find it otherwise. Britain would not be recognisable as itself if all town planning were to be carried out according to one monster national plan worked out for the next X years at ministry level and implemented at the local level by the local councils. Such a pattern is not recognisable for this society, where local interests are still of very great importance and where local initiative is still encouraged and can produce such schemes as Parkhill in Sheffield and the Span developments in London and elsewhere. [39]

Given, then, that it would be inappropriate in this society to work completely from the top downwards, the results for the control of urban development are likely to be varied according to the outlook of the local authorities. In this the traveller about Britain is likely to find 'regional' differences in the urban scene deriving as much from the ideas of the local planners and council architects as from regional-traditional ideas of building. But where he will not find so much difference is in the privately developed areas, where the lack of large-scale development is likely to produce the sameness of Nairn's Subtopia from Southampton to Carlisle. Thus, the future distinctiveness of the urban scene lies largely with the city and county architects and planners who can co-operate in a positive way to produce large areas of development which bear their own stamp. In some cases, as for example in the centre of Liverpool, private enterprise on a large scale may be able to produce a co-ordinated plan for a recognisable area of a town, but such instances are relatively infrequent. Much more frequent is the hotch-potch produced by individual investment in city centres where large office blocks of great financial value are built which, when seen together in an area, are aesthetically unpleasing to say the very least.

To sum up then; in Britain today detailed planning on the macrocosmic scale is not seriously to be considered as part of the national way of life. It smacks too much of the authoritarianism of the Communist state and its five-year plan. The lack of positive control over industrial location and the location of the labour force, coupled with negative rather than positive regulations on the use of land will produce a society in which local municipal and private enterprise rather than state decree will determine much of the future urban pattern of buildings and social life. It would not be otherwise in a democratic society such as Britain is, and is likely to remain. The continued office development in London may raise alarm because of the traffic congestion that ensues and the increase in population commuting from outer suburbs, but only negative action in attempts to control this are to be expected. No Ministry of any type is expected to decree that all future office development *will* take place in Epsom or Slough.

The situation in Britain is, then, that a complex blend of private enterprise, municipal enterprise and governmental policy produces a total urban environment in which this society allows the individual as much freedom as is consistent with the good of other people. As compared with totalitarian states, the individual is still placed before the state. The result is a freedom of action and expression which is far from likely to bring about a stereotyped society of the state-controlled type. From a social point of view the result will be less than perfect aesthetically, especially in many of the privately built suburbs, but it will be a society in which the interplay of different interests will together give a vitality often lacking in the development brought about by one source of control.

In the social structure and organisation which goes with this type of control over urban development there will be demonstrated the voluntary groupings and activities of the democratic society associated with Britain and other Western societies. That is to say that developments in the urban setting will continue to be largely the products of voluntary action on the part of 'entrepreneurs', whether their enterprises are the development of new factories or the organising of new sports clubs. The future will not have the predictability of a totalitarian society (although the plans of totalitarian societies are changed very frequently) and the result will be that the society will be less easy to forecast and the adjustment of the individual to the changes will be largely a problem which he himself has to solve. In the control of urban development, then, in this particular society no radical changes are to be expected. So far the discussion has dealt with control and planning on the large scale, at national and planning authority level. A great deal of attention has been given by sociologists and planners to problems of control of the environment at the more local level, and this will be discussed in the next chapter.

Chapter Six

FOCUS
ON THE NEIGHBOURHOOD

IT is interesting to note that, whilst literature in Britain on urbanism *per se* is difficult to find, writings on the neighbourhood are by no means scarce. This tendency for British sociologists to pay attention to the smaller scale face-to-face groupings rather than the larger secondary groups is rather typical of British sociology and a number of reasons for it may be put forward.

In the first place it is important to note that much of the work done on urban neighbourhoods has been concerned with council estates and the results of movement to them from the older slum areas. It is not often mentioned that the famous study of Kinship in East London is really a comparative study with the obvious intention of pointing out the shortcomings of life in the new L.C.C. estates. But neighbourhood studies in Watling, Becontree and Dagenham, Dagenham revisited, Liverpool, Sheffield, Oxford and so on are all primarily concerned with the effects of moving working class people from outdated central area houses to the new council estates. These studies are in essence studies of social reform and amelioration. The emphasis on the slum and the council estate has left the literature practically bare of studies of middle class privately owned housing areas, or upper class housing areas. The result is that in Britain, the idea of the 'neighbourhood' is almost synonymous with the study of working class housing estates.

A second factor which has had a great influence on the focus on the neighbourhood has been the development of local social organisations, amongst which the community centre is undoubtedly the most important in this particular context. As will be shown later, the community centre movement is inextricably linked in social terms with the neighbourhood unit movement, and the latter is often the background for the promotion of the former.

With these influences at work it is not surprising that the British interest (and to some degree the American too) in the neighbourhood has been one in which the neighbourhood has been seen primarily as a tool for social reform or social work. Objective and impartial analysis of the concept of neighbourhood has been much less to the fore in Britain with the result that a somewhat lopsided set of ideas about the concept of neighbourhood would be gained from the general drift of the literature.

In this chapter we shall attempt two things. Firstly we shall consider the concept of the neighbourhood as a sociological entity and secondly we shall consider the sociological implications of the neighbourhood unit as a planning idea.

THE NEIGHBOURHOOD

Everyone has neighbours, even the people in the Australian outback whose neighbours may be fifty miles away. For the word neighbourhood to have any meaning at all it is necessary to consider some particular criteria which can be applied to make the term useful in urban sociology. A person has neighbours and therefore the limits of his acquaintance may be said to limit his neighbourhood. But such a way of looking at things is obviously not in keeping with the general understanding of the word. A neighbourhood is usually thought of more in geographical terms as a distinct part of a town or city, which may be distinct by virtue of certain boundaries (e.g. made by roads, railways, rivers, parks, etc.) and marked out from other neighbourhoods by a certain homogeneity of housing within the area. As a corollary of the similarity of housing, there can be expected a certain homogeneity of social class within the given neighbourhood. The geographical, or physical, elements and the social ones do not always go together, and indeed the above definition would not always result in two observers delimiting neighbourhoods in any given town being in agreement.

Ruth Glass discusses this problem when she considers two alternative definitions of neighbourhood and the implications of them.[1] In the first definition—'a distinct territorial group, distinct by virtue of the specific physical characteristics of the area and the specific social characteristics of its inhabitants'— she is giving an objective working definition which could be used for drawing boundaries according to reasonably clear physical features and objective social ones such as rateable values, occupational status of residents and so on. Indeed, the 'J' index[2] is a practical way of working out neighbourhoods on such a pattern. Glass's second definition is less clearly objective when neighbourhood is described as 'a territorial group, the members of which meet on common ground within their own area for primary social activities and for organised and spontaneous social contacts'. The terms used in the second definition are much less simple than those of the first in so far as observation is concerned and Glass goes on to suggest indices which can be used to further define such terms as 'primary social activities' and 'organised and spontaneous social contacts'. Maps showing catchment areas for schools, youth and adult clubs and shops of various types are given as examples of this method. If the catchment areas for the different institutions coincide to a large degree and the pattern of catchment areas corresponds to that of distinct territorial groups of people then it can be said that social activities are concentrated within the areas of the territorial groups and the territorial groups therefore qualify as neighbourhoods. In fact, in Middlesborough, about which Ruth Glass wrote, social activities were dispersed rather than concentrated. By observational methods, therefore, the idea of neighbourhood is a difficult concept to elaborate. The general idea is obviously one of things in common—a common type of housing and amenities, some sort of common interests amongst inhabitants and some sort of common pattern of social life. But viewed as a distinct *area* within which these things are to be found the concept is difficult to apply. Most of us who live in towns will use the word 'neighbourhood' at some time or other. The phrases such as 'It wasn't a very nice neighbourhood that they lived in', or 'They have a very nice house in a good neighbourhood' would not be meaningless to the hearer. On the other hand they would be far from precise sociological explanations. All that is being said here is that some vague area round where A or B lives is not very nice or is good.

But the area is an undefined one, apart from the obvious vagueness of such words as 'nice' and 'good'. Districts within a town or city may have names of their own, often derived from old villages swallowed up in the urban growth, but a residential suburb with the name of, say, 'Uppercliffe', is not exactly the same as a neighbourhood. Carpenter[3] makes a distinction as follows. 'The most distinctive characteristics of a neighbourhood are its relation with a local area sufficiently compact to permit frequent and intimate association and the emergence out of such association of sufficient homogeneity and unity to permit a primary or face-to-face social grouping endowed with a strong sense of self-consciousness and capable of influencing the behaviour of its several constituents'. Carpenter then, however, goes on to make qualificatory statements about the neighbourhood which are of considerable interest. He writes,

> The neighbourhood is to be found in towns and cities, especially in residential areas which are not over-densely populated and which possess a population for the most part homogeneous and exhibiting a low rate of mobility. The characteristic processes of urbanism are, however, hostile to the preservation of neighbourhood life in that they promote a high degree of population density, a low rate of permanency of residence and considerable heterogeneity of population. The existence in the city of an intricate network of secondary group associations also tends to break down the primary group spirit, which is the fulcrum [*sic*] of neighbourhood life; as does also the ease with which the urban dweller may wrap himself in the cloak of anonymity and thus escape from the surveillance upon which primary group control depends. With the breakdown of the neighbourhood in cities there have grown up pseudo-neighbourhoods that may be broadly defined as residential areas. Such areas exhibit some similarity to true neighbourhoods in that they may show a considerable degree of homogeneity, especially when identified with particular racial or other ethnic groups, and also in that they operate in a large measure to condition the behaviour of their residents. On the other hand they are far too numerously populated to present anything remotely resembling the close limited primary group community life characteristics of the generic neighbourhood; such uniformities of conduct and attitudes as they display may more accurately be described as products of sectionalized culture patterns.

This particularly lengthy quotation is given here because there is so much in it that enables us to look closely at this difficult concept of neighbourhood.

The essence of Carpenter's initial definition, in the ideal type situation, is that the neighbourhood is a self-conscious primary grouping capable of influencing behaviour. Thus there is awareness of mutual rights and obligations between the group members if they are to be so influenced. This self-consciousness is backed up by homogeneity of the local people and stability of residence as shown by a low rate of mobility. The factor of being 'not over-densely populated' is difficult to make much of since the yardstick by which a neighbourhood is decided to be not over-densely populated is not given. But if the urban development results in a high density, then this, with mobility and heterogeneity, go against the ideal pattern. Secondary group development is seen to detract from the importance of the neighbourhood primary contacts, and social control becomes less effective as anonymity in the larger group becomes more easily obtainable. Thus, the 'pseudo-neighbourhood' according to Carpenter may still demonstrate homogeneity and some conditioning or social control (nothing is said about mobility), but the high density of population militates against the true primary group control which is, rather, replaced by a general uniformity of behaviour of a less personal kind.

Carpenter's ideas on neighbourhood are of especial interest here because he places together so many important factors of the neighbourhood, the one to be dealt with first being the aspect of primary relationships and control. If the neighbourhood is in truth a grouping of people who have primary relationships with each other to such a level that a real social control is exercised over the relationships, then obviously the group must be a small one. Whilst any numerical estimate would be pure guess-work, a figure of over a hundred families would probably be getting towards the limits of such control. Also there must be considered the reasons why primary relationships do ensue between the people; there must be some sort of forces making for interaction. If the neighbourhood group is an isolated one, cut off from other people and having no other contacts available, then it is fairly obvious that relationships within the group will be important, simply be-

cause there are no others to have. Also if the group is composed
of people with special ties that bind the members together
then it may be expected that interaction will be high. The
obvious examples would be the ties of kinship, economic ties
because of economic interdependence, or perhaps because of
religious or ethnic similarities. Whilst Carpenter only actually
instances social and ethnic similarities in the case of the pseudo-
neighbourhoods, it may be supposed that the homogeneity in
his usage applies to social class in its more general form. But
one may certainly expect that the more people have in common
with each other, even if it be only, say, a similarity of age, then
the more things they will be conscious of sharing and the more
this will be likely to make reciprocal understanding possible.
And it is upon reciprocal understanding that the whole of
society is based.

The neighbourhood then is really a small group of people,
rather than an unspecified size of group denoted by the phrase
'not over-densely populated', and it is a group which recognises
its bonds and acknowledges the social controls operating over
the members. The pseudo-neighbourhood, or residential area,
may exhibit some of the characteristics of the ideal type
neighbourhood of Carpenter's definition, but size of population
(rather than density) is likely to restrict the detailed primary
group controls, and all that will be found will be some such
similarities of behaviour, perhaps derived more from general
characteristics such as race or sub-cultural patterns.

The true neighbourhood would obviously be a very small
group of people and it is obviously Carpenter's argument that
it is unlikely to be found in modern urban society. What we
must consider against Carpenter's ideas, is what we do actually
find in modern cities.

The suggestions to be put forward for consideration are based
upon the incontrovertible fact that people of different sexes,
different ages and different social classes have different types
of interests and different physical areas within which interests
are pursued. Overall generalisations about how 'people' act in
the neighbourhoods of the modern city tend to be generalisations which must cover small children still in romper suits right
through to old age pensioners in wheel-chairs. For example,
Roper says of urban life that

Families live in close proximity with little in common . . . The great mobility in the large city tends to keep communities and neighbourhoods in continual flux . . . In the city one does not call upon one's neighbours simply because they live near, nor does one aid in sickness or distress except in emergency cases. The city aids its poor and distressed through impersonal channels. Newspapers take the place of country gossip and one may live for years without knowing one's neighbour.[4]

All these generalisations about city life might be true in some cases, and indeed in many cases, yet everyone knows of neighbours who call simply because they are neighbours and consider it a neighbourly duty to welcome newcomers to a district. Help in sickness and distress is often given in cases other than emergencies. Newspapers may be read, but local gossip does not disappear because of them. Some people may not know their neighbours of years' standing; others will know everything about the people who moved in two weeks ago.

But obviously every instance of the lack of personal relationships in the city can be offset by quoting cases of intense relationships. These contradictory examples do not get us much further. Attempts to define the boundaries of the physical neighbourhoods may be sterile in that they bear so little relation to social relationships. It is more useful to consider social relationships themselves rather than to worry about where neighbourhoods begin and end. To do this one can use a functional type of approach based on the life-cycle of the human being.

For example, if we take as a starting point the young child of pre-school age, the environment at birth, and before mobility develops, is the cot, pram or play-pen, and the neighbourhood is an irrelevant concept to the child itself (though not to the mother as we shall see later) because it (or rather he or she) is not a social creature at all.[5] But when the child becomes mobile and makes its own first social contacts, in playing with other children, then the first relationship with the neighbourhood is made. Here we find the small child playing in garden or on the pavement with other neighbouring children. The contacts made are likely to be restricted to a range of a few houses in either direction and contacts across a road which carries traffic are likely to be more restricted. The relationships made at this stage of development are obviously greatly determined by propinquity, and actual next-door children are likely to become playmates much more than children separated by as few as half a dozen houses, simply because access is so simple and mothers can know where they are. As the children grow a little older and means of transport are given to them (scooters, tricycles and small bicycles) the pavement becomes a means of communication and the network of relationships is extended to houses further along the road. But within the pre-school age range it is customary for pavement edges to form boundaries and the world on the other side of the road may well be a different social group. From random, but fairly routine, observations, I would suggest that the higher the social class the more the child is likely to be restricted in the area covered at this and immediately subsequent stages in the life-cycle. Of course, middle class people tend to live in houses with gardens at relatively low densities, while many lower class people live at high densities in terraces with only pavements and yards. For the latter, then, it follows that there are more chances of contact in a given area and play cannot be restricted to a safe enclosed garden under mother's eye if no garden exists. But in addition to this I would speculate that working class children tend to be given a freedom to roam at an earlier age than middle class ones, and some of the tiny children that one sees in working class areas roaming the streets alone lead one to wonder that so few are involved in traffic accidents. But when the pavement is the only playground then restrictions cannot be imposed even if they are desired.

When the child becomes of school age, at five in this country at the moment, its horizons are widened greatly by the daily journeys to and from the local school. Of course, the child has been shopping and visiting with his parents on innumerable occasions before going to school, but it is at school age that the journeying becomes his own journeying rather than someone else's. For the normal child in this country who attends the local education authority school (private schools raise separate questions) it is usual to attend the school nearest to the home. In some cases a certain amount of zoning of children is done by the education authority when officials visit homes to make censuses of the future school populations. Parents may then be told which school this child should attend when he is five and so a catchment area principle is used for allocating children to the primary schools. In this way the child becomes not only a part of a school group, but also a part of a geographical group. It may well be that the school catchment area is a fairly arbitrary one drawn around the school merely with a compass or a set square and its relation to any social factors is purely fortuitous. In most primary schools there is some mixing of social classes, since few natural neighbourhoods contain only houses with one class of people in them. But the mixing is likely to be less in areas of dense working class bye-law housing, or on council estates, where virtually the whole population is of working class type. In the middle class areas, or the transitional areas where the lower middle classes form a 'buffer zone' between middle and working, there is likely to be more mixture, with some working class housing mixed in with the middle class. The point is that the primary school is the first real social institution in which the child meets his peers on a selection basis not governed by parental control. After a few years of careful choosing of suitable playmates for her offspring, the mother must now stand back and let her child make his own choice from amongst the forty-odd other specimens in his class. An interesting field of social-psychological research is open here as to the factors operating in the making of first friendships. From random observations I would suggest that like does tend to mate with like in most cases, and that social class does have an, albeit unconscious, effect on the friendships made. This is not to suggest that snobbishness is rife at the tender age of five, but perhaps more that children at this age already recognise children with their own type of manners, etiquette and interests. It is by no means irrelevant also to note that gentle parental pressures on their children may affect friendship patterns, and the careful pruning of invitations to tea or birthday parties can have a decided effect on the selections made.

The initial social contacts of the first classes of the primary school often lay the foundations for friendship which last all through the infant and junior schools. If the school is one which 'streams' children at the age of seven, it may well be that a process of social class selection also takes place, since it is claimed by some psychologists and sociologists that even at this early age social class and measured intelligence show some correlation. But for more general social contact, the years in the junior school, between the ages of seven and eleven, are years when the range of interests of the children widen, both socially and physically. It is in this stage that children become very socially conscious and can take part in their first organised groups, such as cubs and brownies, church choirs and so on. In many cases this may mean after-school activities with already established school friends, but it is activity in a new milieu, and with a less authoritarian type of organisation. Also in the local voluntary groups, the children meet children from other schools, perhaps from private schools, and they learn to interact with new types of adults. The essence of these voluntary groups such as cubs and brownies is that they are neighbourhood groups and in going to them the young children are widening their horizons of experience and taking in neighbourhood interests which extend further than just the end of their own road.

In many of the activities associated with the period at primary school the child is learning to stand on his or her own feet in social relationships with other children and adults. But at this stage parental control and guidance, and protection against undesirable or even dangerous social contacts is needed. At the age of eleven in this country a major break in the child's life occurs with its transference to the secondary school. It is not possible to make any complete generalisations since multilateral and comprehensive schemes obviously have very different social effects on the neighbourhoods. But whatever scheme is adopted it is extremely likely that the child at eleven will (a) go to a school with more children than his primary school, (b) go to a school which will bring him into contact with children over a wider geographical range.

It is interesting to note that in the case of the selective authorities, children are usually allowed to rank their preferences for grammar schools and so it may well be that a child gives first vote to a school on the other side of the town. In the case of children not selected for grammar schools there is rarely a choice given and they are expected to attend the nearest secondary modern school as directed by the education authority. This has the result that the grammar school child is likely to mix with a more geographically varied group than the secondary modern child, and thus has opportunities for wider contacts built into his educational system. In the case of comprehensive and quasi-comprehensive systems it is customary for a large comprehensive school to serve a particular catchment area. Often the comprehensive school is 'fed' by a stipulated group of primary schools, so that the child at five years knows which school he will attend right the way through his educational career up to, or beyond, the age of fifteen. In this case there is a distinctive type of enlarged neighbourhood pattern created, and it is easy to delimit the catchment areas for primary and secondary schools.

In terms of social development the secondary school stage is a most interesting one for young people, since it is at this stage that their interests really cover a wider neighbourhood than before. The growing freedom of choice in their activities coupled with freedom of travel, on cycle or unescorted on public transport, means that they are now at a stage when choice can be made as to *where* any chosen activity shall be pursued. For example, if the boy wishes to be a boy scout he may be able to join a school group, a local church group, a local non-church group, or he may decide to join the group of which his best friend at school is a member right away on the other side of town. In informal sport he may decide that the best football or cricket pitches are in a park three miles from home, but with his bicycle to take him there the journey is worthwhile. If the local cinema still exists it may no longer be attractive when one is allowed to go to the big picture houses in the town centre. The essential point being made here is that to the young person the neighbourhood is still meaningful; the local churches, guides, scouts, cinemas, parks and so on still have a meaning. But now they are in competition with other attractions of a similar type, or even a different type, which may be located in other residential areas, or in the town centre, and the mobility of the young person is now becoming very much less limited. There is now competition for the young person's interests and in voluntary associations he need not be limited to his own neighbourhood. As the children grow older and become young teenagers their interests widen and so does their breadth of knowledge of the town or city as a whole. At the age when young people begin to go dancing, it is quite common to begin the first hesitant steps at the local church hall, scout huts or other similar neighbourhood institutions. But as skill develops the interest often turns from the local three-piece in the parish hall to the big bands, bright (or soft) lights of the town centre dance halls and all their more glamorous attractions, not to mention the possibilities of new faces. Thus as the children grow older the neighbourhood fulfils their needs less and less and the opportunities offered by the urban community as a whole have greater attractions. So it may be that in the middle teens, and especially if the young people leave school at fifteen or sixteen to go to work, the daily travel to work may well complete the break with the neighbourhood. It is at this stage that the harassed parent typically laments of his son or daughter that he (or she) is never in, and the charge is made, 'You treat this house like a hotel'. The comparison with an hotel is, of course, too extreme to be real, but the meaning is significant, that the young person uses the home as a centre from which he, or she, will go out to a wide variety of interests, the home having the principal function of providing a place to sleep and eat.

At the stage of life where the young person is employed and unmarried the neighbourhood may well have its fewest functions. Having few ties and many opportunities, young people can make full use of all the facilities of leisure, sport, entertainment and culture that the city has to offer. This is the time of life when the individual can follow his own wishes, not having to worry about responsibilities to other people too much, and it is a time when the seeking of marriage partners takes place.

When young people do marry, and today they are marrying at a fairly early age, they have the immediate problem of where to live. In the working class marriages they are fortunate if they can at once find a house to rent that could be regarded as a possible permanent residence. Rarely are council dwellings available for newly-weds and the renting of private houses is a matter of chance or knowing the right people. House purchase is rarely possible for young people with few savings and below average wages. Some couples live for a time with in-laws, some find themselves rooms of a temporary kind, but few are lucky enough to find a place to 'settle' immediately on marriage. In the middle classes house purchase is likely to be envisaged, but a flat is a more likely start to the marriage until sufficient capital for a mortgage deposit has been saved. Thus two things tend to work against the newly-weds having any strong neighbourhood feeling. The first is the likelihood of them living in an area where flats or rooms are common and where mobility is high. And secondly, today, the wife is likely to continue working for some time after marriage. The first point results in young married couples living in areas where they may well have similarities of interest with other couples of their own recent marital status, but the transience of so much of the residential population militates against any real group feeling. For these young couples mobility is still the great advantage which makes it possible for them to get about, to retain their links with relatives and friends, to keep up their activities in voluntary associations and clubs. When the wife works she may well use the neighbourhood shopping facilities very little, much of the household shopping being done near her work at lunchtime or on the way home. Thus the young couple in rooms in the house converted to flats may have little feeling of neighbourhood and only regard their local district as being convenient for the accommodation it offers, its proximity to work (if in the inner zone) and the transport facilities which it has for getting about the city. Young couples living with in-laws may well be in more permanent residential areas, but for them the temporary nature of the accommodation is unlikely to be forgotten and in the doubling-up within the household the younger couple have no real status of their own at all. They are merely lodgers in someone else's property and as such cannot be expected to have the same local feelings as the proper residents.

The next stage in the life-cycle comes when the wife has her first child, and for analysis purposes we will assume that at this stage the couple either rent or buy more permanent accommodation, even though it is well known how very many couples, especially in London, are not so fortunate as to be able to do this. If the young wife, on producing her first child, gives up work, even if only temporarily, the neighbourhood comes to have a very real meaning for her. From the stage of having no ties at all to hamper her mobility about the city, she suddenly finds herself tied so completely that the home, at times, can become a virtual prison. Mobility is limited by the needs of feeding times and the distance that can be covered when pushing a pram. Transporting the infant on buses becomes a major tactical operation requiring careful thought as to all possible hazards, and the wife whose husband will either lend her his car or provide her with one of her own lives in a different world from her non-car-owning sister. For the normal pram-pushing mother the local shopping expedition may well become the main outing of the day, or even week. What little research has been done on wives going out with their husbands in the evenings shows that this happens much more rarely once children arrive. Only the middle classes seem to accept the idea of paid baby sitters, and in the working classes a relative is almost always required if the baby is to be left. In a recent Birmingham survey in a working class area '89 mothers of children under 12 were asked if they were ever able to go out with their husbands in the evening and what arrangements they made about the care of the children on these occasions. As many as 47 said that they never went out with their husbands alone in the evening; either they took the children as well or their husbands stayed at home to let them go out; more than half said they never went out in the evening at all'.[6] Only 4 respondents mentioned using paid baby-sitters. For the mother with a baby or babies, therefore, the neighbourhood has a very real meaning, yet for the husband who is out at work all day, and who may still be able to maintain some of his outside contacts at pub or club in spite of the young baby, the neighbourhood need not mean very much. He may have a garden to work in at times, but this does not necessarily produce many social contacts, although allotment gardening is a more obvious source of social interaction. But while the baby in the pram may make acquaintances for the mother at the shops, and maybe result in a whole range of new friends being made, the husband is less likely to be brought within this orbit. Reimer suggests that 'Community of interest exists among young married couples who are raising infants or young children of almost the same age', and Gist and Halbert say that 'children are incurably addicted to "neighbouring" and in areas where they are numerous intimate relationships arise between families faced with a common problem of rearing the young'. To some extent this may be true, but studies of working class behaviour in this country tend to show that reliance on the older generation, reliance upon 'mum', is extremely widespread, and in this there may be a different culture pattern between the U.S.A. and England. But even allowing that young people with young children share common problems, it is questionable as to whether *intimate* relationships arise from them. Such relationships as do arise are likely to be limited to the mothers, and the fathers may hardly be touched by them at all. Further, the relationships between the mothers may be limited to the common interests that surround children and child-rearing. For example, mothers of young children frequently have other children to tea with their own offspring, but the reciprocal tea parties are by no means repeated at adult level with reciprocal visits between husbands and wives; the relationships are limited to the children. Finally, it should not be assumed that the social relationships which arise from interaction between children are always amicable ones. Children can be excellent dividers as well as uniters and many an adult coolness can develop from the quarrels of young children, and the problems of the children of 'decent' parents playing with 'rough' neighbours have caused many a local tiff. Without the children the parents may never have had harsh words.

Nevertheless, at the stages when children are dependent creatures in need of adult care and attention, the housewife is likely to find the neighbourhood having a real meaning for her and instances of reciprocal help in baby minding whilst one person goes to the shops, taking neighbours' children to school with one's own and, even, baby-sitting in the evening are common examples of ways in which the mothers free themselves temporarily from the bonds of their children. In new housing areas, particularly when there are large numbers of young parents faced with problems of child-rearing, garden making, council-petitioning for better roads or the provision of a school, reciprocal help is a commonplace and a real feeling of community is readily observable. It is less clear in areas where young couples are in a minority and a young mother may find herself with the only pram in the road and empty houses around her all day where wives are out at work.

When the children are older, and are settled at school for most of the day, the housewife obviously is less restricted in her movements, and when baby-sitters are no longer needed (possibly when the eldest child is left in charge) both parents can have unlimited evenings out if they wish. But at this stage of the life-cycle the parents are getting a little older and are not likely to be wanting to dash back to the local Locarno ball-room where they met fifteen years ago. These couples may enjoy going out together more to the cinema, theatre, restaurant and public house, and in voluntary organisations such as churches, community centres, tennis clubs and musical societies the married couples whose children are 'off their hands' are often the backbone of the organisation, being mature enough and free enough to undertake many duties. In this way the neighbourhood often does have more meaning for these slightly older married couples, and when their children are grown up and married they may well take greater interest in the local activities since their domestic interests have now decreased with their children's departure. But it should be borne in mind that these people are not tied to the neighbourhood, and with present trends they are quite likely to be car owners and so unlimited in their geographic range of interests and activities.

It is when old age begins to make its mark that the wider range of activities will be reduced, particularly when ill-health or a greater sensitivity to inclement weather develops. Old people who do not have their own transport become much more dependent upon local shops and delivered goods, and their needs may become the focus for neighbourly help. In urban life many services for old people, such as home-helps, district nurses and W.V.S. meals-on-wheels are organised on a city wide basis. But equally there are many local clubs for old people and innumerable neighbourly acts on the part of younger neighbours in helping - with shopping, cleaning, gardening, snow-clearance, to mention only a few. When one partner of the marriage dies the dependency of the relict may become very great and neighbourly visits may at times be the only form of real social intercourse that remains. From the dependency of youth the wheel has turned full circle to the dependency of old age.

In this analysis of the life-cycle it has been made apparent that the needs of the individual in regard to the neighbourhood vary tremendously according to sex, age and family status. At times there are few needs which the neighbourhood is the appropriate body to fill; at other times the neighbourhood is a very meaningful concept indeed. But what is essential to the analysis is the continuous recognition that the neighbourhood is a *part* of the town or city; it is a sub-section of the city, not an entity in itself apart from the city. Recognition of this fact is essential for an appreciation of the position of the neighbourhood in the urban structure.

The emphasis upon the importance of primary relationships in the neighbourhood has led to consideration of the neighbourhood as a primary group in itself, and from this comparisons between villages and neighbourhoods have been made. In some cases these have been extremely valuable, at other times (as will be shown) they have been dangerously misleading.

Many years ago the American sociologist E. A. Ross gave an interesting contrast between village and city. He wrote of the village that 'When communication is difficult and slow, you accept as intimates your blood kinsmen and neighbours, because you see them often, you know them best and they are right at hand in case you need them. Even if they are dour and touchy, even if their ways and ideas grate upon you, you fraternise with them for there is no one else to consort with. Even though with them you cannot be quite yourself or follow your bent, you adapt yourself to them from dread of becoming a social outcast'. In the urban neighbourhood by contrast, 'Modern methods of communication and transportation make possible a wide psycho-social and territorial range. The person's activities are not necessarily located in his home community, nor are the participants in these activities his neighbours. Home becomes significant as a place of retirement from the varied stimuli of social activity, and neighbouring tends to be redefined as unwarranted intrusion'.[7] This last phrase is echoed in a much more recent book by Reimer when he says, 'To relax from his working day, the city dweller seeks a residential environment where he will be free from the constant alertness that is forced upon him by mingling with the motley crowd of a heterogeneous urban population. To relax in his private life, the city dweller wants to be with "his own kind" '.[8]

These comments on the neighbourhood may usefully be placed against Carpenter's definition so as to elucidate the principal functions of the neighbourhood. In his ideal type neighbourhood Carpenter describes a 'primary group spirit which is the fulcrum of neighbourhood life', but this is recognised as being broken down by all the processes of urbanisation. Indeed, so much of an ideal type is Carpenter's neighbourhood that it seems almost contradictory to think of it as an urban concept at all. Logically it could be argued that if all the forces of urbanism are 'hostile' to the preservation of neighbourhood life, then how can the neighbourhood be an urban phenomenon? One is led to the conclusion that Carpenter is speaking of a phenomenon that may have existed in the past when towns were small, communications were slow and when all the conditions of which Ross writes were present. But such conditions, which would be typical of the situations described by Flora Thompson in *Lark Rise to Candleford*,[9] are pertinent only to social structures now dead and gone. In a predominantly rural area they may still obtain, but the general picture of the neighbourhood is such that one would have to conclude that it cannot exist in present-day urban society. If this is so, then Carpenter's definition of neighbourhood is an abstraction, and only his definition of the 'pseudo-neighbourhood' or 'residential area' is dealing with reality today. The similarity between the ideal-type neighbourhood and the old-time village is however very close and it may now be of value to make a brief comparason between the village and city so as to put the modern concept of neighbourhood (or residential area of Carpenter) into perspective.

The generalised picture of the rural village before urbanisation had developed in the late nineteenth and early twentieth centuries is of a small community, probably no more than a few hundred people in all, many of whom were interrelated through local marriages. Mobility was slight and the village was relatively isolated, even a few miles' journey being a major expedition. The occupational structure was closely linked to agriculture, its service industries and its by-products. Occupation tended towards a hereditary system and there were close relationships between home, work and leisure. The village had its social hierarchy with squire, parson, schoolteacher, shopkeepers and post office, but social mobility was slight, indeed almost a caste system. Nevertheless relationships were face to face and people knew each other as *whole* people and not just as segments of people in specialised roles. Social control was thus a strong factor and the individual had strong reasons to conform since social isolation or ostracism were very real sanctions. Being born and bred to this environment, though, the individual could adjust fairly readily to it, since no real alternatives were known. The few misfits might leave the village altogether or would become outcasts if they remained.

The contrast with the contemporary city is tremendous. Populations are huge and no individual can possibly know more than a fraction of the inhabitants. Relationship by kin and inter-marriage loses its importance in the community as a whole, though it may have vestiges remaining in some parts. Mobility is great, with both public and private transport, and moving from district to district is a new, important feature. Occupations are diverse, and few are hereditary. Production, distribution, commerce and administration have no such unifying bond as clear and striking as have agriculture and the land. Home has little relationship to workplace and with different occupations within the family, the working members split up all over the city. The social hierarchy of the city is complex and impersonal; classes replace individual statuses and one rarely knows many people as *whole* people. Opportunities for social mobility abound and a person is evaluated for what he is, or what he has, rather than by the ascribed status he derives from his father and family. Social control is less effective, since face-to-face relationships and intimate knowledge of other's business cannot operate over a total community of tens of thousands of people. Anonymity is more easily obtained in the city centre and its institutions, but in the urban ethos it is 'not done' to take too much interest in other people's lives anyway.

Obviously then the village of the past and the city of the present bear little similarity to each other. The differences are historical and concerned with size and complexity of structure.

Comparison between the village and the urban neighbourhood is then a possible next step, since it may be felt that the neighbourhood, being a part of the town, may still demonstrate the characteristics of the village. But the above comparison between village and city must show how misleading such a comparison would be. The urban neighbourhood is not an entity in itself, as is the village, it is merely a part, and a part difficult to define at that, of the whole city, and as our previous life-cycle analysis showed, the neighbourhood is only a 'some functions' unit as contrasted with the 'all functions' of the village (even though the functions may be on a small scale).

Both Ross and Reimer suggest that the neighbourhood is a place of retreat from the *total* urban life; it is a place where the individual can relax, with as little strain as possible, with people of his own sort. This means that he expects to find rest in the neighbourhood from the varied social contacts of city life, and their attendant social adjustments, in a social area where he can expect the people around him to think and act as he himself does. He thus has expectations of a similar outlook on life amongst his neighbours, particularly in so far as life in the neighbourhood itself is concerned. So if people want to go out from the neighbourhood to work in other parts of the city, if they want to spend their leisure time in the city centre, these things do not particularly matter *unless* in some way they affect the neighbourhood. If Mr. Jones across the road goes off to work in his car each morning, wearing his dark suit, white shirt and bowler hat, his actual job does not really matter. But if he suddenly starts going out in greasy overalls, big boots and a cloth cap then it can matter because Mr. Jones is affecting the social status of the area in moving down the scale from an *apparent* non-manual occupation to a manual one. The interesting point is that if he went to his work as a factory hand in a car and business suit probably many people locally would be completely unaware of the dangerous situation that was at hand since so much of the assessment is done through visual evidence. Similarly if the respectable Mr. and Mrs. Smith attended drunken orgies on the other side of town it would not affect the social life of their own neighbourhood at all so long as their behaviour never came to light. If the facts *did* come to light an interesting situation would probably arise. It might be hazarded that some neighbours would be greatly affronted and would cut the Smiths dead; others might well take the view that so long as they didn't hold the drunken orgies in the Smiths' house then it was really no one's business locally. The point at issue is essentially whether the behaviour of a particular person is relevant to the neighbourhood itself. Obviously there are differences of opinion between individuals and between neighbourhoods themselves as to what constitutes correct neighbourhood behaviour, but the essential factor is a recognition that life is not confined to the neighbourhood in anything like the way it is in the hypothetical village.

There are three points to be considered about the urban neighbourhood. Firstly, since it is a fact that cities divide their residential areas according to social class criteria, one must have some knowledge of the social class of any given area. Secondly, one must try to discover what functions the neighbourhood actually provides for the residents. Thirdly, one must try to discover the active behaviour which constitutes neighbourliness.

In a study[10] carried out in an urban district adjacent to Nottingham I attempted some enquiries into these problems. The place was West Bridgford, an urban district of approximately 25,000 population, which lies on the south side of the River Trent. Whilst socially it is mainly a residential suburb of Nottingham it is a local government area separate from the city and it has strong local loyalties and activities of its own. Six different types of housing areas were selected for sample enquiries; older type terrace houses, medium-sized pre-1914 semi-detached houses, pre-1914 large semi and detached houses, modern council houses, modern medium-sized semi-detached houses and modern large detached houses. The occupants of the houses of the samples interviewed were asked about their use of amenities in the town and Nottingham city, their leisure activities, their associational memberships and their neighbourly behaviour. It was interesting to note that whilst the middle class people were much more active in organisations and clubs than were the working classes, the top people in the middle classes (i.e. the most well-to-do in the best residential districts) were less active *locally* and tended more to do shopping and to join activities in the city or the county area. In neighbourly activity the patterns differed between working class and middle class, with the former having more informal neighbouring in the way of 'popping in' to the neighbours, the latter having more formal neighbouring in the way of giving coffee parties or evening entertaining in the home. Thus the neighbourhood means different things to different people and only a detailed typology of behaviour according to certain chosen criteria could do justice to the variety of patterns to be found in various types of neighbourhood.

It is therefore of considerable interest to enquire into the thoughts which lie behind the idea of the neighbourhood as a principle for town planning. Briefly put, the general theme that has been developed is that our modern cities are growing to such a size and such a complexity that some breakdown of them into smaller social units is needed if they are to retain their essentially 'human' characteristics. An official statement made in 1944 put the case as follows,[11] 'Something like half the population of England and Wales lives in towns which have a population of over 50,000. In these larger towns especially a sense of neighbourhood has been lost to great numbers of the inhabitants. The town is generally too large to be fully understood as a social unit, and the neighbourhood, the immediate environment of the many inhabitants, has lost or never had a full identity'. The report notes then that large housing estates built between the wars were just as bad as, if not worse than, older parts of the towns in their inadequacy in stimulating neighbourly feeling. The report continues, 'For the proper social well-being of the large town, then, it is necessary to work out some organisation of its physical form which will aid in every way the full development of community life and enable a proper measure of social amenities to be provided and arranged to advantage in each residential neighbourhood. The idea of the 'neighbourhood unit' arises out of an acknowledgment of the necessity of doing this and offers the means of doing it.'

But the neighbourhood unit has a history which pre-dates 1944 by many years and which throws an interesting light on the thoughts behind it.

THE NEIGHBOURHOOD UNIT

The first appearance of the idea of the neighbourhood unit[12] as a planning concept seems to have been in 1923 when Clarence Perry, a worker in the American community centre movement read a paper entitled 'A Community Unit in City Planning and Development' to a joint meeting of the American Sociological Society and the National Community Centre Association. In the period between 1919 and 1921 Perry had lived in a residential area called Forest Hill Gardens, a suburban housing development in New York begun in 1909 by the Russell Sage Foundation, a famous American philanthropic organisation. Forest Hill Gardens was more than just a number of houses; it had a planned layout which incorporated open spaces, parks and harmonious architectural design and planning so as to produce a co-ordinated physical environment. From his experience there, Perry came to appreciate the values of a locally planned residential area where a common architectural pattern and rational groupings and location of such amenities as schools, playgrounds, shops, parks and so on, worked in with a carefully thought out road pattern designed for pedestrian safety as well as vehicular access, would give social advantages and a sense of locality.

So far as the residents of Forest Hill Gardens went, Perry said that the scheme was 'originally intended to satisfy the environmental needs of a fairly definite social class, and it attracted a more or less homogeneous group of residents'. It was one class, not multi-class. Perry's reflections on the community centre aspect of the development were tinged with disappointment when he recorded that 'reality was far short of the goals set, and political, sectarian and cultural obstacles to the public organisation of community centres were to be dealt with by education and time', a conclusion which seems despondent to say the least. With regard to the neigh-bourhood unit as a *social* grouping, Perry was extremely careful in his statements and only went so far as to say that, 'When residents are brought together through the use of common recreational facilities they come to know one another and friendly relations ensue. Existing developments with neigh-bourhood unit features have consistently produced face-to-face social conditions'. This statement is so hedged about by the conditional 'when' that it is not far from saying nothing. Firstly the residents have to be brought together in the use of common recreational facilities. Supposing they don't want to? If they do get together must it always be assumed that friendly relations will ensue? Evidence from Liverpool would suggest that unfriendly relations can ensue.[13] The production of face-to-face social conditions may be productive of good relations, but we need to know much more about the groups concerned if any conclusion is to be derived. After all, trench warfare in the 1914–18 war produced face-to-face conditions, and the mother of parliaments at Westminster is deliberately designed so that the two main parties may confront each other in a face-to-face situation. Perry's *social* claims for the neighbourhood unit were very careful and extremely modest. His detailed proposals were really much more concerned with the physical layout of residential areas so as to provide the residents with a rational environment for living. In his major work, *Housing for the Machine Age*, an interesting and revealing title, Perry went into great detail over the principles of planning which should underline the neighbourhood unit. Briefly he was concerned with six features: (1) Size, (2) Boundaries, (3) Open Spaces, (4) Institution Sites, (5) Local Shops, and (6) Internal Road Systems. The general plan was to try to reduce local traffic to those vehicles which actually had calls to make in the area, whilst through traffic should by-pass the area by going along major traffic roads which would form unit boundaries. Within the areas, then, the location of shops, schools, churches, etc., would be thought out beforehand, rather than being allowed to locate themselves anyhow. The emphasis was upon the pedestrian, and particularly the young person, within the unit, with easy access and safety being given high priority. What were considered, *a priori*, to be reasonable local needs were to be provided for by the allocation of appropriate sites.

Viewed with the hindsight that one may have today, Perry's proposals may seem rather obvious and unremarkable. But when a look is taken at many of the 'planned 'council estates that were built in Britain before the 1939–45 war (and, sad to say, since it, too) the lack of thought given to the location of amenities and coherent road plans shows how little impact Perry's ideas had for many years. In many towns today the observer can easily find housing estates in which the road layout appears to have been derived from geometrical patterns that look pretty on a drawing board rather than having any relation to contours, shops, traffic routes or anything else. The great crescents so beloved of many pre-war designers ensured little except good healthy exercise for the body in walking the maximum distances possible to get from the home to anywhere else, and exercise for the mind in trying to remember where one was in a featureless area where every house was identical with the rest. Pre-war housing estate studies, too, were virtually unanimous in pointing to the lack of consideration in building roads, schools and shops as the houses went up, and many tenants' associations were the direct outcome of dissatisfaction with these states of affairs.

Estates, then, rather than neighbourhoods, were the products of pre-war development, and there seems no evidence to suggest that the neighbourhood unit theory had made any real impact in this country before the war.

As has been pointed out, a government publication gave it a boost in 1944, and we shall return to consider this report later. But perhaps more important in the chronological order is a report[14] published in 1943 by the National Council of Social Service Community Centres and Associations Survey Group. The report, which was in the form of a small book (or large pamphlet) was the result of work done by a committee of fourteen people (including the chairman). Seven of these people were directly concerned with community associations, one was connected with the Young Women's Christian Association, one was an architect, two were town planners, one was a director of education and one might most usefully be labelled as a member of the Barlow Commission. This committee's report was concerned with the future plans for urban development once the war was won and it came out strongly in favour of town planning on the neighbourhood unit basis, with the community centre as the neighbourhood focal point. Furthermore, the report strongly criticised pre-war housing estates because of the segregation of social classes which ensued, and declared the need for 'social balance' in the neighbourhoods. 'Class distinctions have been emphasised to an undesirable extent by the segregation of rigidly divided income groups into separate residential districts . . . The consequence of this segregation is that the new municipal estates contain relatively few people with varied experience in social leadership and where leaders are lacking it is more than usually difficult to build up community life'. The report therefore recommended that, after the war, 'Every planning scheme should aim at producing one or more neighbourhood units, each fitting into the town to which it belongs and each containing a socially balanced population'.

If we ignore the rather odd terms of the last recommendation with its rather parsimonious desire for 'one, or more', it would appear that this N.C.S.S. group was concerning itself with three interrelated ideas.

1. Neighbourhood units as planned residential areas better thought-out than pre-war municipal estates.
2. Community centres as the foci for the local community life.
3. 'Balanced' social classes, because segregation meant a lack of leaders in working class estates, and, *ergo*, their community centres.

Several important considerations derive from the above points. Of item (1) there is little to say except that this follows closest to Perry's original ideas. On point (2), Perry himself was reticent about the success of the community centre movement in the 1920's. Obviously point (2) is a matter of faith on the part of the community centre research group. Point (3) would appear to be a direct consequence of point (2), in that it can be inferred that the group felt that pre-war community centres on working class municipal estates had often not succeeded because they lacked people with leadership qualities. Since they appear to have assumed that the middle classes would supply the needed leadership, then 'social balance' in the units would be the answer.

Since all experience has shown that urban development tends to produce segregation of the social classes by residential areas, it is obviously a deliberate policy which is required to bring about social balance. Our consideration of the zonal theories in urban development and the production of 'natural

areas' provides plenty of evidence against the natural development of socially balanced areas. The Group argued the case
for social balance on these lines:

> The social mixing of people belonging to different income
> levels has taken place during the war through association not
> only in the fighting services but still more on a neighbourhood
> basis, in the civil defence services. This process will tend to
> become a permanent feature if, as it has been suggested, a
> period of national service is made a part of the normal life of
> every citizen in peacetime, and if the effects of present and
> future taxation and the distribution of the health, education
> and other public services tend to decrease the gap between
> higher and lower ranges of income.

These arguments do not now seem to be very realistic, though
perhaps when the war was still being waged they carried some
emotional charge. But viewed dispassionately it is extra-
ordinarily naïve to speak of the rigid, authoritarian hierarchy
of the armed forces in terms of mixing the social classes—few
examples of greater class differences can be found than between
officers and other ranks. The argument derived from mixing
on the basis for civil defence seems muddled and contradictory
if the neighbourhoods were the segregated ones of which the
Group complains. National service was never suggested
seriously as a permanent feature for women and they, as we
have pointed out, are the ones most affected by the neighbourhood life. The effects of taxation, health services, education,
etc., have been marginal, and if anything the ability to opt
out of national welfare provisions and education have become
hall-marks of social class, whilst the increased prosperity of the
manual classes does not seem to have had the supposed effect.
Thus the arguments put forward for the social mixing derived
from experience up to 1943 seem rather feeble when looked at
twenty years later.

Later in the report, and this is our last quotation, the Group
say this:

> Though physical planning and administrative measures cannot
> by themselves change social relationships, they can, if wisely
> and positively conceived, encourage and facilitate the growth
> of that spirit of fellowship without which true community life is
> impossible. Social barriers will only disappear if people in

different grades [*sic*] find a unity in common interests and purposes. This development can be accelerated by the provision of adequate and distinctive neighbourhood facilities.

Not surprisingly, it is suggested that the common interests can be found in the community association, and in this the socially balanced population can have its leaders and its led.

Unfortunately there are no concrete suggestions as to what the catalytic common interests and purposes are to be that will bring all the people of the neighbourhood together. In one of the few objective studies carried out of community centres, Penelope Hall, in her 1946 study in Salford and Manchester,[15] found only a paper membership in the centres of approximately 3 to 4 per cent of the total population of the estates studied. In her conclusions she wrote,

> Many present-day tendencies, for example: increased mobility, the separation of work interests from home interests, mass entertainment, the growing importance of large compared with small local government units, and the increasing influence of the permanent official in civic and national affairs, all militate against the development of local consciousness and effort. Collectively they give rise to the question as to whether the idea of the neighbourhood unit with a common life focused round the community centre may not be out of tune with the spirit of the age—a wistful looking backward to a tradition which is no longer valid.

Whilst the trends that Miss Hall picks out are all valid ones, she was not to know of the tremendous developments in the ownership of cars which would increase mobility enormously, of the large numbers of married women who would go out to work, and of the impact of television which would bring mass culture into practically every home, replacing the local cinema to the latter's serious decline.

The New Towns Committee, in the same year as Miss Hall's report, gave serious consideration to the question of social segregation and wrote that, 'It is caused, especially in cities, as much by differences of social behaviour associated with differences of income as by the actual differences in income. In some respects, and to some extent, these differences of social behaviour are now less well marked: but they have by no means disappeared, and so long as they continue the tendency to segregation is understandable and will remain.'

The way in which social balance was to be obtained was referred to in a most peculiar way in the report of the Study Group of the Ministry of Town and Country Planning in 1944. They wrote, 'Within the neighbourhood it is strongly recommended that a variety of dwellings should be provided. A great deal of evidence has been submitted[16] indicating that each neighbourhood should be "socially balanced", inhabited by families belonging to different ranges of income groups, or at least not so unbalanced as to be restricted to dwellings and families of one type or income level only, as the case may be.' So far we are on familiar ground, but in the explanation that follows the logic is difficult to follow.

> The careful disposition of amenities such as parks, playgrounds, recreational facilities, community buildings and shopping centres would go a long way to solve the problem of 'social balance', but the main key to a solution would be in the grouping of the various types of dwellings in such a way that they satisfy the desires of the various social groups in the matter of immediate convenience and use, and yet at the same time are part of the neighbourhood. There are practical difficulties in the way of indiscriminately mixing the dwellings of the various income groups. The way to success would be in studying the trends evidenced between the wars, and in so arranging the dwellings within the neighbourhood plan that it is made up of several minor groups of dwellings, each one of which would have its own distinctive character, largely dependent on the size of the dwelling and arrangement of plot plans. The evidence[17] suggests that, on social grounds, these minor groups should provide for 100–200 families.

The whole of this report was given a very searching critical analysis by Leo Kuper, who pointed out many of its inconsistencies. As he says, 'The phrase "evidence suggests" is used when there is ambiguity in the evidence, or it has been inadequately analysed, while the term "social grounds" is wide enough to cover any of a whole range of conflicting criteria'.[18] If we conclude from the extremely vague guidance of the report that the Study Group is advocating a social balance which is gained from building for groups of 100 to 300 families of similar class together, the whole neighbourhood then being the total of the 100–300 sub-groups, then we may be somewhere near a practical proposal. With the suggested total neighbourhood unit population of 10,000 people in all a fairly simple calculation will tell us what proportions of various social classes should be present in the neighbourhood and in the smaller sub-sections, which for simplicity's sake we will take to be 250 dwellings. A calculation such as this was worked out for Sheffield, with the following results.

Using the 1951 Census data we find the following class distribution for Sheffield:

SOCIAL CLASS DISTRIBUTION
PER 1,000 OCCUPIED AND RETIRED
MALE HEADS OF HOUSEHOLDS

Grade 1	Grade 2	Grade 3	Grade 4	Grade 5
25	117	560	132	166

If this distribution is to be applied to a neighbourhood of 10,000 total population of all ages an assumption on household size must be made. We will assume each household to consist of four persons. A neighbourhood of 10,000 people will then, hypothetically, have 2,500 male heads of households, distributed as follows:—

SOCIAL CLASS DISTRIBUTION OF MALE HEADS OF
HOUSEHOLDS IN A NEIGHBOURHOOD UNIT OF
10,000 POPULATION = 2,500 HOUSEHOLDS

Grade 1	Grade 2	Grade 3	Grade 4	Grade 5
63	293	1,400	330	415

A neighbourhood of 2,500 households divided amongst sub-units of 250 households gives ten sub-units. Obviously if each sub-unit were to be socially balanced in accordance with the above distribution it would work out at 6·3 of Grade 1 and 29·3 of Grade 2, together giving about thirty-five middle class families to each sub-unit of 250 total families. But such dilution of resources is not in accordance with the Ministry Study Group's plan, and they suggest 100 to 300 families of *similar* type in the sub-units. This gives something like one and a half sub-units of middle class families (Grades 1 and 2) amongst the total ten sub-units.

These sums are not intended to make fun of the Study Group's proposals; what they are intended to show is that 'social balance' is not composed of an *even* mixture of middle and lower classes, it is a mixture of roughly 14 per cent middle class to 86 per cent lower class. Put together in these proportions the middle classes have to be spread very thin indeed, resulting in Grade 1 families being in a minority of one to forty if mixed in with all other classes. If such a distribution were attempted with a well-established town the relocation of people required to bring it about would necessitate a complete redistribution of housing and population such as has never been seen in our history.

The question of social balance is thus an academic one in so far as present towns are concerned, and even in the new towns and new areas of present towns the abstract ideas of balance have tended to break down against the realities of differences between the occupants of rented houses and owner-occupied houses. One hears relatively little of 'social balance' these days.

Similarly the community centre movement has not become the focal point of neighbourhood life that its proponents had hoped for. If attendance figures are any criterion it might be argued that the local bingo hall, public house or working men's club could probably be considered much more successful.

What has remained, and is put into effect, is the idea of the neighbourhood as an 'amenity' area, with shops, schools, institutions, open spaces and road patterns laid down in accordance with a thought-out plan. This is the essential Clarence Perry unit brought into its fulfilment with convenience being the guiding light. The original sizes of 5,000 and 10,000 populations for the units were essentially, in this country, based on the feeder populations for primary schools, 'either 5,000 to contain one school for children aged 5–7 and one for children aged 8–11, or alternatively a population of 10,000 containing two of each such schools . . . This (latter) neighbourhood would also contain a child population of the age groups 11–15 which would normally require one Secondary (Modern) School'.[19] With this sort of population basis, the planning appears much more practical, but it does not deal with the questions of social interaction, community feeling and so on, which do not seem to have had great results. If we look at some of the arguments put forward on this point we may see why.

One of the most active proponents of neighbourhood planning in this country from the community development side has been L. E. White, who, in two books published by the National Council of Social Service had several points to make. In *Our Neighbourhood*,[20] he wrote, 'The neighbourhood unit is, in fact, the modern urban counterpart of the village, and towns and urban areas can still be broken up into the old constituent villages which were swallowed up by the coming of the Industrial Revolution, or cut off and isolated by a railway or motor road'.

The suggestion of the neighbourhood unit as a modern counterpart to the village of the past is an interesting one, and we shall return to this idea in a later section. The fact that small villages were engulfed by town expansions with the coming of the Industrial Revolution (and long after) is interesting, but not particularly helpful in the modern context. Most suburbs bear a name derived from the old villages or hamlets where there were cross-roads or churches, and even a few cottages may still remain today, but the relevance of this to all the acres of modern housing, shops and schools is hard to see. As for these places being 'cut off' or 'isolated' by railways or motor roads, the reasoning is difficult to see, since both of these are means of communication. Certainly railway tracks form barriers of a sort, although in urban areas there is normally no lack of bridges and cuttings, but motor roads only *reduce* the isolation of the vestigial villages and bring them into touch with the town. Most people are well aware of the differences in communication brought about by the introduction of motor services, especially with trams and buses, and 'isolation' is indeed an odd concept in this situation.

In his book *Community or Chaos*, White writes that the neighbourhood unit is 'a conscious endeavour to recover much that was worth while in the old village tradition and translate it into modern times . . . In contrast with the one-class estates there would be a wise mingling of people to produce a socially balanced community with a diversity of occupations and income levels'.[21] Yet in a later book, when writing about the planning of one-class, or homogeneous, areas in the U.S.A., White says significantly that these plans use 'all the techniques of modern physical planning to reinforce the *natural urge*[22] towards class or social segregation'. If White really does believe that the urge to segregation is a natural one (and all evidence seems to support this as a generalisation) then physical planning alone is unlikely to have very much effect unless the location of dwellings becomes part of an authoritarian pattern of government.

The analogy between neighbourhood unit and village is a misleading one for a number of reasons. Firstly there is the commonplace error of ignoring the historical factor. The neighbourhood of *today* is compared with the village of *yesterday*, and as we saw in the chapters on rural-urban comparison this leads to confusion. But even if some sort of comparison is made the general theoretical analysis is wrong. The suggested size for a neighbourhood unit has been put at a minimum of 5,000 population, with an alternative 'double-unit' at 10,000. These figures would, in some countries, give the place the status of a town at least, and perhaps even a city. Whatever the name would be, 5,000 to 10,000 is a very big village, and for a social group with face-to-face relationships and primary group social controls it is impossible. The neighbourhood unit is not a functional group in the sense that a village is supposed to be in this comparison. The neighbourhood unit is not an industrial-economic unit of interdependent people, indeed it need not even be a local government unit unless deliberately planned as such, and the functions of residence, some leisure, some religion, some education and some shopping emphasise the fact of it being a sub-section of some larger whole.

Nor is the neighbourhood unit isolated in the way that the village is considered to be in the theoretical propositions. Apart from the doubtful validity of claims about the isolation of villages themselves today, it is incorrect to think of neighbourhoods being so 'inward looking' when they are merely parts of the city as a whole. Thus the neighbourhood, being only some-functions does not compete seriously with the larger city centre shops, cinemas and dance halls, and it does not even attempt to provide the essentially urban institutions such as department stores, theatres, concert halls, professional football stadia, museums, small sectarian churches and so on, all of which require large numbers of people to make them viable propositions. The *lack* of these institutions in both neighbourhoods and villages should not lead to the two being regarded as similar areas simply because they lack the same things. Whilst both residents of villages and residents of neighbourhoods may have to go on from their places of residence to visit, for example, a concert hall, the villager moves from one community (his village) to an adjacent larger community (the city) for this purpose. The neighbourhood dweller is a member of the community of the city in the first place, and his neighbourhood is a sub-section of that community.

Obviously, then, from the viewpoint of sociological analysis of village, neighbourhood and city, the concept of *community* is the key one. In the following chapter we shall consider what sociologists, particularly sociologists who are well known for their theoretical contributions to the discipline, have to say on the question. From their writings we shall hope to put the whole problem into a truly sociological frame of reference.

Chapter Seven

A THEORETICAL VIEWPOINT

THE CONCEPT OF COMMUNITY

IN this chapter we shall attempt to derive from the works of a number of well-known sociologists an understanding of the essential features of urban sociology. For this purpose we shall take one concept, that of 'community', as the focal point of the exposition. The reason for using this plan is as follows. We suggest that urban sociology is concerned with a particular aspect of sociology as a whole: it is concerned with people living in particular types of communities which we describe as 'urban'. In sociology we have a basic distinction between 'urban' and 'rural', and we shall try to clarify this distinction. But before tackling the adjectives we feel it best to deal with the noun, and, for our purposes, the most useful noun is 'community'. We shall, therefore, make a detailed analysis of the meaning of the concept of 'community'.

> In everyday conversations we do not (and frequently need not) explain in advance what we mean by such terms as community and crowd . . . we usually have no trouble in grasping the meaning (of a speaker's words) because we know the object of his reference . . When the meanings are not made clear by context, everyday speech is apt to be less communication than the exchange of familiar sounds . . . the 'big words' frequently reach a high level of use and a low level of meaning in the efforts of the platform orator, propagandist or editorial writer.[1]

The word 'community' has reached 'a high level of use and a low level of meaning' with many writers in a variety of fields, and we begin, therefore, with an attempt to raise this word to a higher level of meaning. To raise the meaning of the word or concept of 'community' means that we must subject it to a process of classification. 'The ultimate test of the value of a particular term or concept must be its usefulness for the purpose at hand, namely the description of behaviour so objectively as to be subject to corroboration by other persons.'[2] Thus the word 'community' is valueless as a sociological concept unless it is defined in terms of observable behaviour.

Scientists agree to designate each degree or kind of behaviour which their instruments indicate by specific words or other symbols. These words so defined may then be used to build up more complicated words, the definition of which is, however, always reducible to the readings of standardised instruments . . . Such definitions are called operational definitions . . . Operational definitions, then, are merely definitions which consist as far as possible of words clearly designating performable and observable operations subject to corroboration . . . Now the degree to which the above criteria can be satisfied varies considerably according to the stage of development which a science has reached . . . It is not contended, therefore, that other definitions which are only imperfectly, slightly, or not at all operational may not be valuable in the early stages of a science, or on the frontiers of well-established sciences. They may be useful as first approximations, pending more mature developments. Highly perfected operational definitions are goals to which we strive, rather than tools to be hoped for or conjured up ready-made at the outset of an enquiry.[3]

It cannot be pretended that the term 'community' has as yet been so carefully defined in operational terms that 'the goal' has been reached; as yet sociology has a long way to go before such a claim could be made. Numerous definitions of the word 'community' have been made, but most are in the category of 'conjured up ready-made' and few, if any, can be said to be goals to which the definers have striven. Nevertheless, it is obvious that if a number of definitions of the term show great similarity in the factors included, there must be some trend indicated which will be fruitful to pursue. There is a further problem, however, even when the essential factors have been agreed upon. For example, in very simple terms, a metallurgist who examines two pieces of alloy, such as bronze, may say that piece A and piece B are both bronze in general terms, yet piece A contains a higher proportion of copper than does piece B.

Having identified the component elements or factors, he goes on to describe, or measure, the proportions present of the constituent factors.

With a complex term such as community, we may usefully adopt a similar procedure. Thus we may agree to designate a certain group as a community if factors A, B and so on are present. Having decided upon the factors, it is then our task to measure the amounts present. When we have done this we can then compare communities and, by analysis, show their points of similarity and difference. The problem, then, is of locating the constituent factors and measuring them, at all times doing this in an objective way, open to corroboration by other workers in the same field. If the constituent factors are clearly stated and are open to use by everyone, we are making progress toward our goal of a higher level of meaning; if the factors are not made explicit and remain subjective or undefined, we can only expect the result to be a confusing multiplicity of 'definitions' which will obscure rather than give light.

It is, of course, realised that in a subject such as sociology, in which the phenomena under study are highly complex, the progress will be slow and there can be no *absolute* definition, no final or ultimate word. As research builds up greater knowledge about any subject so it can be described in terms of greater exactitude; so in sociology, if we wish to understand the concept of community more clearly, we require more and more research into all the constituent factors which go to make it up. At this stage of development, however, it is probably more important than anything else that the methods used should be open to general scrutiny. If the facts are presented in an orderly fashion, if everyone who is interested can see how the job has been done and how the conclusions have been reached then progress is being made. Without this completely open method, only a fog of obscurity will descend.

In sociology, community refers to groups of human beings classified according to certain criteria.

The distinctively sociological basis for classification is *interaction*, and strictly speaking, this should be the sole basis of *sociological* classification. When we use geographic proximity, biological relationships, age, colour, etc., as the basis of sociological classifications, we do so because these obvious or relatively easily determinable characteristics are usually correlated in a very high positive degree with the factor in which we are sociologically interested, namely, interaction.[4]

If we intend to study communities as groups distinguished by interaction among their members, we must expect the interaction observed among different groups to be of different types and degrees. At this stage, however, it is the general framework with which we must begin, and for this purpose we will consider definitions of the term community as given by two sociologists. The two chosen, G. A. Lundberg and R. M. MacIver, have been selected from a great number of sociological writers because they differ widely in their approach to the study of society. In their writings there have been manifest differences of opinion, and if, therefore, we can find a measure of agreement between them on the concept of community, we may be fairly sure that other writers on this concept will not show any very great differences in approach.

On the concept of community, then, Lundberg writes,

> We may then agree to designate as a community any plurel[5] which has a given minimum degree of geographic homogeneity and a given minimum degree and kinds of interaction . . . If we agree that community is to be used to designate a plurel with temporal, geographic and interactional dimensions of certain types and degrees, that is entirely satisfactory. The degrees of each component which distinguishes 'community' from an adjoining category should be determined on the basis of practical convenience as research proceeds . . . The interaction dimension may subdivide into all kinds of indexes on the basis of which we infer or measure interaction.[6]

MacIver, who wrote a large book entitled *Community*, gives his definition of the concept in these words,

> By community I mean any area of common life, village or town, or district or country, or even wider area. To deserve the name community, the area must somehow be distinguished from further areas, the common life may have some characteristic of its own such that the frontiers of the area have some meaning . . . wherever men live together they develop in some kind and degree distinctive common characteristics—manners, traditions, modes of speech and so on. These are the signs and

consequences of an effective common life. It will be seen that a community may be part of a wider community, and that all community is a question of degree . . . It is a question of the degree and intensity of the common life.[7]

The reader will perceive at once that Lundberg and MacIver approach the concept from quite different angles, yet there is to be found in their definitions three fundamental points of agreement.

1. That community is allied to geographic area.
2. That community refers to a plurel with a certain common life, or forms of interaction, which distinguish it from other plurels.
3. That community is a relative term—that a community must always be regarded as a community relative to some other group, and thus community is a matter of degree.

If we take these three points of agreement as basic to our study it becomes apparent that in the analysis of the concept of community we must look to the aggregational aspects and to the group aspects, and in the latter we require tools for measuring degrees of interaction. But it is putting the cart before the horse to try to think in terms of degrees before we have even decided what the factors are that must be measured. To make the selection of factors clearer, we shall adopt the use of 'ideal types'.

In setting up an ideal type concept of community we envisage the concept in terms of a number of stated factors, all of which are present to the maximum possible degree. Such a model is extremely unlikely to be found in real life, but for analytical purposes it is of great value. As Von Wiese and Becker point out,

All scientists operate with ideal types or even conscious fictions; the theoretical physicist's world, for example, is an artificially simplified realm in which lines are fictitiously straight, cylinders and spheres are without even microscopic irregularities, and friction is banished utterly. Nobody expects him to formulate a 'law' (a shorthand statement of his observations) relating to the behaviour of a particular knotty, unplaned, kiln-dried, yellow pine two-by-four when struck by a dull axe in the sweaty hands of a 150-pound Italian labourer who receives only thirty cents an hour for his work; ideal-type and empirical are never

confused either by the public or by the physicist himself . . .
Ideal types are therefore only heuristic fictions, and are never
found on land or sea . . . The term derives from Max Weber,
who applied it to various social phenomena which are never
found in an unmixed or 'pure' form, but which for purposes of
conceptual clarity and systematisation are dealt with *as if* they
so existed . . . In speaking of an ideal type Weber does not
mean anything empirically exemplary or 'average'.[8]

Of course, ideal types had been used by scientists well before
Weber's day, but the distinction between 'fact and fiction' was
not always brought out with sufficient clarity.

It may be objected that if ideal types stand for fictions which
can never be observed in the world of fact, then they will tend
to obscure rather than clarify. This argument is considered by
Burgess. 'This objection does not trouble the ideal type analyst
since he maintains that only approximations can be found in
society. The question of measurement then becomes what
degree of approximation. This demand for measurement has
led to a development of scales by which different degrees of the
characteristics may be given values.'[9]

This surely is true: the physicist works out his theories in
terms of perfectly straight lines, completely regular surfaces and
so on, and then in the practical situation sees how reality
differs from the idealised form. For the sociologist it would
appear to be equally valuable to set up an ideal concept of
community so as to encompass all the relevant factors. There is
then a base from which observations in reality can be made.

The main task to be faced in setting up the ideal type for the
concept of community is to discover the factors of the 'common
life' or forms of interaction to be taken into account. If we
agree for definitional purposes that there are, say, five factors
to be considered, we may then say that in the ideal type
community, each of these factors will be present to a 100 per
cent level. Thus, for example, if we decide that the wage-
earner's place of work is a component then we may decide that
all wage-earners in the ideal community will work within that
community. In the real-life situation we can then count the
numbers of wage-earners who work within the community and
the resultant figure gives us a measure for this factor of community.

The following hypothetical example demonstrates this approach.

	Community A				Community B	
	Community A				*Community B*	
	o	Score	100		o	Score 100

Factors		Factors	
A	x	A	x
B	x	B	x
C	x	C	x
D	x	D	x
E	x	E	x

In the above comparison we should say that Community A is closer to the ideal type of community than Community B, according to our definition and measurement. In the above diagram no great problem arises as Community A scores higher on all factors than Community B. If Community A scored much lower than Community B on, say, two factors we should be faced with the problem of deciding what interpretation to make from this result. One possible method would be to weight each factor and to attempt a composite score, adding the measurements for each factor. This raises the problem of whether one can add together different factors to give a final sum which is meaningful, and it may well be argued that this cannot be done. Nevertheless, even if no single measurement can be agreed upon because of the arbitrariness of the weighting procedure, the simple comparison between the two communities on a compound measuring scale is in itself a great advance on merely descriptive analysis.

It will be noted, however, that the hypothetical scale shown above works on a system of 'absent' or 'present'. That is to say, a factor may be wholly absent (o per cent) or fully present (100 per cent) with varying degrees in between. If we were to leave the analysis at this stage we may get some form of comparison, but we should be ignoring the possibility of factors changing in *form* which could be of value in analytical work. For example, if we wished to contrast an agricultural village with an essentially industrial village, we should lose information of value by merely using a basis of work within or without the village. Obviously we should have to take into account the type of work done. Now a scale of 0–100 could be applied to the proportion of workers in agriculture for both villages: one village would score high on this and the other one low. Conversely, a scale of 0–100 on industrial occupations would give a completely reverse picture. From this approach it becomes apparent that if we can agree that some factors can be chosen to which a continuum can be applied, with *contrasting* poles at each end, then an advance in understanding is gained. The method of contrasting ideal types, linked by a continuum, has been used in sociology for many years, particularly in the field of rural-urban sociology. If we apply this method to the concept of community we see more clearly how 'community' is not just a phenomenon which is present or absent, but is a concept which can be applied to the analysis of the *structure* of social groups to highlight the differences between them. In brief, a small hamlet and a large city may both be called 'communities' but obviously they differ in many respects. The data upon which this method will be used will be taken from a representative group of sociologists who have written on the concept of community, and the analysis will show how much agreement is to be found on the essential factors which make up the concept.

GEMEINSCHAFT AND GESELLSCHAFT

The main task to be dealt with in setting up the ideal type for the consideration of the concept of community is that of putting forward the factors of the 'common life', which must be taken into account. For this purpose, the concepts of Gemeinschaft and Gesellschaft, as used by Toennies, will be the starting point for the analysis. The two terms have been translated into the English language as Community and Society and also as Community and Association, but these word-for-word translations tend to confuse; they give the impression that the Gemeinschaft structure is a 'community' structure, whereas the Gesellschaft structure is not. The actual translations of the two words are not of very great importance; it is what Toennies has to say about them that is of primary interest. Toennies' writing has been distinguished by his use of the concepts Gemeinschaft and Gesellschaft as polar types. Placing them at the two ends of a continuum, he says that any group under study may tend more towards the one than the other, though not necessarily 100 per cent of either. As Heberle explains,

> To him (Toennies) Gemeinschaft and Gesellschaft are pure concepts of ideal types, which, as such, do not exist in the empirical world. They can, therefore, find no employment as classificatory concepts. Rather are they to be regarded as traits, which, in empirical social entities, are found in varying proportions. If one should, e.g. define the family as a 'Gemeinschaft', the road to sociological understanding would thereby be barred; it is the peculiar task of the sociologists to find out how far the family in a concrete situation (e.g. the wage earner's family in a great city) approaches more nearly to the type of Gesellschaft than a family in another situation (e.g. on a farm). If one takes the concepts in this sense, it will then be possible to apply them to historical phenomena without doing violence to the logic of the system.[10]

As Toennies' translator, Charles P. Loomis,[11] points out, 'The keystones of Toennies' system are the concepts or ideal types, Gemeinschaft and Gesellschaft, which are based primarily upon natural will and rational will'.

As natural and rational will are fundamental to the understanding of the two ideal types, it is therefore necessary to give some brief explanation of their meaning as expressed by Toennies. He says of them,

> Natural will is the psychological equivalent of the human body, or the principle of the unity of life.
> Rational will is a product of thinking itself, and consequently possesses reality only with reference to its author, the thinking individual.
> Natural will derives from and can be explained only in terms of the past, just as the future in turn evolves from the past. Rational will can be understood only from the future developments with which it is concerned.
> An aggregate or form of the rational will is related to an aggregate of the natural will in the same manner as an artificial

tool or machine built for definite ends or purposes compares with the organic systems and the various organs of the body.

With this brief summary of the concepts of natural will and rational will, we may now proceed to study Toennies' explanation of his concepts of Gemeinschaft and Gesellschaft in detail.

I call all kinds of association in which natural will predominates Gemeinschaft, all those which are formed and fundamentally conditioned by rational will, Gesellschaft.

Real and organic life—this is the essential characteristic of Gemeinschaft. Imaginary and mechanical structure—this is the concept of Gesellschaft.

All intimate, private and exclusive living together . . . is understood as life in Gemeinschaft. Gesellschaft is public life— it is the world itself.

In Gemeinschaft with one's family, one lives from birth bound to it in weal and woe. One goes into Gesellschaft as one goes into a strange country. There exists a Gemeinschaft of language, of folkways, of mores, or of beliefs; but, by way of contrast, Gesellschaft exists in the realm of business, travel or science.

Gemeinschaft should be understood as a living organism, Gesellschaft as a mechanical aggregate and artifact.

The form of unity which binds together the individuals who are members of the two types of group, is shown in the following words. 'In the Gemeinschaft they (the individuals) remain essentially united in spite of all separating factors, whereas in the Gesellschaft they are essentially separated in spite of all uniting factors'.

To demonstrate the unifying bonds of Gemeinschaft, Toennies employs a concept which he calls 'understanding'.

Reciprocal, binding sentiment as a peculiar will of a Gemeinschaft we shall call understanding. It represents the special social force and sympathy which keeps human beings together as members of a totality. The real foundation of unity and consequently the possibility of Gemeinschaft, is in the first place closeness of blood relationship and mixture of blood, secondly, physical proximity, and finally—for human beings— intellectual proximity. In this gradation are, therefore, to be found the sources of all kinds of understanding.

Toennies places great emphasis upon the family as 'the

general basis of life in the Gemeinschaft'. He sees Gemeinschaft existing in village and town life, as these two forms of human groups may be considered as extensions of family life—'here original kinship and inherited status remain an essential, or at least the most important, condition of participating fully in common property and other rights'.

Furthermore Toennies links the individual family, the village and the town with corresponding bases of association. His three gradations of Gemeinschaft are as follows:

1. Family life = concord (understanding). Man participates in this with all his sentiments. Its real controlling agent is the people (Volk).
2. Rural village life = folkways and mores. Into this man enters with all his mind and heart. Its real controlling agent is the commonwealth (in its literal sense).
3. Town life = religion. In this the human being takes part with his whole conscience. Its real controlling agent is the church.

To bring out the contrast with these three gradations of Gemeinschaft, Toennies then gives his three gradations of Gesellschaft.

1. City life = convention. This is determined by man's calculations. Its real controlling agent is Gesellschaft *per se*.
2. National life = legislation. This is determined by man's calculations. Its real controlling agent is the state.
3. Cosmopolitan life = public opinion. This is evolved by man's consciousness. Its real controlling agent is the republic of scholars.

Toennies then goes on to show that,

within each of these categories a predominant occupation and a dominating tendency in intellectual life are related in the following manner:

Gemeinschaft

1. Home (or household) economy, based upon liking or preference, viz. the joy and delight of creating and conserving. Understanding develops the norm for such an economy.
2. Agriculture, based upon habits, i.e. regularly repeated tasks. Co-operation is guided by custom.
3. Art, based upon memories, i.e. of instruction, of rules fol-

lowed, and of ideas conceived in one's own mind. Belief in the work and the task unites the artistic wills.

Gesellschaft

1. Trade based upon deliberation; namely, attention, comparison, calculation, are the basis of all business. Commerce is deliberate action *per se*. Contracts are the custom and creed of business.
2. Industry based upon decisions; namely of intelligent productive use of capital and sale of labour. Regulations rule the factory.
3. Science, based upon concepts, as is self-evident. Its truths and opinions then pass into literature and the press and thus become part of public opinion.

From these illustrations taken from Toennies' work it can be seen what he considers to be the most important components of his contrasting ideal types. It will also become apparent to the reader that his concepts of Gemeinschaft and Gesellschaft bear a strong resemblance to other dichotomies employed by sociologists. For example there is Spencer's evolutionary theory of 'from indefinite, incoherent homogeneity to a definite, coherent heterogeneity'. We may also note the almost identical concepts used by Durkheim in mechanical and organic solidarity, and Weber when he used communal and associative relationships (Vergemeinschaftung and Vergesellschaftung) which in fact were derived from Toennies' works.

The sociological importance of Toennies' concepts is commented on by Talcott Parsons, when he writes of the essential differences between Gemeinschaft and Gesellschaft,

The main criterion seems to be . . . that of the way in which it is possible to speak of the parties having a 'purpose' in entering into or adhering to the relationship. In the Gesellschaft case it was a specific limited purpose, a specific exchange of goods or services, or a specific immediate end held in common. In the Gemeinschaft case it is never this. (These are, of course, polar types so there is a transition between them.) If it is possible to speak of an 'end' for which a party enters into the relation, or for which it exists, this is of a different character. In the first place it is of a general, indefinite character, comprising a multitude of subsidiary specific ends, many of them as yet entirely undefined . . . In so far as such a relationship is entered into by voluntary agreement it is an agreement to pool interests over a certain more or less well-defined general area of life. There are usually certain rather definitely understood minimum points . . . but even these do not define the relationship in the same sense that the specific ends of the parties do in the contractual sense.[12]

With regard to the institutional aspects of the concepts, Parsons has several important points to make.

In the Gesellschaft relation the parties to the relationship are held to obligations, morally in the first instance, but enforced by sanctions if necessary. But in this case the obligations are typically limited by the terms of the contract, that is, in entering into the relationship a party has assumed certain specific positively defined obligations. And, above all, in any new situation that may arise the presumption is against the inclusion of a new obligation unless it can be shown to be in 'the contract' or implied in its terms. The burden of proof is on him who would require the performance of an obligation not obviously and explicitly assumed.

Gemeinschaft obligations, on the other hand, are typically unspecified and unlimited. If specified at all it is in the most general terms, e.g. marriage vows . . . The burden of proof is on him who would evade an obligation arising in any (particular) contingency . . . Though the obligations attached to a Gemeinschaft are unspecified and in the above sense unlimited, in another they are limited. But it is an entirely different kind of limitation from that given in the Gesellschaft relation. This is a corollary of the fact that the same person stands in a plurality of Gemeinschaft relations and others involving ethical obligations. Hence the claims of any one are limited by the potentially conflicting claims of others. There is implied a hierarchy of values, and a *valid* reason for refuting an obligation claimed by the other party to a Gemeinschaft relation is its incompatibility with a higher obligation . . . But the point is that the higher obligation here must be explicitly invoked; in the Gesellschaft case such considerations are irrelevant.

This brings forward an important aspect of Gemeinschaft relations—the idea of a hierarchy of Gemeinschafts to which the individual belongs. Taking Toennies' illustration we could say that the Gemeinschaft of blood (family) will rank higher than the Gemeinschaft of physical proximity (the agricultural village), which in turn will rank higher than the Gemeinschaft of intellect (or religion) associated with the town. The interactional implications of these types of Gemeinschaft relationship will further guide us in adopting criteria for the determination of community.

The last aspect of Parsons' commentary on Toennies which we shall consider here is the importance of attitudes in the Gemeinschaft. In his analysis of the institutional aspects referred to above, Parsons writes of Gemeinschaft,

> Certain things will be regarded as indispensable minima for the relationship to exist at all . . . But in general, institutional sanction is concerned rather with attitudes than with specific acts . . . The acts formally forbidden are those held to be particularly incompatible with the 'proper' attitudes, those formally enjoined a minimum expression of such an attitude . . . In so far as acts fall within a system of Gemeinschaft relations they constitute particular modes of expression of deeper-lying, more permanent attitudes . . . What carries the relationship is not these *ad hoc* elements taken alone, but the relatively permanent and deep-seated attitudes of which these may be held to be expressions. It is owing to this fact that we always inquire into the attitudes behind an act within a Gemeinschaft relationship as we do not in the other cases.

It might be added that in inquiring into the attitude behind the act we should expect to find something akin to Giddings' 'Consciousness of kind'—'a state of consciousness in which any being . . . recognises another conscious being as of like kind with itself'.[13]

At this point we may pause to consider what help we have received from Toennies and Parsons in our course towards the clarification of the concept of community.

The simplest way to present the information gained will be in tabular form, giving what Toennies calls 'corresponding and opposite concepts', and then continuing this list from the further analysis as given by Parsons.

CORRESPONDING AND OPPOSITE CONCEPTS

Gemeinschaft	*Gesellschaft*
Natural will	Rational will
Self	Person
Profession	Wealth
Land	Money
Family law	Law of contracts[14]
Organic	Mechanical[15]
Private life	Public life
Individuals united in spite of all deparating factors	Individuals essentially separated in spite of all uniting factors.
(Hierarchy)	(Hierarchy)
1. Family-household economy	1. Trade (City)
2. Rural agricultural village economy	2. Industry (State)
3. Town as area of intellectual proximity—religion and art	3. Cosmopolitan life. Science becoming basis of public opinion
Inherited status	Achieved status
General indefinite purpose, largely undefined	Specific limited purpose
Obligations unspecified and unlimited, or only general	Obligations limited by contract
Burden of proof on person *evading* obligation	Burden of proof on person *requiring* performance of obligation
Evocation of higher Gemeinschaft obligations to evade lower ones	No hierarchy of obligation—only terms of the contract are important
Acts important only as expressions of deeper attitudes	Attitudes are irrelevant—acts are the only important factors

In this table we have set down the main factors of Gemeinschaft and Gesellschaft as extracted from the writings of Toennies and Parsons and in so doing we have used the concepts as ideal types and as polar categories. In doing this we are using the concepts as Toennies intended them to be used. To repeat what Heberle says, 'To him (Toennies) Gemeinschaft and Gesellschaft are pure concepts of ideal types, which, as such, do not exist in the empirical world'.[16]

The objection has been raised that these concepts represent stages of historical development but for our present purposes the historical aspect has no relevance. If, for example, the Gemeinschaft relationship as applied to the village unit was more commonly found in older times, or in primitive societies, this is of no direct concern to us in the present context. We are here using the two concepts as ideal types which may be applied for the analysis of groups in modern society. If it appears that modern society is showing a tendency to move from Gemeinschaft relationships to Gesellschaft relationships, and that recognition of this trend will be of value in working towards a clearer analysis of the concept of community, then we shall make use of this information *for our own purpose*. We are not here making a historical study, but if historical data are of value, then they will be included.

FURTHER POLAR TYPES

Having considered at some length the contribution of Toennies to our problem, we may now turn to a consideration of the information that can be gained from other writers on this topic. In this survey we shall pass from one writer to another, finally summing up by means of a further table, as employed for Toennies and Parsons.

From the work of Herbert Spencer[17] we may extract the antithetical concepts of 'indefinite, incoherent homogeneity' and 'definite, coherent heterogeneity'. We may consider these to be ideal types, the two poles at each end of the continuum describing social organisation.

Emile Durkheim in his 'Division of Labour', employs the concepts of mechanical and organic solidarity. These again are polar ideal types, bearing a strong resemblance to Gemeinschaft and Gesellschaft. Referring to these concepts of mechanical and organic solidarity Durkheim writes,

> The first binds the individual directly to society without any intermediary. In the second, he depends upon society because he depends upon the parts of which it is composed . . . In the first, what we call society is a more or less organised totality of beliefs and sentiments common to all the members of the group: this is the collective type. On the other hand, the society in

which we are solidary in the second instance is a system of different, special functions which definite relations unite.

Thus Durkheim shows the two polar types, but then, bringing the concepts nearer to reality he goes on to say,

> These two societies really make up only one. They are two aspects of one and the same reality, but none the less they must be distinguished . . . The first can be strong only if the ideas and tendencies common to all members of the society are greater in number and intensity than those which pertain personally to each member. It is as much stronger as the excess is more considerable.[18]

The likeness of mechanical and organic solidarity to Spencer's concepts of homogeneity and heterogeneity and Toennies' Gemeinschaft and Gesellschaft is brought out in the following sentences.

> Societies where organic solidarity is preponderant . . . are constituted, not by a repetition of similar, homogeneous segments, but by a system of different organs each of which has a special role, and which are themselves formed of differentiated parts . . . This social type rests on principles so different from the preceding that it can develop only in proportion to the effacement of that preceding type. In effect, individuals are here grouped, no longer according to their relations of lineage, but according to the particular nature of the social activity to which they consecrate themselves. Their natural milieu is no longer the natal milieu, but the occupational milieu. It is no longer real or fictional consanguinity which marks the place of each one, but the function which he fills.[19]

Durkheim then has a word to say about geographic aspects of groups which is particularly appropriate to the examples given by Toennies.

> Territorial divisions have something artificial about them. The ties which result from cohabitation are not as profoundly affective of the heart of men as are those arising from consanguinity. Thus, they have a much smaller resistive power. When a person is born into a clan, he can in no way ever change the fact of his parentage. The same does not hold true of changing from a city or a province . . . Territorial divisions are thus less and less grounded in the nature of things, and,

consequently, lose their significance. We can almost say that a people is as much more advanced as territorial divisions are more superficial.[20]

It should be particularly noted that Durkheim's writing in the above extracts is in the tradition of evolutionary theory. Indeed he makes explicit his belief that 'as we advance in the scale of social evolution mechanical solidarity grows slacker'.[21] Nevertheless, if we put to one side theories of social evolution, we can see that the conceptual framework devised by Durkheim is of value in our study of contemporary community.

C. H. Cooley, in his study of social organisation, adds further weight to the general argument so far developed. In his references to primary groups, he describes structural conditions which are very similar to those given by Durkheim in his concept of organic solidarity.

> By primary groups I mean those characterized by intimate face-to-face association and co-operation. They are primary in several senses, but chiefly in that they are fundamental in forming the social nature and ideals of the individual. The result of intimate association, psychologically, is a certain fusion of individualities in a common whole, so that one's very self, for many purposes at least, is the common life and purpose of the group.[22]

Then, giving illustrations on a rather smaller scale than Toennies, Cooley suggests, 'The most important spheres of this intimate association and co-operation . . . are the family, the play-group of children and the neighbourhood or community group of elders'.[23]

The durability of the ties of the primary group are brought out in a way that reminds us of Durkheim's comments on the clan. 'Primary groups are primary in the sense that they give the individual his earliest and completest experience of social unity, and also in the sense that they do not change in the same degree as more elaborate relations, but form a comparatively permanent source out of which the latter are ever springing.'[24]

The trend towards the Gesellschaft or mechanical[25] solidarity is noted by Cooley in the following way.

> The action of the new communication is essentially stimulating, and so may, in some of its phases, be injurious. It costs the

individual more in the way of mental function to take a normal part in the new order of things than it did in the old. Not only is his outlook broader, so that he is incited to think and feel about a wider range of matters, but he is required to be a more thorough-going specialist in the mastery of his own function; both extension and intension have grown. General culture and technical training are alike more exigent than they used to be, and their demands visibly increase from year to year, not only in the schools but in life at large.[26]

The next writer to whom we turn is Max Weber and, as he was greatly influenced by Toennies, we must discriminate in selecting from his work so as to avoid overloading the general argument. In explaining his conceptual framework, Weber writes,

> A social relationship will be called 'communal' (Vergemein-schaftung) if and so far as the orientation of social action, whether in the individual case, on the average, or in the pure type, is based on a subjective feeling of the parties, whether effectual or traditional, that they belong together. A social relationship will, on the other hand, be called 'associative' (Vergesellschaftung) if and in so far as the orientation of social, action within it rests on a rationally motivated adjustment of interests or a similarly motivated agreement, whether the basis of rational judgment be absolute values or reasons of expediency. It is especially common, though by no means inevitable, for the associative type of relationship to rest on a rational agreement by mutual consent. In that case the corresponding action is, at the pole of rationality, oriented either to a rational belief in the binding validity of the obligation to adhere to it, or to a rational expectation that the other party will live up to it.[27]

The importance of the comments made by Parsons on Toennies are here quite obvious. Weber makes his designation of communal relationships more precise by the following statement.

> It is by no means true that the existence of common qualities, a common situation, or common modes of behaviour imply the existence of a communal social relationship . . . A communal relationship . . . does not even exist if they (people in a similar situation) have a common 'feeling' about this situation and its consequences. It is only when this feeling leads to a mutual

orientation of their behaviour to each other that a social relationship arises between them, a social relationship to each other and not only to persons in the environment. Furthermore, it is only so far as this relationship involves a feeling of belonging together that it is a 'communal' relationship.[28]

If for 'a feeling of belonging together' we substitute Giddings' 'consciousness of kind' the similarity of approach is obvious.

The last writer to whom we turn in this brief survey is L. T. Hobhouse, from whose work we extract various comments on social development. Hobhouse writes,

> The equality which the primitive enjoys is the equality of the undifferentiated and unenterprising, while his freedom is somewhat illusory, for the primitive man, though he may have no individual superior, has little chance of any personal life apart from his group, and little initiative apart from its traditions. It is *solidarity* rather than free *co-operation*[29] which is the character of the primitive groups. But this solidarity with such elements of freedom and equality as it allows is more and more completely lost as communities become organised on the principle of subordination.[30]

The similarity of approach between this statement and Durkheim's thesis is so striking that one might almost believe the above passage was written by Durkheim himself. Hobhouse's major contribution to the present argument, however, is his reference to the concept of community. He writes,

> The whole population owning a common rule may be designated a community. The name, however, would suggest something more than a rule in common. It would suggest a common sentiment and a common interest . . . As a matter of cold nomenclature, it will be convenient for purposes of comparison to give the term community the widest possible extension, and therefore to consider all populations living under a common rule as political communities, though they have only the bare bones of a common life. The entire population of a territory, large or small, will then constitute a community if it owns a common rule . . . The community proper must be an assignable body of people possessing accordingly distinct limits . . . Common government . . . is not essential to a community. What is essential is a common rule habitually observed through-

out a population of distinct structure with assignable limits. This distinctive unity does not prevent a community from being part of a larger community. To be distinct it must have rules, or the power to make trules of its own, and these it may enjoy, although its relations to other parts, and perhaps some internal matters of common importance, have to be determined by mutual consultation, or in a common parliament. Community and sovereignty are quite distinct conceptions.[31]

One further point worthy of note is that the community 'is not a voluntary association which men can enter and leave as they choose, but its organisation is a necessity of social life, and imposes itself accordingly on the reluctant'.[32] In closing on Hobhouse it is worth noting that he recognises the degree of abstraction which his thesis involves, and he makes the point of saying that, 'We cannot simply define the community as an organism, but it is general to attribute to it a certain kind and degree of organic character'.[33] And recognising the difficulties arising from the use of such abstractions Hobhouse justifies this method on the grounds that 'an idealised type, however, has its value in science as indicating a line of comparison'.

With this return to the specific employment of ideal types, we may end the series of quotations from selected writers. Of necessity many writers have been omitted from this brief survey and all the references given have been merely selections from, in many cases, vast volumes. Our object throughout has been to demonstrate the great similarity in theoretical approach to the concept under study, and it is therefore appropriate that at this stage we should attempt a brief synthesis before venturing further.

The two most outstanding features in the methodology described are the use of ideal types and the use of dichotomies. Of the first enough has been said at this stage: of the second, some further discussion is desirable. There is always a danger, particularly in a subject so complex as the structure of society, that the use of a dichotomy will result merely in a sorting out into 'is' and 'is not'. This danger need not arise if the purpose of the analysis is held on to clearly from the beginning. The setting up of polar contrasting ideal types is merely a step taken towards giving greater clarity of exposition in the initial stages. The important part of the process is in the linking of the two poles by a continuum. Thus, if we return for a moment to the earlier stages of our consideration of the concept of community, we then decided that the problem of definition was primarily a problem of deciding what factors or elements went together to make up the concept, and then of ascertaining the degrees. If we employ the diagrammatic form to illustrate this approach, we can show how the ideal type continuum can be used to advantage. For example, let us say that the information so far gained from the writings of the sociologists from which we have quoted suggests that the important factors of community are, as before, A, B, C, D and E. If we could then agree that each factor can be depicted by polar contrasting ideal types linked by a continuum, we could employ the method of contrast which we earlier suggested was desirable. In doing this we are therefore able to move away from the initial stage of scoring on a 1 to 100 per cent basis and we are now employing what may be termed a multiple factor analysis according to the ideal type method of approach. In all the evidence gained from sociologists quoted, there is a common theme running through of contrasting polar types. Gemeinschaft and Gesellschaft were the first principal examples used, but it was very noticeable that the other writers used the same method also. We may now, therefore, list the contrasts put forward by these writers as we did for Toennies and Parsons. Taking the main points only, in the order of the writers as they were discussed, we get the following list:

Gemeinschaft Type	Gesellschaft Type
Spencer	
Indefinite, incoherent, homogeneity	Definite, coherent, heterogeneity
Durkheim	
Mechanical solidarity	Organic solidarity
Individual bound directly to society without any intermediary	Individual depends upon society because he depends on the parts of which it is composed

Society is a more or less organised totality of beliefs and sentiments common to all members of the group	Society is a system of different, special functions which definite relations unite.
Is strong only if ideas and tendencies common to all members are greater in number and intensity than those personal to each member	Reverse operates: strength lies in different organs each of which has a special role
Natal milieu, consanguinity, real or fictional	Occupational milieu, the function of which the individual fulfils

Cooley

Importance of primary group in forming the social nature and ideals of the individual. A certain fusion of the individualities in a common whole, so that for many purposes one's very self is the common life and purpose of the group	Communication makes outlook of the individual broader, but he is required to be more of a specialist in the mastery of his own function. General culture and technical training become more exigent, and demands on the individual increase
Primary groups as comparatively permanent source from which more elaborate relations spring	The more elaborate relations increase

Weber

Communal relationship (Vergemeinschaftung). Orientation of social action based on a subjective feeling of the parties that they belong together.	Associative relationship (Vergesellschaftung). Orientation of social action rests on rationally motivated adjustment of interests or agreement.

Hobhouse

Solidarity	Free co-operation
Equality of the undifferentiated and unenterprising. Little chance of personal life apart from the group, and little initiative apart from its traditions	Greater personal opportunity results in community becoming organised on the principle of subordination.

If we add this list to the one compiled by Toennies and Parsons, we now have a body of knowledge gleaned from a representative selection of sociologists, referring to the polar type concepts. If we take the left-hand column we have suggestions as to the elements to be considered in analysing the concept of community and for each factor we have a contrasting partner in the right-hand column, giving us the other end of the continuum. Having compiled these two lists we may now proceed to an analysis of the main points of agreement which appear to be the most important. From Lundberg and MacIver we saw that the main factors in the concept of community are those of the geographic area and the common life. As yet we have not developed this theme to any great extent but it may now be appropriate to do this.

Geographic area, according to Lundberg, is not a fully sociological factor, but it may be a secondary factor of great importance. From the references made to primitive cultures by Hobhouse it would appear that small isolated groups tend more to the Gemeinschaft type than groups which are in free communication with outside influences. Thus it would appear that the important aspect of the geographic factor is the degree of isolation of the group and from this we may further suggest the importance of distinct boundaries.

But although the geographic aspect is of importance, the aspect of common life is of greater sociological importance and we must therefore turn our attention to a more detailed consideration of this factor.

By using the method of contrast between Gemeinschaft and Gesellschaft, we can see that Gemeinschaft is much more difficult to analyse than is Gesellschaft. From Toennies and Parsons we get the description of Gemeinschaft having only a general indefinite purpose, the obligations upon members being unspecified or unlimited, or at most only general. This fits in well with the writings which have an evolutionary aspect to them, and which stress the 'indefinite, incoherent homogeneity', the 'equality of the undifferentiated and unenterprising', and so on. But unless the concept of Gemeinschaft is merely an archaic idea, only useful today in the study of 'primitive society', there must be some facets of our modern society which display the noted characteristics.

MacIver writes, 'Community is something wider and freer than even the greatest associations; it is the greater common life out of which associations rise, into which associations bring order, but which associations never completely fulfil[34] . . . Community is not broken up into its associations. Community is prior to its associations. It is communal will which creates associations'.[35]

If we accept MacIver's point that the community is a form of framework upon which the associations hang, we can see that it is general, but the associations are specific. We must then take a somewhat different view from Durkheim, who believed that mechanical solidarity is, as it were, pushed aside by the growth of organic solidarity; as he puts it, organic solidarity 'can develop only in proportion to the effacement of that preceding type' (mechanical solidarity).[36]

Perhaps this is one of the problems of trying to think in terms of dichotomies without allowing for a joining continuum and the possibility that the contrasted polar types, in a complex society, need not always be mutually exclusive. If we accept MacIver's postulates it seems that the associations can only come into being from a basis of order which is that of community. If we accept Durkheim's postulates the growth of associations must in due course replace the bases of community with a completely new form of social structure. Without going into social theories involving the laws of nature, or the theory of social contract (or even the Brave New World), we can readily appreciate how this abstract thinking can lead to mental confusion.

It may, therefore, help to simplify the position if we set up a postulate that will attempt to bridge the gap. The postulate is that the growth of associational relationships will result in a decline in the force of communal relationships, but can never destroy them completely without in so doing destroying themselves. We may contrast, for example, a small, isolated, primitive society with a modern, highly complex, western society. In the primitive society we expect to find a small homogeneous isolated society with strong traditions which bind the individual actions. With this we anticipate a low state of technological development and little or no social change. In the western society the group loyalties of the individual become more numerous and separate from each other. Achieved status and class structure become important factors in the life of the society. Capitalism and industry give rise to the importance of contractual relationships and 'rational' interests. The geographical aspects of the groups decline in importance.

All these Gesellschaft relationships cannot exist without an underpinning of the Gemeinschaft ones. Toennies, for example, contrasts the family-household economy with trade, the village economy with industry and both these are useful devices, since they illustrate in more concrete form the differences between his more abstract concepts such as natural and rational will, or self and person. Parsons, in using the marriage and family relationships for illustration gives a useful example with obligations limited by contract. These, and others, are all useful heuristic devices for bringing out the desired contrasts.

In modern society, then, the emphasis tends to fall greatly upon the Gesellschaft relations since modern society is a large complex social structure. But within this society and lying below all the contractual, rational and associational interaction of the members, there must still be the deeper relationships which are not specific to any given situation. In his recent book on the family, Fletcher attempts to put the case for the family as a unit, still today embodying many of the essential Gemeinschaft components: it is not, in his view, an outmoded and discredited relic of by-gone days. Whilst the family remains as it is, a group of people with intimate personal relationships unspecified by any systematic code of rules, the importance of inheritance, ascribed status and the differences in socialisation patterns of infants cannot be ignored. Whilst societies still demonstrate irrational patterns of beliefs in customs, mores, religion, patriotism, prejudice and so on, there are large areas of life where there is a 'totality of beliefs and sentiments common to all members of the group' rather than a society which is a 'system of different, special functions which definite relations unite'. The occupational milieu, what you do, may be increasingly important as society goes on, but the social milieu, who you are, is still very much there today. Thus it is fallacious to think always, as Durkheim suggests, of the Gesellschaft replacing the Gemeinschaft to the extinction of the latter. If this were to happen then people would live in a society which was marked by complete rationality of every behavioural act and the society would probably become extinct since no one would be so irrational as to mate with the opposite sex and rear the ensuing offspring.

Thus to think always of Gemeinschaft and Gesellschaft situations as being mutually exclusive can be misleading and it is wise to recall that the dichotomies used for polar types are *ideal* types which have no real place in this living world. Reality lies somewhere along the linking continuum and does not conform to neat abstract patterns. In a real-life situation elements of Gemeinschaft and Gesellschaft are blended together, as for example in the industrial company where the kinship network influences the composition of the board of directors. The nearer any real-life industrial firm is to complete rationality of organisation, the nearer it would approach the ideal Gesellschaft. But in the application of this ideal to urban life the ideal type would only be attained by the exclusion of the family and all that goes with it. An urban society without family and kinship would be an odd case of the baby having been thrown out with the bath-water.

Perhaps the theoretical structure used by so many of these theorists can be better employed if a direct acknowledgment is made of the evolutionary, or dynamic, element involved in the dichotomies. Obviously the social change is from Gemeinschaft to Gesellschaft and never the other way round. The rational, contractual and associational elements of modern society increase rather than decrease. Towns and cities tend to become larger, as do populations of countries; technologies become more complex and production and consumption rates increase. As societies become urbanised and industrialised, so the *overall* structure is better described in terms of Gesellschaft characteristics. But for all the complexity of a society of fifty million people, the face-to-face relationships between kinfolk, friends, and even neighbours do not entirely disappear. Irrational, customary usages still influence actions (as in parliamentary election voting) and moral codes are still taught to children, if taught at all, as dogma rather than reasoned argument by most parents. And it is from the background of traditional usage, the irrationalities of our legal, religious, economic and familial institutions that the associational elements are derived.

Irrational prejudices against coloured people, foreigners, Jews, Catholics, married women and so on still form the basis upon which society carries out its discriminatory acts. Contractual relationships in employment are still more likely between whites than between whites and blacks, and inter-marriage between white and black is blocked by feelings derived from Gemein-schaft, not Gesellschaft. Thus Weber's 'feeling of belonging together' which typifies the Vergemeinschaftung relationship is crucial here. People can have a feeling of belonging together in a variety of ways and at different levels, from the marriage relationship to the crowds at a political rally, but in Weber's concept the latter would be excluded because of the limitations of the relationship here involved. As he says 'common qualities, a common situation, or common codes of behaviour' are not sufficient to qualify for Vergemeinschaftung. Athletes may have common qualities, people in a shipwreck may share a common situation, negroes and whites may have common codes of behaviour; none are enough for this concept to apply. Weber is, in fact, very much in line with MacIver when the latter says of community, 'Its unity reaches deeper than the co-ordination of its associations ... It is the communal will which creates associations'.

The problem, then, is one of deciding what things are held in common between people, not because of local circumstances or events, but because the people concerned think of themselves essentially as together before thinking of themselves apart. And the difficulty here lies in the fact that the frame of reference is a relative one. If, for example, one takes the case of the small isolated rural village, then the people who live in it may think of themselves as belonging together with reference to the county or region in which they live. But this would not neces-sarily extend to a feeling of belonging together in the kinship relations, since people would be related to some in the village and not to others. Even in the kinship network some people would have the closest of ties, such as between spouses and between parents and children; others would have less close ties. Thus the problem is essentially a problem of ever-widening frames of reference, rather like a set of concentric circles. The nuclear family feel they belong together *vis-a-vis* the village. The village feels it belongs together *vis-a-vis* the county or

region. Before communications were so extended it would probably have been reasonable to say that the region felt it belonged
together *vis-a-vis* the country as a whole; today this is dubious.

It is noticeable that this approach to the problem becomes
less satisfactory as soon as its goes beyond the very small
primary group of the village, and it is the smallness of size that
gives the Gemeinschaft relationship its peculiar characteristics.
The group of people constituting the county or region fall away
from the criteria because, obviously, they do not really match
up to Weber's requirements of the essential feelings of belonging
together rather than being apart basically, but united because
of certain features, or situations.

The Gesellschaft relationship is, then, one which deals with
certain aspects of those groups which have grown beyond the
primary face-to-face size and structure, and only elements, or
traces, of the Gemeinschaft are found within it, and in some
cases these are instances of pseudo-Gemeinschaft which should
not be confused with the real thing.

To illustrate this, one may take the case of the comparison
drawn between urban neighbourhoods and the highly idealised
villages. This strove to find points of similarity which could be
used to bolster the arguments for establishing planned neighbourhoods which would be real living social units. But the
analogies failed because the population scale was wrong and
because it is apparent that the people in the neighbourhood do
not think of themselves as this undifferentiated whole which is
so essential to the Gemeinschaft. The people of an urban
neighbourhood can think of themselves as being of that district
rather than of the city as a whole, and can think of themselves
as being of the city rather than the region or even country,
but these are quite different conceptual frameworks. Both
neighbourhood and city fail to qualify as Gemeinschaft situations; they are too big, too complex and diverse in construction
and the whole nature of their pseudo-Gemeinschaft appearances
lies in comparing them to larger units so as to make this sort of
relationship look as if it exists. In the true Gemeinschaft the
members of the relationship do not need this relationship to the
wider circle. Thus the people who stand in relationship to each
other by the bonds of marriage, kinship and village extended
kinship can, in effect, say 'Yes, we do have a feeling of belonging

together because our relationships with each other stem from inter-marriage and close, personal, face-to-face primary relationships. Obviously the feeling is stronger in the nuclear family than in the extended one, but it is there in the village because we feel that our relationships with each other stem from this essential bond between us'. In the neighbourhood or city the people can only say, 'Well, yes, I suppose that I feel more a sense of belonging to the part of the city where I live because I know more people there and I have friends and neighbours there and, obviously I don't know other neighbour-hoods as well as I do my own'. But the neighbourhood dweller cannot say, 'Yes, in spite of all things that separate us I still feel that we who live in Uppercliffe are bound together in weal or woe and recognise ourselves as essentially different from all the rest of the city'. This sentiment is obviously unrealistic and demonstrates quite clearly that the neighbourhood is not in the same category as the ideal type village. The lesson to be learned from this comparison is that the Gemeinschaft concept is useful *only* if applied to relationships and groups which are essentially small and self-consciously of a nuclear type. As soon as the unity of the group is only discernible by comparison with a larger one, the concept loses its value.

It is interesting to note how the previous discussion of macro-cosmic and microcosmic views of social relationships has relevance here. In discussing urban society in the macrocosmic way, attention is inevitably directed to the intricate network of secondary relationships which make possible the industrialised, urbanised society which typifies so much of modern life. But, in recognising that man does not live by secondary relation-ships alone, the microcosmic view comes into use and attention is directed more closely to the personal relationships which still occur at face-to-face level in the urban setting. It was noted in our discussion of Wirth's statement on urbanism that he over-did the emphasis on secondary relationships and gave too much of an impression that city life consisted of nothing but secondary associations. Perhaps influenced by this somewhat gloomy approach to urban life, which was by no means restricted to Wirth, the protagonists of the community centre movement attempted to utilise the concept of neighbourhood as a peg upon which to hang their plans. In essence, the neighbourhood was likened to the ideal type village of the Gemeinschaft category, but as the analysis of this chapter has demonstrated, this was quite fallacious.

In the next, and final, chapter I shall try to draw together the many threads that have run through these chapters and to make tentative conclusions.

Chapter Eight

CONCLUSIONS

WHEN a field so wide as urban sociology has been the focus of attention in a single book it would be arrogant, and highly misleading, to attempt to drawn any very firm conclusion. This chapter, therefore, will merely be a short summary of some of the main points covered and some pointers to areas which require more detailed study.

In the early chapters an attempt was made to throw light on some of the key features of urbanism by using the traditional rural-urban dichotomy. Both descriptive and quantitative approaches were used, and the results were interesting in their variety. It was noted in the descriptive analysis how difficult it was not to get tangled up with a mixture of rural and urban, and past and present. When the comparisons were kept fairly strictly to both rural and urban in the present, the differences were less than when the comparison was between the past village and the present city.

In the study of the limited statistics for certain social indices in this country, the hypotheses under test were by no means uniformly supported by the evidence. It was recognised that the data presented were often extremely limited by the types of categories available, but nevertheless some hypotheses were quite obviously refuted whilst others showed no worth-while rural-urban differences at all. In this analysis the compact nature of this country was noted, and the differences between Britain and the U.S.A. made some American situations totally inapplicable to this country. One interesting point which did come from the data was the way in which the *types* of towns affected statistical indices. In particular the effects of 'retirement towns' in the south were noted several times. Also the importance of London and the south-east as population magnets could not be overlooked, and the north-south differences were noted on several occasions. In all, the quantitative approach was interesting in showing how factors other than rural-urban appear to be of importance in British society.

When we turned to consider urban society *per se* it was noticeable how many of the descriptions of urban characteristics carried with them an implicit comparison with rural characteristics. Indeed, it became more and more apparent that descriptions of urban life depended upon *either* a rural-urban comparison *or* an urban historical comparison. The three-category analysis of urbanism showed how the city could be viewed in 'the large' as a social system with particular social forces operating, or could be viewed much more from the viewpoint of the individual with emphasis upon the adjustment of the person to the social system.

In the next two chapters we considered the large scale and small scale problems of urban life by using town-planning as the hook upon which to hang the macrocosmic, and the neighbourhood unit as the hook for the small scale or microcosmic. In these analyses it was seen that town planning is essentially limited in its scope by historical developments and the general ethos of the society in which it operates, whilst neighbourhood unit planning was seen to be largely based upon a variety of value judgments held by social workers.

In the theoretical analysis, where the polar ideal types of Gemeinschaft and Gesellschaft were first employed and then added to by excerpts from selected writers, it was seen that the dichotomy was highly involved with a historical, or evolutionary, perspective which was not always made as obvious as it might have been. Further, it was noted how, in looking at the community from the dichotomous viewpoint the problem of urban development was not satisfactorily solved. Our own analysis favoured MacIver rather than Durkheim in this, and demonstrated that the theoretical categories used were, in fact, better guides if it was allowed that the one type could be present in addition to the other, rather than only *in its place*.

This analysis leads us back to the problem which seems to be at the heart of the analysis of urbanism in modern society. Sociology is essentially, at base, a study of social change. For all the studies which may, through necessity, have to be cross-sectional ones of society as it is *now*, these studies are only meaningful if they are contributions to a study of the *process* of society. Obviously both historical and comparative studies are of value in gaining understanding of a given social situation, but it does seem that the historical method gives more attention to the dynamics of the situation, and, *a priori*, it would seem to be the most likely method for predictive attempts, since it is a method which is directly involved in the time scale. This is not to say that the comparative study is valueless. Far from it; the comparison between two groups, whether they be complete cultures or selected housing estates, enables us to gain understanding because of the highlighting of differences between the groups. But in the barely developed realm of experimental sociology[1] it is interesting to note that the projected experiment and the ex-post-facto experiment both use the time scale as an integral part of the design, the former working from the present to the future, the latter working back from the present to the past. The so-called cross-sectional design purports to be a study comparing two groups *now*, but it is clearly shown in the design that the past is of importance, and this design is by far the least satisfactory design of the three.

This argument is not intended to be a mere panegyric in favour of a more openly stated historical approach to sociological problems. C. Wright Mills made a stimulating appeal, or directive, for this in his work on the Sociological Imagination. We need not try to précis his case, though we must acknowledge its cogency whilst noting a certain bias of the author in favour of his own value judgments. What is important in the context of the study of urban sociology is to straighten out some of the tangled paths which appear to be in use in approaching this field of study.

As Nels Anderson has pointed out,[2] the world today has interesting problems of urbanism and urbanisation, and Anderson is concerned that urbanisation should be studied carefully, since this is a process which is occurring at a fantastic rate all over the globe. The problems differ in scale and in form according to the actual locations chosen, but all show similar developments. The dynamic process of urbanization is a world-wide phenomenon. How then can it best be studied?

A description of an urban setting is meaningless unless the description is limited to those factors which are of value in increasing our understanding of the social structure and processes under study. No sociologist asked to study an urban community would go around measuring the size of people's hats or noting the colour of their eyes; these factors would have no apparent relevance to the phenomenon of urbanism. The sociologist asked to report on an urban community would want to collect *relevant* data. The question then is essentially one of determining the relevance of certain data as against others, and relevance can only be determined by a clear statement of the question or questions for which we want answers.

Our analysis so far suggests that there are two criteria of relevance operating; the comparative and the historical. We may want to know, for example, how Middlesborough compares with Maidstone in certain characteristics such as housing, health, mortality, etc. These data, added to data for other towns, other cities and other rural areas will give us a picture *now* of differences between towns and differences between urban and rural as aggregates. So far, so good. We know now how these two categories differ. Apart from answering questions about comparative factors in the two towns, what value are they to sociological theory? Doubtless the functionalist would argue that an understanding of the interrelationships of the different factors in urban and rural locations is of great value. This is true, but limited. The picture is only of rural and urban at any one moment, and rural and urban are extremely changeable phenomena as we well know. If rural and urban were institutions in a primitive isolated society in which social change was practically nil, we might feel satisfied with the findings. But a description of these differences in modern Britain is a mere snapshot when a moving picture is more desired.

Thus it may be that the comparative method, derived so greatly as it is from the work of anthropologists with isolated primitive societies, is of less direct value to the sociologist concerned with modern rapidly developing societies. For a comparative method to be of real value in a modern society such as we are dealing with in Britain, it is necessary to think more in terms of comparison in the experimental situation than direct comparison as such. Thus, in the classic situation of the projected experiment, where two groups are matched on all

217

relevant variables and then a new factor is introduced to the experimental group, the whole emphasis of study is upon the change which occurs after this has happened. The new factor and the changed situation are thus linked together in a relationship which is as near 'causal' as can be obtained, and this is an improvement on a mere correlation derived from a less controlled non-experimental situation. The experimental situation has in it a dynamic element which enables the observer to say that if to a given situation 'A' a new element 'X' is introduced, then the new situation 'B' will arise. The difference between A and B is then attributable to the element X.

The comparative method does not have this time element in it and the predictions that can be made are predictions of a typological character. Thus a here-and-now comparison between communities of different size may enable the observer to note that the elements A, B, C to n are present in various communities in various ways or to various degrees. If it is found that correlations exist between certain elements in certain sizes of communities then a certain predictability may be achieved. Given size of community as a standard factor it may be possible to say, from collated observations that if factor A is present in such a way, then factor B is likely to be present also.

This predictability of associated factors fits in with the polar types continuum used in a static manner. In pointing to manifestations of some characteristics there is the prediction that others will be present also. Thus it could be that from observations of communities along the rural-urban continuum the observer is able to note that, for the factors A to n, there is a progression that can be demonstrated. From this two types of predictions can be made. The first, as has just been noted, says that if factors A, B and C are present in particular forms, then E and F will also be present in particular forms. This is a type of 'Gestalt' prediction which fills in the gaps which could be filled in by observation. That is, the factors E and F *could* be observed if desired, but the Gestalt makes this work unnecessary. The second type of prediction is a dynamic one and would take the form of predicting what a community would be like, *other things being equal*, if it were to move along the continuum from rural to urban. This prediction is a prediction with a time element in it, and the 'other things being equal' element becomes much more unlikely, necessary though it is.

Quite obviously these two types of predictions are based upon the same data, the only differences being that the first type is a static, comparative prediction, whilst the second is a dynamic, historical prediction. But, bearing in mind for the second one the caveat 'other things being equal', the historical aspect becomes somewhat unreal, since change in time is essentially the reverse of things being equal. To put this discussion in the form of an example that would be fairly near to real life, it might be that research established that the most useful factors for comparing rural and urban communities were A: Size of population, B: Proportion of employed concerned with agriculture, C: Standardised birth rate, D: Standardised death rate from tuberculosis. From these four factors (which represent a possible n factors) we discover correlations which enable us to predict with reasonable accuracy that given data on one factor we can fill in the other three. That is to say, we discover the Gestalts. We can then use the prediction in time to say that if, for example, the size of population is increased from 500 to 5,000, then it will follow that the proportion of employed concerned with agriculture, the standardised birth rate and the standardised death rate from tuberculosis will also change to certain predictable figures, 'other things being equal'. The principal reason for things not being equal is that a growth of population from 500 to 5,000 is unlikely to occur overnight, and so, for example, changes in agricultural technology, or in medical science, may make for changes in the other factors. Our ability to predict the likely effects of inventions not yet made, or techniques not yet developed, is very obviously extremely low and such predictions are beyond the abilities of anyone except the astrologer. What does seem to occur in real life is that the social scientist, not being a crystal-ball gazer, attempts to use an amalgam of the historical and functional approaches for what are quite admittedly low-level predictions. Given types of social structures which bear a relation to each other (such as rural and urban communities obviously do) the sociologist analyses the situation in the here-and-now so as to unravel the intricate web of relationships and thus gain a better understanding of the principles underlying the structure. In the case of the rural-urban continuum a number of major 'strands' have been suggested, and some have proved to be useful and important, others have not been so good. But as the observer moves along the rural-urban continuum he may learn to expect certain structural changes to occur. This understanding enables him to give some predictions if he is asked what the likely outcome would be of introducing some new element into a given structure. The most obvious example of this case is the neighbourhood unit concept which attempts socially to impose a rural structural pattern onto an urban situation. As has been demonstrated, many of the assumptions of the neighbourhood unit were sociologically unsound, and much less is heard of it today than ten to fifteen years ago. As for 'social balance', this also would appear to be an ideological concept which, given the present form of our society, is sociologically unsound. People may *wish* for social balance, but this is quite different from predicting the likelihood of its attainment *unless* our society alters very greatly.

In the broader field of town planning, it is unlikely that our society will impose a great number of controls which, if they were to be used, could make for the solution of what are generally accepted social problems. For example, the movement of population to the south-east, the continuing growth of an already bloated Greater London, are problems that *could* be dealt with more effectively if industrial location were directed by government control of a mandatory nature, and even more so if the government took powers to direct people to work in particular places. But, given our present type of society, such strict measures are not very likely. 'Freedom' would undoubtedly be held to be in jeopardy if such legislation were passed. What is much more likely to occur, using the information at hand and the likelihood of social change within the present framework, is that some increased development of regional planning will come about, and this will be linked more closely with overall economic and social planning. But the actual form that this will take will be determined by political considerations, the obvious one being the particular political party in power at any given time.

As for the sociology of urbanism itself, greater attention will obviously have to be given to the effects of new technological developments and social developments as they affect urban life. Amongst the obvious and important ones, none stands out more clearly than the increasing ownership of private transport, particularly of the family motor car.[3] With increased general ownership of cars and among the middle and upper classes of a second car, a transport revolution is now occurring, and its social repercussions for city and neighbourhood, for village and countryside are enormous and as yet virtually unstudied by sociologists. A further revolution is occurring in retail distribution with the development at a great pace of self-service shops and supermarkets. The most recent stage is the possibility of emulating American ideas with the out-of-town large shopping centre, a plan for which is to be studied by the Department of Town Planning of Manchester University.[4] Undoubtedly shopping is an important social activity, greatly affected by civic design, new forms of shops, working wives and aging populations, but research in this field by sociologists is practically nil.[5]

A further development which is now being discussed in the national press is the increase in holiday cottages in villages in the more beautiful parts of the country and on the coasts. If increasing prosperity leads to considerable buying of holiday cottages in such villages, then the phenomenon of the village which is half empty for most of the year will become more common.

The above suggestions are matters which warrant serious sociological attention, but they are merely additions to the long list of studies in urban sociology yet to be carried out. Our knowledge of the social effects of high density development is sketchy in the extreme, yet multi-storey flats are a recognised part of practically every town development scheme today. Urban society has a tremendous potential for providing for increased leisure, yet we know very little about the leisure patterns of urbanites. Mass media have taken mass culture to the remotest villages, yet we know little of their effect on rural social life.

Indeed, if the young promenaders at the closing concert at the Albert Hall are really to build Jerusalem in England's green and pleasant land, they will, at the moment, do so with very little insight gained from British sociology.

NOTES

1. INTRODUCTION TO THE PROBLEM

[1] M. Ginsberg, 'The Problems and Methods of Sociology', in F. C. Bartlett *et al.*, *The Study of Society*, London, 1939.

[2] Ruth Glass, 'Urban Sociology', *Current Sociology*, Vol. 4 No. 4, 1955.

2. DESCRIPTIVE COMPARISON OF RURAL AND URBAN

[1] It is recognised that there are criticisms of the rural-urban contrast method, and these will be discussed in the summing-up on the next chapter.

[2] Thomas Sharp *in* 'Design in Town and Village', London, H.M.S.O., 1953, p. 1.

[3] Although it must be recognised that the Northern industrial towns are having a current vogue with novels such as *Saturday Night and Sunday Morning* and *A Kind of Loving*, and plays such as *A Taste of Honey*. The latter, however, being a play about a Salford schoolgirl who is made pregnant by a negro sailor and who then goes to live with a young homosexual is not an attempt to depict the ordinary, everyday life of urban dwellers.

[4] T. L. Smith, 'The Urban and Rural Worlds', in T. L. Smith and C. A. McMahan, *The Sociology of Urban Life*, New York, 1951, p. 43.

[5] P. A. Sorokin and C. C. Zimmerman, *Principles of Rural-Urban Sociology*, New York, 1929, p. 15.

[6] T. Sharp, *Town Planning*, Chap. 2, Pelican Books, 1940.

[7] L. Wirth, 'Urbanism as a Way of Life', *American Journal of Sociology*, Vol. 44, July, 1938.

[8] 'Area attached to a dwelling-house'.

[9] Ministry of Health, 'Design of Dwellings', London, H.M.S.O., 1944.

[10] Op. cit., p. 16.

[11] R. C. Angell, *The Integration of American Society*, New York, 1941, p. 190-1.

[12] Ibid., p. 191.

[13] In the village in which I lived it was customary for everyone who turned up at the Annual Meeting of the local church to be elected onto the Parochial Church Council.

[14] See G. D. Mitchell, 'Social Disintegration in a Rural Community', *Human Relations*, Vol. 3, No. 2, 1950.

[15] T. L. Smith and C. A. McMahan, op. cit., p. 51.

[16] D. J. Wheeler suggests five household categories for survey purposes in market research in 'A New Classification of Households', British Market Research Bureau Ltd., London, 1955.

[17] R. E. Park, 'The Urban Community as a Spatial Pattern and a Moral Order', in E. W. Burgess: *The Urban Community*, Chicago, 1925, pp. 35-6.

[18] Note the areas of greatest population growth between the 1931 and 1951 and 1961 Censuses.

[19] N. P. Gist and L. A. Halbert, *Urban Society*, New York, 1948, p. 264.

[20] R. C. Angell, op. cit., pp. 20-1.

Notes

3. RURAL–URBAN COMPARISON: A QUANTITATIVE APPROACH

[1] Registrar General's Statistical Review, 1960, Part 1, p. ix.

[2] O. D. Duncan and A. J. Reiss, *Social Characteristics of Urban and Rural Communities*, New York, 1956.

[3] Unless specific mention otherwise is made, 'this country' is defined as England and Wales.

[4] Occupational Tables, p. 620.

[5] Possibly attributable to American armed forces located in this region.

[6] The Standardised Mortality Ratio shows the number of deaths registered in the year of experience as a percentage of those which would have been expected in that year had the sex/age mortality of a standard period (1950–2) operated on the sex/age population of the year of experience.

[7] The 'Counties' are actually Executive Councils, which in a few cases include county boroughs within them, e.g. Oxford County and City, Gloucester County and City.

[8] See B. Benjamin, 'The Population Census as a Source of Social Statistics', p. 54 in A. T. Welford *et al.*, *Society*, London, 1962, for comment on this point.

[9] G. P. Wibberley, *Agriculture and Urban Growth*, London, 1959, p. 48.

[10] C. A. Moser and Wolf Scott, *British Towns, a Statistical Study of their Social and Economic Differences*, London, 1961.

4. URBAN SOCIETY

[1] G. P. Wibberley, 'Changes in the Structure and Functions of the Rural Community', *Sociologia Ruralis*, Vol. 2, No. 2, Winter 1960.

[2] H. Hoffsommer, 'Rural Sociological Interdisciplinary Relations within the field of Sociology', *Rural Sociology*, Vol. 25, 1960.

[3] L. Nelson, *Rural Sociology*, New York, 1948.

[4] Charles T. Stewart, Jnr., 'The Urban-Rural Dichotomy: Concept and Uses', *American Journal of Sociology*, Vol. LXIV, September, 1958.

[5] L. Wirth, 'Urbanism as a Way of Life', *American Journal of Sociology*, Vol. 44, No. 1, July 1938.

[6] For brief statements on these theories, see N. P. Gist and L. A. Halbert, *Urban Society*, New York, 1956, and E. E. Bergel, *Urban Sociology*, New York, 1955.

[7] See the general theme of J. Jacobs, *The Death and Life of Great American Cities*, London, 1962.

[8] R. M. MacIver and C. H. Page, *Society*, London, 1952, p. 219.

[9] The Annual Abstract of Statistics for 1960 shows that of 7,850,000 employed women in Great Britain, 4,090,000 were married, so that the majority of employed women are now married women. Of 13,130,000 total married women this makes 31 per cent in employment.

[10] R. Fletcher, 'The Family and Marriage', Penguin Books, *Britain in the Sixties* Series, 1962.

[11] In its report for 1961–2, Stevenage Development Corporation say of the recently opened 'Locarno' dance hall, 'It's popularity is beyond question'. They also note a 26-lane bowling centre under construction. New Towns Act, 1946, Reports of the Development Corporation for the period ended 31st March 1962, H.M.S.O., 1961, Cmnd. 266.

[12] R. Dewey, 'The Rural-Urban Continuum; Real but Relatively Unimportant', *American Journal of Sociology*, Vol. LXVI, No. 1, July 1960.

[13] R. Lynd, *Knowledge for What?*, Princeton, 1945, p. 83.
[14] T. L. Smith and C. S. McMahan, *The Sociology of Urban Life*, New York, 1951.
[15] *Which?*, May, 1963.
[16] S. Reimer, *The Modern City*, New York, 1952, p. 111 and p. 134.
[17] B. Jackson and D. Marsden, *Education and the Working Class*, London, 1962.

5. THE CONTROL OF URBAN DEVELOPMENT

[1] W. Ashworth, *The Genesis of Modern British Town Planning*, London, 1954, p. 9.
[2] Local Government Board, Statistical Memoranda and Charts, relating to Public Health and Social Conditions (1909), p. 9 (quoted in Ashworth).
[3] Ashworth, p. 11.
[4] Rev. G. Lewis, 'The State of St. David's Parish: with remarks on the moral and physical statistics of Dundee', 1841. Quoted in Ashworth, p. 18.
[5] Ashworth, p. 118.
[6] Ashworth, p. 163.
[7] P. A. Graham, *The Rural Exodus*, London, 1892, p. 9.
[8] A. F. Weber, *The Growth of Cities in the 19th Century*, New York, 1899.
[9] Re-issued in 1902 as *Garden Cities of Tomorrow*, and new edition in 1946.
[10] Howard (1946 edition), p. 20.
[11] Ibid., p. 34.
[12] Ibid., p. 35.
[13] Ibid., p. 26.
[14] Ibid., p. 54.
[15] Mumford, ibid., p. 33.
[16] Mumford, ibid., p. 32.
[17] R. K. Kelsall, *Citizens' Guide to New Town and Country Planning*, Oxford, 1949, p. 79.
[18] Ashworth, p. 181.
[19] Ashworth, p. 188.
[20] Ashworth, p. 191, quoting T. Adams, *Recent Advances in Town Planning*, p. 53.
[21] Ashworth, p. 202.
[22] G. C. M. M'Gonigle and J. Kirby, *Poverty and Public Health*, London, 1936, pp. 201–2.
[23] Royal Commission on the Distribution of the Industrial Population: Report. Cmd. 6153, London, 1940.
[24] Expert Committee on Compensation and Betterment, Final Report, Cmd. 6386, London, 1942.
[25] Report on the Committee on Land Utilisation in Rural Areas, Cmd. 6378, London, 1942.
[26] See Kelsall, op. cit., pp. 90–2.
[27] Ashworth, p. 231.
[28] New Towns Act, 1946.
[29] F. J. Osborn and A. Whittick, *The New Towns*, London, 1963, p. 342.
[30] Op. cit., p. 183.
[31] Lecture to the Sheffield University Architectural Society, by L. Hugh Wilson, consultant architect for Cumbernauld New Town, November, 1963.
[32] *Source:* Annual and Monthly Digest of Statistics.
[33] Donald L. Foley, 'British Town Planning: One Ideology or Three?', *British Journal of Sociology*, Vol. II, 1960, p. 219.
[34] Ibid., p. 216.
[35] Foley (op. cit.), notes that 'the town planning professionals, in thinking of

Notes

themselves as technicians, may sometimes be disinclined to think it within their province to venture too far into the realms of the social and/or regional'.

[36] D. A. N. Perks, 'Social Change in Minehead', B.A. Dissertation, Department of Sociological Studies, University of Sheffield (Unpublished).

[37] Peter Self, *Cities in Flood*, London, 1957, p. 65.

[38] Ibid., pp. 65–6.

[39] Span Developments now have plans for building a complete village at Hartley in Kent (*Daily Telegraph*, 7th January 1964).

6. FOCUS ON THE NEIGHBOURHOOD

[1] R. Glass, *The Social Background of a Plan*, London, 1948.

[2] P. G. Gray, T. Corlett and P. Jones, 'The Proportion of Jurors as an Index of a District', *Social Survey*, London, 1951.

[3] N. Carpenter, *Encyclopaedia of the Social Sciences*, New York, 1933, pp. 357–7.

[4] Marion Wesley Roper, *The City and the Primary Group*, Chicago, 1935.

[5] That is to say, not social outside the home environment.

[6] *Responsibility in the Welfare State*, Birmingham Council of Christian Churches, 1961, p. 27.

[7] E. A. Ross, *Principles of Sociology*, New York, 1938 edition.

[8] S. Reimer, *The Modern City*, New York, 1952.

[9] Flora Thompson, *Lark Rise to Candleford*, Worlds Classics, London, N.D.

[10] Peter H. Mann, 'Community and Neighbourhood with Reference to Social Status', Ph.D. Thesis, University of Nottingham, 1955.

[11] Site Planning and Layout in Relation to Housing; Report of a Study Group of the Ministry of Town and Country Planning in *Design of Dwellings*, Ministry of Health, H.M.S.O., London, 1944.

[12] For a useful annotated bibliography of this concept, see James Dahir, *The Neighbourhood Unit Plan*, New York, 1947.

[13] Liverpool University, Department of Social Science, 'Neighbourhood and Community', Liverpool, 1954, section on 'The Liverpool Estate'.

[14] National Council of Social Service, *The Size and Social Structure of a Town*, London, 1943.

[15] M. P. Hall, *Community Centres and Associations in Manchester*, Manchester 1946.

[16] None of which is cited.

[17] Also not cited.

[18] L. Kuper, 'Social Science Research and the Planning of Urban Neighbourhoods', *Social Forces*, Vol. 29, No. 3, March 1951, p. 241.

[19] *Design of Dwellings*, p. 59.

[20] L. E. White, *Our Neighbourhood*, N.C.S.S., London.

[21] L. E. White, *Community or Chaos*, N.C.S.S., London, 1950.

[22] My italics.

7. A THEORETICAL VIEWPOINT

[1] R. M. MacIver and C. H. Page, *Society*, pp. 3–4.

[2] G. A. Lundberg, *Foundations of Sociology*, p. 23.

[3] G. A. Lundberg, *Social Research*, New York, 1949, pp. 88–90.

[4] G. A. Lundberg, *Foundations of Sociology*, p. 360.

[5] Any plural number of things to which we respond as a whole, in contradistinction from the single units of which the whole is composed.

Notes

[6] Ibid., pp. 361–2.

[7] R. M. MacIver, *Community*, London, 1924, pp. 22–3.

[8] L. Von Wiese and H. Becker, *Systematic Sociology*, New York, 1932, pp. 21–2.

[9] E. W. Burgess, 'Research Methods in Sociology', in G. Gurvitch and W. E. Moore, *20th Century Sociology*, New York, 1945, p. 31.

[10] R. Heberle, 'The Sociology of Ferdinand Toennies', *American Sociological Review*, Vol. 2, No. 1, February, 1937.

[11] All the following quotations are from *Fundamental Concepts of Sociology* (Gemeinschaft and Gesellschaft) by Ferdinand Toennies. Translated and supplemented by Charles P. Loomis. New York, 1940. This book has been more recently published in Great Britain under the title *Community and Association*, London, 1955.

[12] T. Parsons, *Structure of Social Action*, New York, 1937, p. 687 et seq.

[13] F. H. Giddings: *The Principles of Sociology*, New York, 1916, p. 17.

[14] So far from Toennies' list.

[15] Not to be confused with Durkheim's terminology.

[16] R. Heberle: Op cit.

[17] H. Spencer, *First Principles*, London, 1911, p. 396.

[18] E. Durkheim: *The Division of Labour*, Glencoe, 1947, p. 129.

[19] Ibid., p. 181–2.

[20] Ibid., p. 186–7.

[21] Ibid., p. 152.

[22] C. H. Cooley, *Social Organisation*, New York, 1927, p. 23.

[23] Ibid., p. 24.

[24] Ibid., p. 26-7.

[25] Using Toennies' terminology.

[26] Ibid., p. 98.

[27] M. Weber: *Social and Economic Organisation*, London, 1947, p. 124.

[28] Ibid., p. 126.

[29] My italics.

[30] L. T. Hobhouse, *Social Development*, London, 1924, p. 34.

[31] Ibid., pp. 41–2.

[32] Ibid., p. 59.

[33] Ibid., p. 71.

[34] *Community*, p. 24.

[35] Ibid., p. 130.

[36] *Division of Labour*, p. 182. Yet he does believe that they are 'two aspects of the one and same society'.

8. CONCLUSIONS

[1] See especially E. Greenwood, *Experimental Sociology*, New York, 1951 and F. Stuart Chapin, *Experimental Designs in Sociological Research*, New York, 1947.

[2] Nels Anderson, 'Urbanism and Urbanization', *American Journal of Sociology*, Vol. 65, 1959–60, p. 68.

[3] The adjective 'family' here denoting a vehicle capable of transporting a whole family as one unit as against a limited vehicle such as a motor scooter.

[4] *The Guardian*, 18th September 1963.

[5] See the article by W. G. McClelland, 'The Supermarket and Society', *Sociological Review*, Vol. 10, 1962, p. 133.

INDEX

227

Index

Index

Index

St. Helens, 56, 116
St. Just, 43
St. Marylebone, 36
St. Pancras, 36
Salford, 176
Salt, Titus, 125
Saltaire, 126
Sampson, Anthony, 94
Saturday Night and Sunday Morning, 222
School and neighbourhood, 173 ff., 220
Scott Committee, 134, 224
Scunthorpe, 118
Sector theory, 75, 95
Self, Peter, 143, 225
Sharp, Thomas, 4, 11, 222
Sheffield, 65, 66, 76 ff., 91, 112, 116, 134, 149, 178
Sheffield University, 87
Shopping, 93, 102
Sinclair, Upton, 5
Size of community and rural-urban differences, 12
Skelmersdale, 140
Slough, 148
Smith, T. L., 6, 19, 222
Smith, T. L. and McMahan, C. A., 222, 224
Social balance and neighbourhood, 173 ff., 220
Social class, 67, 110
Social differentiation and rural-urban differences, 18
Solidarity, 194, 198, 204, 226
Sorokin, P. A. and Zimmerman, C. C., 7 ff., 64, 222
Southampton, 134, 147
Southport, 92
Southwood-Smith, T., 125
Span Developments, 126, 147, 225
Spencer, Herbert, 194, 198, 204, 226
Standard regions, 28
Standardised mortality ratios, 48, 223
Steinbeck, John, 5
Stepney, 36
Stevenage, 43, 135
Stevenage Development Corporation, 223
Stewart, Charles T., Jnr., 70, 223
'Stockbrokers' Tudor', 11
Study Group of the Ministry of Town and Country Planning, 177 ff., 225
'Subtopia', 147

Surveyors' Institution, 129
Swindon, 144
System of interaction and rural-urban differences, 18

Taste of Honey, A, 222
Tax payers, 63
Teignmouth, 134
Territorial divisions, 199
Thetford, 144
Thompson, Flora, 166, 225
'Three Magnets, The,' 121
Toennies, F., 26, 190 ff., 226
Town and Country Planning Act, 1932, 130, 135
Town and Country Planning Act, 1944, 135
Town and Country Planning Act, 1947, 141
Town and Country Planning Association, 137
Town Development Act, 1952, 143
Town Planning Institute, 129
Transitional zone, 73, 79
Transport, 66

'Understanding,' 192
Unwin, R., 125
Urban ethos, 105 ff.
Urban social structure, 96 ff.
Urban superficiality, 110
Urban tolerance of eccentricity, 109
Urban work, 9
Urbanism as a problem, 2, 5, 6
Urbanism as a way of life, 71 ff., 97

Value judgments, 3
Vice area, 72
Village, 4, 5
Von Wiese, L. and Becker, H., 187, 226
Voting behaviour, 61 ff.

Wallasey, 116
Walsall, 116
Wandsworth, 36
Watling, 131, 149
Weber, A. F., 29, 64, 121, 224
Weber, Max, 188, 201, 205, 210, 226
Weekly Budget, The, 121
Welford, A. T., 223
Welwyn, 125, 130, 135
Western civilisation, 4

Index